Music, Menus & Magnolias

Charleston Shares Its
Culture and Cuisine

An Offering of
The Charleston Symphony Orchestra League
Charleston, South Carolina

On the front cover:

A Church Steeple

This is the steeple of St. Michael's Episcopal church, the oldest church in Charleston.
From its beginning, Charleston has been nicknamed the "Holy City," as it represented
religious freedom and a safe haven for Christians who were persecuted during the
Reformation. Also, upon sailing into Charleston the first thing people noticed were the
many church steeples. To Charlestonians, the nickname symbolizes the reverence they
have for Charleston.

On the back cover:

The U.S. Customs House

This classic design building was completed in 1879, thirty years after construction
began. It took 19 Acts of Congress to appropriate the funds, many design changes, and
years of idleness before it was ready for occupancy.
The Charleston Symphony Orchestra performs on its steps for special occasions. While
the building abounds in history, it is the memories of these beautiful concerts and the
anticipation of more to come that make this building special to us.

Inset:

Maestro David Stahl conducting the Charleston Symphony Orchestra.

Printed in the USA by

WIMMER
The Wimmer Companies, Inc.
Memphis

Dedication

As the Charleston Symphony Orchestra
celebrates its 60th Season, members of the
Charleston Symphony Orchestra League
wish to recognize two special people for their dedicated support of the
Orchestra and its league of volunteers.
We want this couple to know how much we love them and
appreciate all they have done for the Orchestra and for music
in Charleston.

Their energy, time, effort, personal sacrifice, optimism, generosity
of spirit, vision, creativity, contagious
enthusiasm, good nature, sense of humor, and their love
of music combined with their love of Charleston
have served as inspiration to all who know them.
They epitomize all that leaders should be.

This is not only a dedication,
but also an expression of appreciation and gratitude to

Marion and Burt Schools

whose love of music and enthusiastic support of the
Charleston Symphony Orchestra and
Charleston Symphony Orchestra League
have affected us all.

Thank you,
Marion and Burt Schools,
from the
Charleston Symphony Orchestra League

THE COMMITTEE

CO-CHAIRMEN
Nancy Herrmann
Jane Graham Carver

EDITOR
Nita Swann

BUSINESS STAFF
Betty Howell - Secretary
Billie Floyd - Treasurer
Susan Spencer - Office Manager

PRODUCTION AND DEVELOPMENT
Gail Maginnis - Chairman
Marion Schools - Assistant Chairman
Terry Ritchen - Musician Liaison
Louisa Hawkins - Recipe Selection Chairman
Marlies Tindall - Recipe Tasting Chairman

ADMINISTRATIVE SUPPORT
Janette Moody - Chairman
Marlene Williamon - Assistant Chairman
Joanne Ayers - Fanya Azar
Johanna Bowen - Evelyn Cathcart
Betty Lee Johnson
Phyllis Miller - Mary Pings
Ian Purches - Judy Purches
Debbie Williamson

ADVERTISING AND MARKETING
Lorelle Burke - Chairman
Hilde Hottendorf - Retail Sales Chairman
Jean Matthews - Wholesale Sales Chairman

MUSIC, MENUS, & MAGNOLIAS

Prelude

In Charleston, South Carolina, a city steeped in tradition and proud of its heritage, there is, and forever must be, a symphony orchestra. As surely as food nourishes our bodies, the music of our orchestra nourishes our souls.

As the twentieth century winds towards its close and regional orchestras throughout the country are either struggling for existence or fading completely away, all of us in the Charleston Symphony Orchestra League are determined that our orchestra will remain. Life without it would be too dismal to imagine.

Many of you may be familiar with an old proverb that says, "If of thy worldly goods thou art bereft, and of thy meager store two loaves alone to thee are left, sell one. And with the dole buy hyacinths to feed the soul."

Our orchestra is our hyacinth. It brings us great joy.

There must never be a season when the music doesn't begin, when our conductor doesn't lift his baton on opening night and send the strains of the Star Spangled Banner, and our spirits, soaring through the concert hall.

And it is to this goal that we have created this cookbook. It is a marriage of two things we love best--food and music. We wanted this book to be unique, beautiful, and definitely user-friendly. We want you to display it proudly and use it often.

By purchasing this book, you have helped us assure the fact that the Charleston Symphony Orchestra will not be silenced.

Music, Maestro, please!

ACKNOWLEDGEMENTS

**The CSOL wants to especially thank all of the people
who have submitted recipes for this cookbook:**

Carol Allen
Margaret Allen
Nancy Allen
Sue Almeida
Leona Altman
Jeanne Averill
Joanne Ayers
Viki Baena
Kate Barnett
June Beerman
Barbara Belknap
Evelyn Bell
Ledlie Bell
Mary Bell
Jim Bennett
Joan Benson
Carol Berque
Carolyn Betz
Shirley Bissett
Arthur Blair
Herbert Blomstedt
Judy Boehm
Linda Bondurant
Johana Bowen
Sharon Bowers
Rosemary Bowman
Donna Brandt
Marcia Bryant
Barbara Burbage
Lorelle Burke
Mimi Cannon
Fran Carek
Jane Carver
Seabie Carver
Geraldyne Cassidy
Evelyn Cathcart
Elizabeth Chamberlain
Elizabeth Chandler
Sheila Christie
Jack Clarkson
Lucie Cogswell

Joan Cole
Therese Comerford
Ann Connellee
Ethel Corcoran
Marsha Cotter
Norma Jeann Crews
Candace Culberson
Donna Cyr
Annelle Davidson
Gisela Dawson
Patricia Deaton
Dorothy Diesing
Katherine Doak
Howard Drew
Louise Drew
Maida DuPlessis
Joyce East
Lorraine Cox Easterby
Sandra Eastman
Elizabeth Easton
Vadene Echols
Cindy Edgar
Darrell Edwards
Tacy Edwards
Ruth Eldredge
Peggy Gale
Holly Galos
Evonne Garrett
Tina Garrett
Pat Garvin
Trudy Gary
Dottie George
G. Robert George
Jill Goldman
Thora Golz
Janet Gopsill
Margaret Grazis
Walter Griffith
Erma Grooms
Virginia Gwinn
Chalmers Haas

Billie Hall
Dottie Halsey
Jeannette Hard
Ashley Harris
Louisa Hawkins
Gloria Hedden
Barbara Heddinger
Phyllis Heizer
Mary Kahler Hench
Teri Lynn Herbert
Nancy Herrmann
Nina Hershon
Aileen Hock
Mary-Lou Hockersmith
Jean Hodges
Azile Holman
Hilde Hottendorf
Ruth Houghton
Betty Howell
Virginia Howell
Mary Nance Huff
Maureen Huff
Sissy Hunter
Tara Hyatt
Carlotta Hyers
Barbel Irons
Helen Jacobs
Gregory Jones
Rosemary Judge
Lynn Jutzeler
Betty Karl
Kathy Keene
Katherine Kelsey
Lucy Kennedy
Michael Lam Kester
Lee Kidd
Zachary M. Kilpatrick, Jr.
Marilyn Kohn
Jodi Lamson-Scribner
Julia Lamson-Scribner
Pamela Lamson-Scribner
Michael Lan Kester
Marjorie Lasko
Mary Ellen Lees
Martha Lent
Judy Lester
Charlotte Libater

Patricia Lightsey
Liz Lipscomb
Robbie Litke
Christine Lloyd
Margaret Lorince
Gail Maginnis
Michael Maginnis
Phoebe Marti
Donna Mastrandrea
Marilyn Matthesen
Jean Matthews
R.C. Matthews
Gloria Maynard
Gwen McCurdy
Rebekah McNeill
Janet Meaburn
Marianne Mead
Joan Middleton
Anne Miller
Phyllis Miller
Martha Millhouse
Joanne Moody
Peg Moore
Ginger Morgan
Mary-Claire Morgan
Mary Moser
Ballard Murphy
Lee Belle Murray
Melissa Myers
Jean Neumeyer
Joyce Nichols
Dottie Nordstrom
Terry O'Connell
Libby Olson
Barbara Patrick
Emily Pearson
Jane Pease
Patsy Pettus
Eloise Pingry
Mary Pings
Barbara Polk
Katie Porter
Judith Purches
Gloria Qualls
Lottie Quarterman
Emily Remington
Jeanne Rice

Tara Ring
Flo Riordan
Ed Ritchen
Terry Ritchen
William Ritchen
Hope Robinson
Paula Robison
Maizie-Louise Rubin
Virginia Russell
Marion Schools
Kathleen Schuyler
Alice Schwartz
Frances Schwartz
Lucy Seger
Susan Sievert
Louise Sill
Catherine Sippell
Lindsey Skolds
Linsey Marie Skolds
Aline Smith
Linda H. Smith
Sue Sommer-Kresse
Cynthia Spano
Merle Sparkman
Dorie Spaulding
Susan Spencer
Trude Spicer
Jerry Spivey
Jean Spurlock
Cecil Stack
Carol Jackson Stafford
David Stahl
Karen Stahl
Marian Stansell
Myrtle Staples
Ross Steinberger
Barbara Sunday
Nita Swann
Deborah Syrett
Cheryl Taylor
Julia Terry Templeton
Peggy Theoharous
Joan Thomas
Peggy Thomason

Marlies Tindall
Elizabeth Tomorsky
Sharon Unser
Laurie Van Deventer
Mary Elizabeth Van Every
Jean Vance
Linda Vandergrift
Linda von Grotthus
Jean Wade
Millie Wald
Don Wallace
Adelaide Waller
Henrietta Walton
Virginia Weckel
Sylvia Weeks
Mary Whyte
Chris Willhemsen
Marlene Williamon
Etta June Williams
Linda Wills
MaryEllen Witter
Betty Womble
Liz Woolley
Eleanor Zeltman
Mary Zimmer
David Zinman
Mary Zinman
Mary Zobel

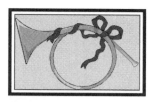

SPECIAL ACKNOWLEDGEMENTS

Those who have tested, tasted, selected, input and proofed recipes — without your help there would not be a cookbook.

In addition, the Charleston Symphony Orchestra League is deeply grateful to the following people who have given so generously of their time and talents to make this cookbook possible:

Photography:
Norman Lorusso - Multi Media Creative Services

Graphic Design:
Lorelle Burke - Creative Director, Burke & Lawrence Advertising
Sheila Davidson - Graphic Designer, Sheila Davidson Designs
Michael Meads - Graphic Designer, Michael Meads Designs

Food Stylist:
Dottie P. Hardin - Piggly Wiggly Carolina Company

Photography set assistants:
Clarice Hutchins - Pastry Chef
Michael Kennedy - Art Director, Piggly Wiggly Carolina Company
Christina Lorusso - Florist, Extra Touch Floral Service
Debbie Pulaski - Deli Sales Promoter, Piggly Wiggly Carolina Company

Props and Accessories:
Brittains of Charleston
Luden's Marine Supplies

Charleston History:
Laura Wichmann Hipp, Charleston Tea Party Walking Tours

Computers and Meeting Space:
The Citadel

And for help and generosity in getting this project underway:
Greenbax Enterprises, Inc.

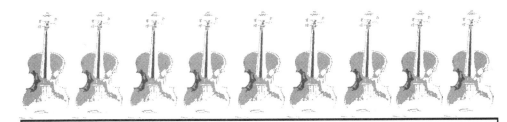

Favorite Recipes

Table of Contents

Appetizers, Beverages & Snacks

Parmesan Canapés

Sante Fe Cheesecake

Chutney Cheese Ball

Green Chile Pie

Zucchini Antipasto

Spinach Crescents

Almond Mushroom Pâté

Red Caviar Dip (see photo)

Hot Crab Dip

Porgy's Cheese Roll

and More

The Pineapple Fountain

The pineapple is the symbol of southern hospitality. Ships sailing from

the West Indies would carry pineapples, which were then an exotic fruit.

For port cities the pineapple became a treasured delicacy. It was con-

sidered a true sign of hospitality if one shared a pineapple with friends.

The fountain is located in Waterfront Park.

Menus

Having Friends in for a Drink

Bruschetta

Santa Fe Cheesecake

Spicy Snack Crackers

Marinated Shrimp

Date Nut Balls

Chocolate Nut Candy Bits

Parmesan Canapés

Makes about 30 canapés

1 cup shredded (not grated) Parmesan cheese, firmly packed	⅛ teaspoon cayenne pepper
1 medium onion, grated	1 loaf party rye or pumpernickel bread, thinly sliced
½ cup mayonnaise	

+ Mix all ingredients.
+ Spread about a level tablespoonful on each bread slice. (This may be done a couple hours ahead of serving if refrigerated.)
+ Just a few minutes before serving, place under a preheated broiler until bubbly.

Good for a cocktail party, since they can be made ahead.

Sherry Cheese

Makes about 2 cups

1 pound Cheddar cheese	¼ teaspoon paprika
⅜ cup Golden Sherry	¼ teaspoon hot pepper sauce
¼ to ½ cup mayonnaise-type salad dressing	½ teaspoon Worcestershire sauce
½ teaspoon dry mustard	3/16 teaspoon garlic powder
¼ teaspoon ground (cayenne) red pepper	

+ Grate cheese finely.
+ Add other ingredients and combine thoroughly.
+ Refrigerate until ready to use.
+ Serve with crackers or celery ribs cut into 3-inch pieces.

This recipe was inspired by an appetizer that was served for many years at a wonderful "old Charleston" restaurant on Market Street.

Bruschetta

Serves 6 to 8

Variation I - Very easy

1 loaf Italian or French bread, sliced ⅜ to ½ inch	½ cup Parmesan cheese, grated
½ cup light mayonnaise	1 teaspoon (or more) garlic powder

Variation II

Use the same ingredients as Variation I plus

½ 14-ounce can artichoke hearts, chopped

Variation III

4 to 6 Roma tomatoes, sliced	1 garlic clove, crushed
6 to 8 Greek olives, pitted and chopped	¼ pound feta cheese, crumbled

- For Variation I, toast bread (in oven) on one side. Spread the other side with a mixture of mayonnaise, cheese and garlic powder. Broil 3 to 4 inches from heat for 2 to 4 minutes, or until mixture bubbles. Serve immediately.
- For Variation II, follow the same directions as above, but include the chopped artichokes in the spread mixture.
- For Variation III, toast bread slices on one side. On the other side, rub the crushed garlic clove over the top. Put 1 to 2 slices tomato (according to size of bread), some chopped olives and crumbled cheese on the untoasted side. Broil 3 to 4 inches from heat for 2 to 4 minutes, or until cheese just starts to melt. Serve hot.

To pit and chop olives, place olives in a freezer bag. Gently pound each olive with a rolling pin (or edge of a bread board) until pit "slips." Open bag and remove contents. Discard pits and chop any extra-large pieces.

Santa Fe Cheesecake

Serves 12

1½ cups crushed tortilla chips

¼ cup butter or margarine, melted

2 8-ounce packages cream cheese, softened

2 eggs

1 8-ounce package Monterey Jack cheese, with jalapeño, shredded

1 4-ounce can chopped green chilies, drained dash of red pepper (optional)

1 8-ounce package sour cream

½ cup green onions, chopped

½ cup each red, yellow, and green peppers, chopped

½ cup tomatoes, chopped

½ cup black olives, chopped

- Preheat oven to 325°.
- Combine tortilla chips and melted butter. Spread in bottom of lightly-greased 9-inch springform pan.
- Bake for 15 minutes. Cool.
- Beat cream cheese at medium speed until smooth.
- Add eggs, 1 at a time, beating well.
- Add cheese, chilies, and red pepper.
- Spread over baked tortilla chips and bake another 30 minutes.
- Cool completely.
- Before serving, spread top with sour cream, onions, peppers, tomatoes and olives.
- Chill and serve with tortilla chips.

Well worth the time it takes!

Walnut Cheese Cookies

Makes about 4 dozen

½ pound butter	2 cups Cheddar cheese, grated
2 cups flour, sifted	1 cup walnuts, chopped
⅓ cup sugar	
1 teaspoon salt	

- Preheat oven to 350°.
- Combine butter, flour, sugar and salt and blend until particles are very fine.
- Add cheese and mix well with a fork.
- Add chopped walnuts.
- Press dough into a long roll about 1½ inches in diameter.
- Wrap in plastic wrap.
- Chill for about 30 minutes (sometimes they are easier to handle if chilled in freezer).
- Cut into rounds about ¼ inch thick.
- Place on ungreased cookie sheet and bake for 10 to 12 minutes, or just until the edges are lightly browned.

Bake 2 to 3 days ahead for best flavor.

Chutney Cheese Ball

Makes 12 generous servings

2 8-ounce packages cream cheese	2 teaspoons curry powder
½ cup chutney, cut up	1 teaspoon dry mustard
½ cup almonds, pecans or coconut, chopped	

- Mix all ingredients together.
- Refrigerate overnight.
- Make into a ball and roll in nuts or coconut.
- Serve with crackers.

This recipe seems very simple, but it tastes wonderful.

Green Chili Pie

Makes about 40 appetizers

⅓ cup green chilies, chopped (use hot, if desired)

12 ounces Cheddar cheese, shredded

6 eggs, slightly beaten and salted

- Preheat oven to 350°.
- Grease bottom and sides of 10-inch baking dish with butter.
- Sprinkle green chilies evenly over bottom of dish.
- Cover with cheese, then with eggs.
- Make sure eggs are distributed evenly over cheese.
- Bake uncovered for 30 minutes.
- Let stand for 5 minutes before cutting into small squares.
- Remove from pan and insert a toothpick into each square.
- Serve warm.

Vegetable Relish Dip

Makes 5 to 6 cups

4 large tomatoes, peeled and chopped

6 to 8 green onions, chopped

2 6-ounce cans black olives, chopped

2 4-ounce cans green chilies, chopped (or substitute jalapeño peppers to make it HOT)

5 tablespoons olive oil

4 tablespoons vinegar

2 teaspoons garlic salt

pepper to taste

- Mix well and refrigerate.
- Serve with plain corn chips.

Tastes better when made the day before using.

Zucchini Antipasto

Serves 8 to 10

4 medium zucchini (scrubbed well, not peeled)	½ cup fresh mint, shredded
⅓ cup olive or corn oil	salt and pepper to taste
3 cloves garlic, minced	¾ cup red wine vinegar

- Cut zucchini lengthwise into thin slices, and cut these crosswise, 1 to 2 inches long.
- In a large skillet, heat half of the oil and sauté half of the zucchini slices until golden, turning once.
- Repeat with remaining oil and zucchini.
- Drain each batch on paper towels.
- In a 10x6-inch dish, arrange ⅓ of sautéed zucchini on bottom layer. Sprinkle with ⅓ of the garlic, mint, seasonings and vinegar.
- Make 2 more layers in the same manner.
- Cover and refrigerate overnight.
- Before serving, spoon some of the marinade over the top, or turn the whole antipasto into a serving dish.
- Serve with crusty bread.

Mushroom Pâté

Makes about 16 servings

½ pound fresh
mushrooms, finely
chopped
½ cup onion, finely
chopped
1 tablespoon oil
1 8-ounce package
cream cheese

¼ cup Parmesan
cheese, grated
½ cup fresh parsley,
minced
2 tablespoons soy
sauce

- Sauté mushrooms and onion in oil for 2 minutes.
- Remove from heat and stir in cream cheese until blended.
- Add remaining ingredients and stir to combine.
- Cover and refrigerate at least 3 hours or until thoroughly chilled.
- Serve with small slices of French bread.

Spinach Rolls

Makes about 80 appetizers

2 10-ounce packages
chopped spinach,
thawed and squeezed
dry
1 cup mayonnaise
1 cup sour cream
½ to 1 cup bacon bits or ham

6 green onions,
chopped fine
1 1-ounce package
ranch dressing mix
8 flour tortillas, regular
size (use thinnest
ones)

- Mix together all the ingredients except for the tortillas.
- Spread mixture on the tortillas and roll up.
- Chill at least 3 hours.
- Slice diagonally into ⅓-inch slices.
- May be made the day before.

Very tasty. Very pretty.

Hummus and Chickpea Dip

Makes 1 cup

1 5-ounce can chickpeas (garbanzo beans)
1 large clove garlic, crushed
   salt to taste

4 to 6 tablespoons tahini (pureed sesame)
5 to 6 tablespoons lemon juice
   dash of olive oil
   parsley, chopped
   paprika to garnish

- Drain chickpeas.
- Place in blender or processor.
- Add crushed garlic, salt, tahini and lemon juice.
- Blend to creamy paste.
- Add a little olive oil to give a smoother texture and better taste.
- Turn into a bowl and garnish.
- Serve with pita bread pieces for dipping.

Authentic Middle Eastern recipe acquired while living in Saudi Arabia. Delicious and also lowfat.

Corn Dip Appetizer

Makes about 3 cups

1 16-ounce can whole kernel corn, drained
¼ cup green pepper, finely chopped
¼ cup red pepper, finely chopped

1 tablespoon onion, grated
¼ cup sour cream
½ cup mayonnaise
1 2-ounce jar chopped pimiento
½ teaspoon salt

- Mix all ingredients and chill well.
- Serve with party rye or wheat bread.

May also be used as a salad, presented on a lettuce leaf.

Spicy Snack Crackers

Makes 2 pounds

1 cup corn oil	1 1-pound box small
1 tablespoon dill weed,	square cheese
chopped	crackers
1 teaspoon garlic salt	1 11-ounce box oyster
1 2-ounce package	crackers
ranch dressing mix	

- Mix together corn oil, dill weed, garlic salt and ranch dressing.
- Let stand for 1 hour, stirring frequently.
- Combine crackers in large bowl.
- Pour liquid mixture over crackers and toss well.
- Toss again and again, every few minutes, until all moisture is absorbed.
- Store in airtight container.

An addictive snack!

Ham Rolls

Makes 3 to 4 dozen

½ pound ham, shredded	1 medium onion,
or minced	minced
1½ pounds Cheddar	mustard
cheese, grated	small rolls

- Thoroughly mix together the ham, cheese and onion.
- Add enough of your favorite mustard to make spreadable.
- Spread on small rolls, wrap in foil and refrigerate, or freeze, if desired.
- Bake at 375°, unwrapped, until cheese melts and rolls are hot, approximately 20 minutes, or 30 minutes if frozen.

Men, especially, enjoy these because they are a little heavier than some "cocktail" fare.

Vegetable Pizza

Makes enough for a crowd

2 8-ounce cans
crescent rolls
2 8-ounce packages
cream cheese,
softened
1 1-ounce package
ranch dressing mix

1 cup mayonnaise
broccoli flowerets,
very finely cut
green pepper, very
finely chopped
1 tomato, diced and
seeded
carrots, grated
2 tablespoons black
olives, chopped

- Preheat oven to 400°.
- Spread dough onto cookie sheet that has sides.
- Bake for 10 minutes.
- Allow to cool.
- Mix cream cheese, ranch dressing and mayonnaise until smooth.
- Spread onto cool crust.
- Top with vegetables.
- Cut into squares.

Makes a very pretty presentation. Recipe halves beautifully.

Almond-Mushroom Pâté

Makes 3 cups

3	tablespoons butter	1	cup almonds, toasted
1	onion, finely chopped	2	tablespoons balsamic
3	cloves garlic, finely		vinegar
	chopped	1	teaspoon salt
¾	pound mushrooms,	½	teaspoon pepper
	chopped	2	teaspoons olive oil
½	teaspoon thyme		

◆ Heat butter in large pan.

◆ Sauté onion, garlic, mushrooms and thyme over medium-low heat until quite brown.

◆ Toast almonds in microwave 5 minutes, stirring every minute, until lightly browned.

◆ Cool 10 minutes.

◆ Put into food processor with olive oil and process until smooth.

◆ Add mushroom mixture, vinegar, salt and pepper.

◆ Process until smooth or still slightly chunky, whichever you prefer.

◆ Transfer to serving bowl and refrigerate, covered, several hours or overnight.

◆ Serve with party rye bread.

To make a pretty platter, serve with saga bleu cheese and ginger crisps, along with a ripe pear and some grapes.

Sausage Snacks

Makes 60 to 70 slices

1 pound hot or mild Italian sausage

1 pound lean ground beef

1 pound Velveeta cheese, shredded

1 green pepper, chopped

1 red pepper, chopped (optional)

1 2-ounce jar pimientos, chopped

2 loaves cocktail pumpernickel or rye bread, sliced

- Preheat oven to 350°.
- In large skillet, cook sausage. Pour off fat.
- Add beef. Brown. Pour off fat.
- Stir in peppers and pimiento. Remove from heat.
- Stir in cheese until melted.
- Spread mixture on bread.
- Bake on cookie sheet for 10 minutes.
- May be cut into triangles for bite-size snack.

May be prepared ahead and frozen. Reheat frozen slices on a baking sheet for 10 minutes at 350°.

Tracy's Pâté with Currants

Makes 2 to 3 cups

2	small celery stalks with leaves	½	teaspoon nutmeg, grated
4	whole peppercorns	¼	teaspoon ground cloves
6	cups water		
1	teaspoon salt	¼	cup onions, chopped
1	pound chicken livers	1	small garlic clove
	pinch of cayenne	¼	cup brandy
½	pound sweet butter	½	cup dried currants
2	teaspoons dry mustard		

- Boil celery, pepper, water, and salt. Reduce heat, simmer 10 minutes.
- Add livers, simmer 10 minutes (livers should be slightly pink inside).
- Drain; discard all but livers.
- Place livers in food processor; add all but currants. Blend until smooth.
- Put in bowl, add currants and mix.
- Put in oiled mold (it will firm up in refrigerator).
- Chill at least 4 hours before unmolding.
- Serve with crackers.

Hard boiled eggs will peel easily if cracked and placed in cold water immediately after cooking.

Chicken Pâté

Makes about 3 cups

1½ cups chicken, cooked and finely ground

1 cup almonds, finely chopped

¼ cup green onions or chives, finely chopped

3 tablespoons crystallized ginger, finely chopped

1½ tablespoons soy sauce

1 tablespoon wine vinegar

½ teaspoon Worcestershire sauce

½ cup mayonnaise (may use lowfat mayonnaise)

1 cup sour cream, or plain or lowfat yogurt

- Combine all ingredients, except sour cream and garnish, in a large bowl. Blend thoroughly.
- Cover and refrigerate for 24 hours.
- Shape into crescent, oval or circle (can be frozen at this point).
- Frost with sour cream.
- Garnish with parsley or surround with flowers.
- Serve slightly chilled with crisp crackers.

With lowfat mayonnaise and yogurt, this pâté is a healthy alternative to the traditional liver pâté.

Danish Appetizer Meatballs

Makes about 25 meatballs

Meatballs

¾	pound ground beef	1	10-ounce can
¼	pound sausage		condensed
1	small onion		consommé
½	cup fine dry	¼	teaspoon pepper
	breadcrumbs	⅛	teaspoon marjoram
3	tablespoons	⅛	teaspoon nutmeg
	shortening	2	eggs
1	teaspoon salt	½	cup evaporated milk

Sauce Piquant

1	cup liquid (juices	2	tablespoons flour
	remaining after	3	tablespoons water
	cooking meatballs	2	tablespoons sweet
	plus water; see below)		pickle relish

- To make meatballs, combine all ingredients except consommé and shortening.
- Shape into balls and brown in hot shortening.
- Drain well. Pour consommé over meatballs and simmer 15 minutes.
- Transfer meatballs into a chafing dish.
- For Sauce Piquant, pour all liquid from frying pan into a measuring cup, then add enough water to make 1 cup.
- Heat to boiling.
- Blend 2 tablespoons flour with 3 tablespoons water and stir into hot liquid.
- Cook, stirring, until thickened. Boil 1 minute.
- Stir in sweet pickle relish.
- Pour sauce over meatballs and serve warm.

A classic meatball recipe that is always a favorite.

Shrimp Mold

Makes about 25 servings

1	8-ounce package cream cheese	1	pound shrimp, cooked and chopped
1	3-ounce package cream cheese (may use lowfat)	½	cup celery, finely diced
3	tablespoons mayonnaise-type salad dressing (may use light)	1	onion, finely chopped
		1	green pepper, finely chopped
		2	hard-boiled eggs, diced
½	package gelatin, dissolved in 2 tablespoons cold water		salt and pepper
		2	teaspoons hot sauce (optional)
			parsley

- ◆ Combine all ingredients, except parsley and a few shrimp, and pour into oiled mold.
- ◆ Chill.
- ◆ Decorate with parsley and remaining shrimp.
- ◆ Serve with crackers.

Curry Shrimp Mix

Serves about 12 to 16

1	8-ounce package cream cheese (lowfat)	¼	cup chopped chutney
2	teaspoons curry powder	½	cup sour cream (fat-free)
¼	teaspoon garlic powder salt	1	cup cooked shrimp, cut into small pieces

- ◆ Combine all ingredients.
- ◆ Chill.
- ◆ Serve with crackers or toast points.

Salmon Cheese Ball

Serves 6 to 8

1 7¾-ounce can pink salmon
1 8-ounce package cream cheese
5 ounces mild Cheddar cheese
2 tablespoons onion, minced
1 tablespoon dried parsley flakes
1 tablespoon lemon juice
1 or 2 teaspoons liquid smoke
¾ teaspoon celery salt
½ teaspoon garlic powder
½ cup pecans, chopped

+ Mix together all ingredients, except pecans.
+ Shape into a ball.
+ Chill for several hours.
+ Roll ball in pecans.
+ Serve with crackers.

Marinated Shrimp

Serves 6

2 teaspoons sugar
2 teaspoons salt
½ teaspoon dry mustard
2 tablespoons Worcestershire sauce
¼ cup catsup
½ cup vinegar
½ cup oil
1 small onion, thinly sliced
1 bay leaf
2 pounds shrimp, cooked and cleaned

+ Mix together sugar, salt, mustard, Worcestershire sauce, catsup, vinegar and oil.
+ Put in covered container with shrimp, onion and bay leaf.
+ Marinate at least 24 hours.

Crab Surprises

Makes 40 pieces to serve 15 to 20

5 English muffins
¼ cup butter or margarine, melted
1 5-ounce jar sharp pasteurized process cheese spread
¼ teaspoon garlic powder
½ teaspoon seasoned salt
1½ teaspoons mayonnaise
1 7½-ounce can crabmeat
dash of hot red pepper sauce
parsley flakes

- Preheat oven to 425°.
- Split muffins in half and cut the halves into quarters.
- Mix rest of ingredients (except parsley flakes).
- Spread on muffins and sprinkle with parsley flakes.
- Bake for 15 or 20 minutes.

Can be frozen and reheated in microwave.

Simple Shrimp Spread

Makes about 2 cups

1 8-ounce package cream cheese, softened
¼ cup sour cream
1 tablespoon lemon juice
3 tablespoons green onion, thinly sliced
¼ to ½ teaspoon crushed red pepper flakes
1 tablespoon cream, half-and-half or milk
2 4¼-ounce cans tiny shrimp, drained and rinsed
parsley, chopped

- Beat cream cheese and sour cream until smooth.
- Stir in all other ingredients.
- Add chopped parsley for appearance.

This makes a good dip for vegetables or is excellent as a sandwich or cracker spread. Wonderful with melba toast or cracked pepper crackers.

Snow Stacks

Makes 24 to 30

1 pound white cooking
  chocolate or vanilla
  flavored chips
1 cup salted peanuts

1 cup slim pretzels,
  broken into small
  pieces

- Melt chocolate in microwave.
- Stir in peanuts and pretzels.
- Spoon onto cookie sheet lined with wax paper.

A very quick, delicious snack. Your bridge club will think you worked hours.

Party Orange Sticks

Makes 96

1 loaf white bread, very
  thinly sliced
2 sticks butter, well-
  softened

1 cup sugar
  rind of 2 deep orange-
  colored oranges,
  grated

- Preheat oven to 225°.
- Cream together butter, sugar and orange rind.
- Spread onto bread slices.
- Cut each slice into 4 strips. (Pizza cutter works well.)
- Place on an ungreased cookie sheet.
- Bake for 1 hour, or until bread is browned and crisp.
- Store in airtight container.

These rapidly disappeared at the Symphony League's New Members' Tea.

Hot Buttered Rum for All Winter Long

½ gallon vanilla ice cream
¼ pound butter
1 pound light brown sugar

1 teaspoon ground cloves
1 teaspoon nutmeg
1 teaspoon cinnamon

- Mix well with blender or mixer.
- Store in freezer until ready to serve.
- To make 1 serving, place 3 heaping tablespoons in 1 cup boiling water with 1 shot of your favorite dark rum.

Great for a cold night in front of a roaring fire.

CSOL Tea Party Punch

To serve 20:

2 quarts cranberry cocktail juice
3 quarts unsweetened pineapple juice
1 quart orange juice

1½ cups frozen lemon juice (not concentrate)
2 quarts diet lemon-lime soda
4 teaspoons almond extract, or to taste

To serve 120:

2 gallons cranberry cocktail juice
6 46-ounce cans unsweetened pineapple juice
1 gallon orange juice

4 7½-ounce bottles frozen lemon juice (not concentrate)
3 67-ounce bottles diet lemon-lime soda
2 1-ounce bottles almond extract

- In large punch bowl, mix the ingredients in the order listed.
- Garnish with ice cubes containing fresh mint leaves or strawberries.

"Pièce de Résistance" Cheese Pie

Serves 12

½ cup pecans, coarsely
   chopped
2 tablespoons
   margarine
½ teaspoon salt
1 8-ounce package
   cream cheese,
   softened
2 tablespoons milk
1 2½-ounce jar sliced
   dried beef, cut into
   fine slivers

1 small green pepper,
   diced
2 tablespoons
   dehydrated onion
   flakes
1 teaspoon cream-style
   horseradish
¼ teaspoon coarse black
   pepper
½ cup dairy sour cream

- Preheat oven to 350°.
- In frying pan, melt margarine. Add nuts and salt. Toss lightly for several minutes.
- Remove to sheets of paper toweling. Blot dry and set aside.
- In a medium bowl, blend cream cheese and milk well. Stir in dried beef, green pepper, onion flakes, horseradish and pepper.
- Fold in sour cream.
- Spoon into 8-inch tart pan or small baking dish.
- Top with pecans.
- Just before serving, bake 20 to 25 minutes.
- Serve with party rye bread slices or crackers.

Can be made a day ahead and refrigerated. For large party, double recipe.

Orange Hummus

Makes 24 servings

2 cans (about 2 cups) chickpeas	¼ teaspoon paprika
¼ teaspoon ground cumin	½ cup orange juice
¼ teaspoon ground coriander (can use fresh cilantro)	¼ cup tahini
	1½ to 1¾ teaspoons salt
	1 to 2 tablespoons cider vinegar
¼ teaspoon ground ginger (can use fresh)	3 to 5 medium garlic cloves, crushed
¼ teaspoon dry mustard	3 to 5 scallions, minced (whites and greens)
¼ teaspoon turmeric	1 to 2 teaspoons soy sauce

- Combine all ingredients in a food processor or blender.
- Serve with pita squares.

Different Deviled Eggs

Makes 12 to 24 servings

1 dozen eggs, hard-boiled	¼ teaspoon salt (carefully, to taste, as ranch dressing mix is salty)
4 tablespoons mayonnaise	
1 tablespoon Worcestershire sauce	¼ teaspoon pepper
	paprika
1 teaspoon dry mustard	fresh parsley
4 tablespoons dry ranch dressing mix	dill sprigs

- Slice eggs in half lengthwise and carefully remove yolks.
- Mash yolks, then mix with mayonnaise, Worcestershire sauce, mustard, ranch dressing mix, salt and pepper.
- Stuff egg whites with mixture and garnish with paprika, parsley and dill sprigs.

For picnic, place each half in colorful baking cup.

Mozart's Magic Fruit (Marinated Fruit)

Serves 6 to 8

1½ cups cantaloupe balls
1½ cups honeydew balls
1½ cups fresh pineapple
     chunks
  1 11-ounce can
     mandarin oranges,
     drained
  1 cup fresh
     strawberries,
     stemmed

  1 6-ounce can frozen
     lemonade, thawed
     and undiluted
¼ cup orange
     marmalade
  2 tablespoons orange-
     flavored liqueur
     mint leaves

- Combine cantaloupe, honeydew balls, pineapple chunks, mandarin oranges, and strawberries in a large serving bowl.
- In a small bowl, combine lemonade, marmalade, and liqueur. Stir well.
- Pour over fruit and toss gently.
- Cover and chill 2 hours before serving.
- Garnish with mint leaves.

This is very attractive served in small, stemmed, dessert dishes for brunch or dinner.

Spiced Nuts

Makes 3 to 4 cups

1 egg white	¼ teaspoon salt
1 pound pecan or walnut halves	½ cup sugar
1 tablespoon cold water	½ teaspoon cinnamon

- Preheat oven to 250°.
- Beat egg white slightly. Add water and beat until frothy, but not stiff.
- Fold in nuts.
- Combine sugar, salt and cinnamon. Add to nuts and mix well.
- Spread in buttered 9x13-inch pan.
- Bake for 1 hour.
- Use spatula to remove nuts from pan.
- Place on platter or wax paper.

Stuffed Mushrooms

Makes 18 appetizers

18 medium-size mushrooms butter, melted	¼ cup Parmesan cheese, grated
1 3-ounce package cream cheese, softened	2 tablespoons milk
	18 almond slices

- Preheat oven to 350°.
- Wipe the mushrooms with a damp cloth to clean.
- Remove the stems and brush the caps with butter, inside and out.
- Beat the cream cheese until light, then beat in the Parmesan cheese and milk.
- Fill the mushroom caps with the cheese mixture and top each with a sliced almond.
- Bake for 15 minutes or until lightly browned.

Easy and very tasty.

Marinated Medley

Serves a crowd

Vegetables

1 cauliflower head, cut into bite-size pieces

6 carrots, sliced round

½ pound fresh mushrooms, sliced if large

1 bunch fresh broccoli, cut into bite-size pieces

3 or 4 celery ribs, cut into 1-inch pieces

1 14-ounce can artichoke hearts, drained and cut in fourths

1 6-ounce can ripe olives, drained and pitted

1 9-ounce jar stuffed green olives

1 tablespoon salt cherry tomatoes

Marinade

2 teaspoons garlic juice

¾ cup oil (can use the oil from the olives, if desired)

1 teaspoon black pepper

½ cup red wine vinegar

2 teaspoons dry mustard

2 teaspoons salt

1 tablespoon oregano flakes (not ground)

- To prepare vegetables, bring a large pot of water to boil on stove. Add salt.
- Blanch cauliflower, carrots, mushrooms, broccoli, and celery individually, until crisp-tender. (Each vegetable will take about 2 to 3 minutes, except the mushrooms, which will take about 1 minute.)
- Remove from water and hold.
- Add the artichoke hearts and olives to the drained vegetables.
- Mix all marinade ingredients and pour over vegetables.
- Chill for 24 hours.
- Before serving, garnish with halved cherry tomatoes.

Spinach Crescents

Serves 6 to 8

Filling

1 pound spinach, finely chopped
⅓ cup raisins

¼ cup pine nuts
2 tablespoons oil
1 clove garlic, chopped
½ teaspoon salt

Pastry

2 sheets prepared pastry (can use phyllo, if desired)

1 egg, beaten

- Wash the spinach and cook until tender in a covered pan.
- Drain off excess liquid and chop.
- Cover the raisins with boiling water and simmer for 5 minutes.
- Drain, chop and add to spinach together with the pine nuts.
- Heat the oil in a skillet, add the chopped garlic and sauté until brown.
- Add the spinach mixture and salt and sauté 2 to 3 minutes.
- To prepare pastry, preheat oven to 400°.
- Roll out sheets to ⅛-inch thick and cut into 4-inch rounds.
- Place a tablespoon of spinach mixture in the center of each round, moisten edges of pastry and fold in half. Press edges with a fork to seal.
- Brush with beaten egg.
- Bake for 15 to 20 minutes or until golden brown.

For a lighter pastry, use phyllo. The filling also makes an excellent filling for baked tomatoes.

Red Caviar Dip

Serves 12

1 pint sour cream
1 8-ounce package
   cream cheese, at
   room temperature
½ teaspoon lemon juice

2 teaspoons onion,
   grated
   hot pepper sauce, to
   taste
1 8-ounce jar red caviar

- Blend together the sour cream, cream cheese, lemon juice, onion and hot pepper sauce.
- Carefully fold in the caviar, reserving a little for garnish. Do not crush eggs.
- Serve with crackers.

Crab Canapés

Makes about 30 canapés

1 7½-ounce can
   crabmeat, drained
1 cup Swiss cheese,
   grated
½ cup mayonnaise
1 tablespoon green
   onion

1 teaspoon lemon juice
¼ teaspoon curry
   powder
1 10-biscuit can
   refrigerator biscuits
1 8-ounce can water
   chestnuts, sliced

- Preheat oven to 375°.
- Separate biscuits into 3 layers and place on large ungreased cookie sheet.
- Mix crabmeat, cheese, mayonnaise, onion, lemon juice, and curry powder in a bowl.
- Spoon 1 teaspoon crabmeat mixture onto each biscuit round.
- Top with a slice of water chestnut.
- Bake for 12 minutes or until golden brown.

Mendham Pâté

Serves 20 to 40

1 10½-ounce can beef consommé
1 ¼-ounce envelope plain gelatin
½ pound liverwurst

4 ounces cream cheese
   a bit of onion, grated
2 drops Worcestershire sauce
1 to 2 dashes garlic salt
   green olives, sliced

- Heat consommé and dissolve gelatin in it.
- Oil a mold (approximately 1 quart or less).
- Arrange the sliced olives on the bottom of the mold.
- Pour a thin layer of the consommé on the olives and put in freezer for 5 minutes (until consommé hardens).
- Put liverwurst and cream cheese in blender together with the rest of the consommé and other seasonings. Blend until smooth.
- Pour over hardened olive mixture.
- Chill at least 2 hours.
- Remove from mold before serving.
- Serve with crackers.

This recipe will keep, refrigerated and covered, for 3 weeks.

Porgy's Cheese Roll

Serves 20 to 40

8 ounces goat cheese
8 ounces cream cheese
1 cup black olives,
  chopped

1 tablespoon olive oil
½ teaspoon salt
  paprika
1 cup walnuts, finely
  chopped

- Soften the 2 cheeses.
- Blend with other ingredients, reserving 3 tablespoons of the walnuts. Mixture will be soft.
- Chill slightly, then form into 2 rolls and chill until firm.
- Garnish with reserved walnuts and serve with garlic melba toast.

Hot Crabmeat Dip

Makes approximately 1½ cups

1 tablespoon milk
1 8-ounce package
  cream cheese
1 8-ounce package
  crabmeat (can use
  fresh)

1 tablespoon
  horseradish
1 tablespoon onion,
  finely chopped
1 3-ounce package
  almond slivers
  plain crackers

- Preheat oven to 350°.
- Add milk to the cream cheese and cream.
- Flake the crabmeat into the cream cheese.
- Add horseradish and onion. Mix well.
- Place in a 1-quart casserole.
- Cover with almond slivers.
- Bake for 30 minutes or until hot and bubbly.
- Serve with crackers.

This recipe was submitted by Ed Ritchen, Conductor for the Charleston Symphony Youth Orchestra.

Breads Brunches & Cheese

Angel Biscuits (see photo)

Lemon Blueberry Muffins (see photo)

Lemon and Ginger Muffins (see photo)

Apricot - Almond Coffee Cake

Yummy Apple Pancakes

Plantation Shortcake

Crab Almond Quiche

Cheese Soufflé

Cheese and White Wine Casserole

and More

Sweet Grass Baskets

Sweet grass baskets have been made in Charleston for many generations by the Flower Ladies, a very beloved and respected group of black women. The baskets are made from grasses that grow wild in the Charleston area. Unfortunately, due to development these grasses are becoming more difficult to find. These baskets have their origin in Africa where they are made exactly the same way. To this day, they are only made in Africa and Charleston.

<u>Sunday Brunch</u>

Marinated Fruit

Breakfast Casserole

Country Scalloped Apples and Sausage

Grits and Cheese

Sour Cream Banana Bread

Lemon and Ginger Muffins

Apricot Bread

Makes 1 large loaf

2 3-ounce packages cream cheese, softened
⅓ cup sugar
1 tablespoon all-purpose flour
½ cup dried apricots, chopped

2 eggs
1 teaspoon orange peel, grated
½ cup orange juice
½ cup water
1 17-ounce package quick nut bread mix

- Preheat oven to 350°.
- Combine cream cheese, sugar, and flour.
- Add apricots.
- Beat in 1 egg and the orange peel. Set aside.
- Combine the second egg, slightly beaten, with the orange juice and water. Add this to quick bread mix, stirring until moistened.
- Turn ⅔ of the bread batter into greased and floured 9x5x5-inch loaf pan.
- Pour cheese mixture over top.
- Spoon on remaining batter.
- Bake for 1 hour.
- Cool 10 minutes, then remove from pan.
- When cool, wrap in foil and refrigerate or freeze until ready to serve.

Sour Cream Banana Bread

Makes 1 large loaf

½ stick margarine
1 cup sugar
2 eggs
1 teaspoon vanilla
2 cups flour
1 teaspoon baking
  powder

1 teaspoon baking soda
¾ teaspoon salt
1 cup bananas, mashed
1 cup sour cream
½ to ¾ cup nuts, chopped

- Preheat oven to 350°.
- Cream margarine and sugar.
- Add eggs and vanilla.
- Sift dry ingredients and add quickly. Mix just to combine.
- Add banana, sour cream, and nuts with spoon.
- Spoon into greased loaf pan and bake until a toothpick comes out clean, about 50 minutes for a large loaf.

Slices toast well.

Brown Bread

Makes 1 large loaf

2 cups buttermilk
2 teaspoons baking
  soda
½ cup brown sugar
¼ cup molasses

2 cups graham or whole
  wheat flour
1 teaspoon baking
  powder
1½ cups all-purpose flour
½ teaspoon salt

- Preheat oven to 350°.
- Combine baking soda and buttermilk.
- Mix all ingredients together.
- Pour into greased loaf pan.
- Bake for 1 hour.

Tastes even better a few days later.

Bishop's Bread

Makes 1 large loaf

1½ cups all-purpose flour, sifted
1½ teaspoons baking powder
¼ teaspoon salt
⅔ cup semi-sweet glazed chocolate bits
2 cups walnuts, coarsely chopped
1 cup dates, finely chopped
1 cup candied cherries, halved
3 eggs
1 cup granulated sugar

- Preheat oven to 325°.
- Sift flour, baking powder, and salt.
- Stir in chocolates, walnuts, dates, and cherries until well coated.
- In a large bowl, beat eggs well with mixer.
- Gradually beat in sugar.
- Fold in flour mixture.
- Pour into a greased 10x5x3-inch loaf pan lined with wax paper.
- Bake for 1½ hours, or until done.
- Cool in pan on wire rack.
- Wrap in foil to store or freeze.

Corny Cornbread

Makes 12 squares

2 eggs, beaten
1 8¾-ounce can whole kernel corn, drained
1 8½-ounce can corn, cream-style
8 ounces sour cream
2 8½-ounce boxes cornbread mix
1 stick margarine, melted

- Preheat oven to 350°.
- Mix eggs, corn, and sour cream.
- Add cornbread mix and melted margarine.
- Bake for 35 to 40 minutes in a greased 13x9-inch baking pan.

Blueberry Walnut Bread

Makes 2 large loaves

3 eggs, beaten
2 cups brown sugar
2 teaspoons baking soda
2 cups buttermilk
4 cups flour

2 teaspoons baking powder
6 to 8 ounces fresh blueberries
1 cup walnuts, chopped

- Preheat oven to 350°.
- Combine eggs and brown sugar.
- Dissolve baking soda in buttermilk.
- Sift together flour and baking powder.
- Add buttermilk and flour alternately to sugar and egg mixture.
- Add blueberries and walnuts.
- Pour into 2 greased loaf pans.
- Bake 35 to 45 minutes.

Cornbread from Scratch

Makes 18 2-inch squares

¾ cup yellow cornmeal
⅓ cup self-rising flour
2½ teaspoons baking powder
½ teaspoon salt

2 tablespoons sugar
1 egg
1 cup milk
2 tablespoons corn oil

- Preheat oven to 425°.
- Mix together all dry ingredients.
- In separate bowl, mix milk and egg. Add to dry mixture.
- Add oil and mix.
- Grease an 8x10-inch pan. Heat pan in oven before adding mixture.
- Bake for 20 minutes.

Honey Wheat Bread

Makes 3 loaves

2 ¼-ounce envelopes
  active dry yeast
4 cups very warm water
3 tablespoons honey
1 tablespoon butter or
  margarine

1 tablespoon salt
5 cups bread flour
5 cups whole wheat
  flour

- Sprinkle yeast over very warm water (comfortably warm when dropped on the wrist). Stir to dissolve.
- Stir in honey and butter.
- Let stand until bubbly.
- Stir in salt, 1 cup bread flour and 1 cup whole wheat flour. Stir well.
- Continue adding flour until 10 cups have been used.
- Turn out on lightly floured surface and knead 10 minutes, until dough is smooth and elastic.
- Place in large greased bowl, turning to bring greased side up.
- Cover and let rise 45 minutes to an hour.
- Punch down and divide into 3 parts.
- Pat out each part to make a 12x8-inch rectangle.
- Roll up from the short end and place in greased 8x4x3-inch pans.
- Cut slashes, 1 inch deep, on top of loaves.
- Cover and let rise in a warm place for about 10 minutes.
- Bake loaves in 400° preheated oven for 15 minutes.
- Lower heat to 350° and continue baking for about 30 minutes, or until the bread sounds hollow when tapped.
- Remove from pans.

Pumpkin Bread

Makes 3 large loaves

3⅓ cups flour
3 cups sugar
2 teaspoons baking soda
1½ teaspoons salt
1 teaspoon cinnamon
1 teaspoon nutmeg
1 cup oil
4 eggs
2 cups pumpkin pie filling
⅔ cup water

- Preheat oven to 350°.
- Sift together all of the dry ingredients.
- Make a well and add the remaining ingredients. Mix thoroughly.
- Grease and flour 3 large aluminum foil loaf pans.
- Fill each pan ⅔ full.
- Bake for 60 to 75 minutes, or until a toothpick inserted in the middle comes out clean.
- Let cool and wrap in foil.
- Freezes well.

This is great as a dessert if topped with vanilla ice cream or yogurt.

Spoon Bread

Serves 6

2 cups water
1 cup ground cornmeal
1 teaspoon salt
2 tablespoons butter or margarine
3 eggs, separated
1 cup milk

- Preheat oven to 400°.
- Combine water and cornmeal in saucepan.
- Cook mixture over low heat, stirring constantly until thick.
- Remove from heat and add butter.
- Combine egg yolks and milk and add to mixture.
- Fold in egg whites.
- Pour in buttered 4-quart baking dish.
- Bake for 25 minutes or until center is done.

Orange Bread

Makes 1 loaf

2 tablespoons butter or margarine, melted
¾ cup orange juice
2 tablespoons orange peel, grated
½ cup dates, finely chopped
1 cup sugar
1 egg, slightly beaten
½ cup pecans, coarsely chopped
2 cups all-purpose flour, sifted
½ teaspoon baking soda
1 teaspoon baking powder
½ teaspoon salt

- Preheat oven to 350°.
- Combine butter, orange juice, orange peel, dates, sugar, egg, and pecans.
- Mix and sift remaining ingredients.
- Stir together and mix well.
- Turn into greased loaf pan.
- Bake for 50 minutes, or until done.

Freezes well.

One pound of coffee makes forty five cups. Two pounds of butter will butter one hundred rolls. One bushel of potatoes, mashed or boiled, will serve one hundred twenty five to one hundred and forty people.

Pinch Bread

Makes 1 large round loaf

1	cup milk, scalded	4½	cups flour
½	cup shortening	1	cup brown sugar
½	cup sugar	1 to 2	teaspoons cinnamon
1	teaspoon salt	½	cup walnuts or
2	¼-ounce packages		pecans, chopped
	yeast	1	stick butter or
2	eggs, beaten		margarine, melted

- Combine milk, shortening, sugar, and salt until the shortening is melted. Cool until lukewarm.
- Soften yeast in this mixture.
- Add beaten eggs and then the flour.
- Knead until smooth (about 5 to 7 minutes).
- Place dough in a large greased bowl, turn, and cover with plastic wrap.
- Let rise until double (about 1 hour).
- Punch down dough and divide into egg-size pieces (about 32).
- Combine brown sugar, cinnamon, and walnuts.
- Roll each piece of dough in melted butter or margarine and then the brown sugar mixture.
- Put in 2 layers in a tube pan.
- Let rise until double in size (about 1 hour).
- Bake at 350° for 40 minutes.

If the tube in the pan is removable, line the pan with foil to keep the butter from dripping out of the pan.

Irish Soda Bread

Serves 8

2 cups all-purpose flour, sifted
½ teaspoon baking soda
2 teaspoons baking powder
1 tablespoon sugar
½ teaspoon salt

3 tablespoons butter or margarine, softened
¼ cup raisins
¼ cup currants
2 teaspoons caraway seeds
1 cup buttermilk or sour milk

- Preheat oven to 350°.
- Sift the flour, baking soda, baking powder, sugar, and salt together.
- Cut in butter or margarine.
- Add raisins, currants, caraway seeds, and milk. Mix thoroughly.
- Knead on a floured breadboard for 2 to 3 minutes.
- Spread evenly in greased 9-inch pie pan. Cut a cross on top with sharp, floured knife.
- Bake for 30 to 45 minutes or until golden brown.

Serve warm with butter and a cup of tea.

Yogurt Bread

Makes 2 loaves

2 cups warm water (105° to 110°)	½ teaspoon salt
2 tablespoons dry granular yeast	1 cup plain, fat-free yogurt
¼ teaspoon ground ginger	2 cups oat bran
2 tablespoons molasses or honey	¼ cup wheat germ
	5 cups unbleached all-purpose flour

- Mix together water, yeast, ginger and molasses or honey.
- Let stand for 5 minutes.
- Add salt and yogurt, mix thoroughly.
- Add oat bran, wheat germ, and flour.
- Knead dough until firm and elastic, about 10 minutes.
- Divide dough and put in 2 well-greased 8x4x3-inch bread pans.
- Cover and let rise until dough is to top of pans (30 minutes to 1½ hours).
- Uncover and bake at 350° for 45 minutes.

Angel Biscuits

Makes 7 to 8 dozen

1 ¼-ounce package dry yeast
2 tablespoons warm water
⅓ cup powdered sugar

5 cups all-purpose flour
1 teaspoon salt
1 teaspoon soda
1 cup shortening
2 cups buttermilk

- Dissolve yeast in warm water.
- Sift flour with other dry ingredients.
- Cut in shortening.
- Mix yeast mixture with buttermilk, then mix in dry ingredients.
- Knead only a few times. Cover and let rise until doubled.
- Roll out and cut with 1½-inch biscuit cutter.
- Bake at 400° for 15 minutes.

You may bake for 8 minutes, then cool and freeze. Later, thaw and bake for another 8 minutes.

Cinnamon Buns

Makes 16 buns

1 8-ounce package crescent rolls	½ cup nuts, chopped (optional)
¼ cup butter, softened	½ cup powdered sugar
4 teaspoons sugar	1 tablespoon milk
2 teaspoons cinnamon	

- Preheat oven to 375°.
- Open and separate crescent rolls.
- Brush thoroughly with butter.
- Combine sugar and cinnamon.
- Sprinkle rolls with sugar mixture.
- Place 1 heaping teaspoon of nuts on wide end of dough.
- Roll up, starting at wide end.
- When roll is complete, pinch ends together.
- Cut each roll to make 2 small buns.
- Bake on cookie sheet for approximately 10 to 12 minutes.
- Blend powdered sugar with milk.
- Top warm buns with sugar icing.

Lowfat Popovers

Makes 12 muffins

1 cup flour	1 teaspoon cinnamon
2 teaspoons orange zest (or lemon zest)	1 cup skim milk
2 teaspoons poppy seeds	3 egg whites
	1 tablespoon oil

- Preheat oven to 450°.
- Whisk together all ingredients.
- Pour batter into greased muffin tins.
- Bake at 450° for 15 minutes.
- Reduce heat to 350° and bake for another 30 minutes.

Danish Puffs

Makes 12 to 15

Bread

2 sticks butter, divided	1 cup boiling water
2 cups all-purpose flour, sifted and divided	1 teaspoon almond extract
2 tablespoons cold water	3 eggs

Icing

2 cups confectioners' sugar, sifted	⅛ teaspoon salt
1 teaspoon butter	1 teaspoon vanilla
4 tablespoons cream or milk	almond slivers

- Preheat oven to 400°.
- Cut 1 stick butter into 1 cup flour until it resembles coarse meal.
- Add cold water and stir until well-blended (May use hands to mix).
- Divide dough in half.
- Press each half into 3x12-inch strip and put on ungreased cookie sheet.
- Combine boiling water and remaining stick of butter in saucepan and bring to a boil.
- Add almond extract.
- Remove from heat.
- Stir in remaining cup of flour.
- Add eggs, 1 at a time, beating well after each addition.
- Spread over dough.
- Bake for 35 to 45 minutes. Dough will puff up, then fall.
- For icing, combine confectioners' sugar with butter, cream, salt and vanilla. Frost while hot.
- Decorate with almond slivers.

Cheese-Filled Rolls

Makes 10 rolls

½ cup walnuts, finely chopped
2 tablespoons Parmesan cheese, grated
1 tablespoon basil leaves
1 10-ounce can flaky biscuits

1 4-ounce package provolone or mozzarella cheese, cut into ten ¾-inch cubes
3 to 4 tablespoons margarine, melted

- Preheat oven to 375°.
- Combine nuts, Parmesan cheese, and basil. Blend well and set aside.
- Separate dough into 10 biscuits.
- Partially split each biscuit horizontally.
- Insert 1 cube of cheese into the center of each biscuit. Firmly press edges together to seal in cheese.
- Dip biscuit in margarine then roll in nut mixture, lightly pressing nuts into the dough.
- Place in 10 ungreased muffin cups.
- Bake for 12 to 16 minutes, until golden brown.

Lemon Blueberry Muffins

Makes 24 large muffins

2 cups all-purpose flour, unsifted
2/3 cup sugar
1 teaspoon baking powder
1 teaspoon baking soda
1/2 teaspoon salt
    pinch of ground cloves
2 cups fresh blueberries
1/2 stick butter
1 8-ounce container plain, lowfat yogurt
1 large egg
2 teaspoons lemon rind, grated
1 teaspoon lemon extract
1 teaspoon vanilla extract

- Preheat oven to 375°.
- Combine, flour, sugar, baking powder, baking soda, salt and cloves.
- Add blueberries and toss to coat with flour mixture. Set aside.
- Melt butter and let cool.
- Mix butter, yogurt, egg, lemon rind, and extracts. Combine with dry ingredients.
- Stir until moistened. Do not overmix.
- Fill well-greased large muffin pans and bake for 20 to 25 minutes.
- Sprinkle with granulated sugar and remove from pan when cool.

Lemon and Ginger Muffins

Makes 12 regular or 48 miniature muffins

½ cup butter
1 cup plus 2
  tablespoons sugar
2 large eggs
2 tablespoons ginger
  root, peeled and
  chopped

2 tablespoons lemon
  rind, grated
1 teaspoon baking soda
1 cup buttermilk
2 cups flour
¼ cup lemon juice

- Preheat oven to 375°.
- Grease muffin cups.
- Beat butter and 1 cup sugar until fluffy.
- Beat in eggs, 1 at a time.
- Add ginger and lemon rind.
- Stir baking soda into buttermilk.
- Fold flour into ginger mixture alternately with buttermilk.
- Scoop into greased muffin tins.
- Bake 15 to 20 minutes, depending on size of muffin cups.
- Mix lemon juice and 2 tablespoons sugar together while muffins bake.
- Stir until sugar dissolves.
- Cool muffins 3 to 5 minutes in pan.
- Remove muffins from pan and dip tops and bottoms in lemon juice mixture.

Raisin Bran Muffins

Makes 4 to 5 dozen muffins

1 15-ounce box raisin bran cereal	4 eggs, beaten
3 cups sugar	1 cup vegetable oil
5 cups flour	1 quart buttermilk
5 teaspoons baking soda	½ cup apricots, chopped
1 teaspoon salt	½ cup dates, chopped
	1 cup pecans, chopped

- Preheat oven to 350°.
- In an extra large bowl, combine raisin bran, sugar, flour, baking soda, and salt.
- Add eggs, oil, and buttermilk. Mix well.
- Fold in fruits and pecans.
- Pour into containers and store in refrigerator until ready to use.
- When ready to bake, spoon into greased muffin pans. Fill ⅔ full.
- Bake 20 to 30 minutes, or until they are a deep golden brown.

This is also good using dried fruit bits instead of the apricots and dates.

Sweet Potato Muffins

Makes 36 muffins

1¼ cups sweet potatoes, mashed	1 cup raisins
2 cups sugar	½ cup walnuts
1½ cups oil	½ cup pecans
4 eggs	½ cup confectioners' sugar
3 cups flour	dash nutmeg
2 teaspoons cinnamon	

- Preheat oven to 350°.
- Combine sweet potatoes, sugar, oil, and eggs in bowl. Mix well.
- Add flour and cinnamon. Mix just until moistened.
- Fold in raisins, walnuts and pecans.
- Fill buttered muffin cups ¾ full.
- Bake for 15 to 20 minutes.
- Cool slightly and sprinkle each muffin with powdered sugar.
- Top each muffin with a dash of nutmeg.

Anything that grows underground--potatoes, beets, carrots, etc.--should be put on to cook in cold water. Anything that grows above ground--peas, beans, etc.-- should be started in boiling water.

Apricot-Almond Coffeecake

Serves 12

2	sticks butter	¼	teaspoon salt
2	cups sugar	1	8-ounce carton sour cream
2	large eggs		
1	teaspoon almond extract	1	cup sliced almonds (or pecans)
2	cups all-purpose flour	1	10-ounce jar apricot preserves
1	teaspoon baking powder		

* Preheat oven to 350°.
* Beat butter at medium speed with electric mixer for about 2 minutes, or until creamy.
* Gradually add sugar, beating at medium speed for 5 to 7 minutes.
* Add eggs, 1 at a time, beating just until yellow disappears.
* Stir in almond extract.
* Combine flour, baking powder and salt.
* Add flour mixture to butter mixture alternately with sour cream, beginning and ending with flour. Mix at low speed, just until blended, after each addition.
* Place about ⅓ of the batter into a greased and floured 12-cup Bundt pan.
* Sprinkle with half of the almonds and dot with half of the apricot preserves.
* Top with remaining batter, sprinkle with remaining almonds and dot with remaining preserves.
* Bake for 55 minutes, or until a wooden pick inserted in the center comes out clean.
* Cool 20 to 30 minutes, then remove from pan and let cool completely on a wire rack. Handle gently while warm.

Freezes well.

Sour Cream Coffeecake with Macadamia and Coconut Streusel

Serves 10 to 12

Cake

¾ cup butter
1¼ cups sugar
2 eggs
2½ cups all-purpose flour
2 teaspoons baking powder
1 teaspoon baking soda
½ teaspoon salt
1½ cups sour cream
2 teaspoons orange zest, grated

Streusel

¼ cup flour
¼ cup butter
½ cup sugar
1 cup macadamia nuts, chopped (unsalted or with the salt rinsed off)
1¼ cups coconut, shredded

- Preheat oven to 375°.
- Cream butter and sugar.
- Beat in eggs.
- Mix together flour, baking powder, baking soda, and salt.
- Add to butter mixture and blend well. Do not beat.
- Stir in sour cream and orange zest.
- For the streusel, cream together the flour, butter, and sugar.
- Toast the coconut in the oven for 10 minutes.
- Reduce oven temperature to 350°.
- Mix the creamed mixture with the coconut and nuts.
- Spread half the batter in a 10-inch Bundt pan, greased and lightly floured.
- Distribute half the streusel on top.
- Add remaining batter and distribute remaining streusel on top.
- Bake for about 50 minutes, or until a toothpick comes out clean.

Crumb Cake

Makes 36 to 40 squares

Cake

½ cup butter, softened
¾ cup sugar
2 eggs
2 teaspoons vanilla
2 cups flour

4 teaspoons baking powder
¼ teaspoon salt
1 cup milk

Topping

1 cup butter
1 cup sugar

3 cups flour
2 teaspoons cinnamon

- Preheat oven to 350°.
- Cream butter and sugar.
- Add eggs and vanilla.
- Mix together flour, baking powder, and salt.
- Add dry mixture and milk alternately to the butter mixture and beat well.
- Pour into a greased 9x13-inch pan.
- For topping, mix together all topping ingredients until coarse and add to top of cake.
- Bake for 35 to 40 minutes.

Cinnamon French Toast

Makes 6 slices

2 eggs
¼ cup milk
1 tablespoon sugar
1 teaspoon cinnamon

1 small, uncut loaf cinnamon swirl bread from the deli
margarine for frying

- Beat eggs, milk, sugar, and cinnamon in shallow bowl.
- Cut cinnamon loaf into 1-inch slices.
- Dip the slices into egg mixture.
- In large frying pan, brown each side in hot, melted margarine over medium-high heat.
- Serve immediately with maple syrup.

Aunt Lucy's Pineapple Crumb Cake

Serves 10 to 12

Cake

2 cups butter (or margarine)
2 cups sugar
5 eggs
2 teaspoons baking powder

1 pound graham cracker crumbs
½ cup milk
1 cup coconut
1 teaspoon vanilla
1 cup pecans, chopped

Filling

½ cup butter (or margarine)
1 16-ounce box confectioners' sugar

1 8-ounce can crushed pineapple, drained
1 cup pecans, chopped
1 teaspoon vanilla

- Preheat oven to 275°.
- Cream butter and sugar.
- Add eggs, 1 at a time, beating after each addition.
- Add remaining ingredients and mix well.
- Bake in 3 greased and floured 9-inch cake pans for 30 minutes, or until done.
- Let cool on racks.
- For filling, cream butter and sugar.
- Add drained pineapple, chopped pecans, and vanilla.
- Spread between layers of cake.

Yummy Apple Pancake

Serves 4

Pancake

½ cup milk
2 eggs
½ cup flour

¼ teaspoon salt
1 tablespoon butter

Topping

¼ cup brown sugar,
    packed
1 tablespoon butter
½ teaspoon vanilla

1½ cups apples, thinly
     sliced
¼ cup walnuts, chopped
¼ cup raisins

+ Preheat oven to 450°.
+ Combine milk, eggs, flour, and salt.
+ Heat heavy, ovenproof 9-inch skillet in oven until very hot.
+ Add butter to coat skillet.
+ Pour in batter immediately.
+ Bake on lowest rack at 450° for 10 minutes.
+ Reduce to 350° and bake another 10 minutes.
+ For topping, melt butter and sugar on top of stove.
+ Add vanilla and other ingredients.
+ Cook until apples soften.
+ Pour apple mixture over pancakes.
+ Cut into wedges and serve.

Gingerbread Waffles with Lemon Sauce

Makes 16 squares

Waffles

¼ cup butter or margarine

½ cup brown sugar, packed

½ cup molasses

2 eggs, separated

1 cup milk

2 cups flour

1½ teaspoons baking powder

1 teaspoon cinnamon

1 teaspoon ground ginger

½ teaspoon ground cloves

¼ teaspoon salt

Lemon Sauce

3 eggs

1 cup sugar

¼ cup lemon juice

1 teaspoon lemon rind, grated

dash salt

2 tablespoons butter or margarine, melted

- Cream butter and brown sugar.
- Beat in molasses, egg yolks, and milk.
- Add flour, baking powder, cinnamon, ginger, cloves, and salt.
- Beat egg whites until stiff. Fold into creamed mixture.
- Bake in preheated waffle iron.
- To prepare sauce, combine all ingredients in top of double boiler.
- Cook, stirring over simmering water for about 15 minutes, until slightly thickened.
- Serve warm or cool.

Excellent when served with butter and syrup.

Pancakes from Scratch

Makes about 2 dozen

2 cups flour, sifted	3 tablespoons butter or
3½ teaspoons baking	shortening, melted
powder	1 egg
1¾ cups milk	1 teaspoon salt
	3 tablespoons sugar

- Sift flour, baking powder, salt, and sugar together in bowl.
- Put egg in another bowl and beat for about ½ minute.
- Add milk to beaten egg and pour over dry ingredients.
- Beat only until well blended, about ½ minute. Scrape bowl often.
- Quickly blend in melted and cooled butter.
- Bake on preheated griddle, turning only once to brown on both sides.

For thinner pancakes, use 2 cups milk.

For apple pancakes, sift ½ teaspoon cinnamon with flour and add 1 cup finely chopped pared apple.

Brunch Casserole

Serves 12

4 cups bread cubes, firm white or French
2 cups Cheddar cheese, shredded
⅓ cup onion, chopped
¼ cup green pepper, chopped
1 4½-ounce jar mushrooms, sliced
½ cup tomatoes, peeled and chopped

10 eggs, beaten
4 cups milk
1 tablespoon parsley, chopped
1 teaspoon dry mustard
¼ teaspoon onion powder
¼ teaspoon pepper
8 to 10 slices bacon, cooked and crumbled

- Arrange bread cubes in bottom of a well-greased 9x13-inch baking dish.
- Layer cheese, onion, green pepper, mushrooms, and tomatoes on top of bread.
- Combine remaining ingredients, except bacon. Mix well.
- Pour egg mixture over bread and cheese layers.
- Sprinkle bacon evenly over top.
- Cover and refrigerate overnight, or up to 24 hours.
- Remove cover.
- Bake at 325° for 50 to 60 minutes, or until center is set.
- Allow to stand 5 minutes before serving.

Country Escalloped Apples and Sausage

Makes 8 to 10 servings

3 pounds Granny Smith or McIntosh apples	1 cup granulated sugar
¾ cup butter, melted	1 cup brown sugar
1 teaspoon cinnamon	2 cups fine breadcrumbs
2 pounds small sausage links	

- Preheat oven to 350°.
- Generously grease a deep 4-quart casserole with melted butter.
- Peel apples and cut into 1-inch slices.
- Combine sugars.
- Brown sausage and blot all grease.
- Layer about ⅓ of apples, cinnamon, sausage, sugars, and breadcrumbs.
- Repeat layering 2 more times, ending with a "spoke" of sausages covered with sugar and cinnamon.
- Bake, covered, for 20 minutes.
- Uncover and continue baking until apples are soft, about 25 minutes.

Aunt Helen's Quiche

Serves 6

1 cup Swiss cheese, grated	4 eggs
8 slices bacon, cooked and crumbled	½ cup biscuit baking mix
⅓ cup onion, chopped	⅛ teaspoon salt
2 cups milk	⅛ teaspoon fresh black pepper

- Preheat oven to 350°.
- Sprinkle cheese, bacon, and onions in the bottom of a well-greased 9-inch pie tin or quiche pan.
- Blend rest of ingredients in blender and pour over bacon mixture.
- Bake for 50 to 55 minutes.

Crab Almond Quiche

Serves 6

Pie Crust
+ Make pastry for a 9-inch pie shell or use a deep-dish, frozen pie crust, thawed for 20 minutes.

Quiche Filling
1 cup (¼ pound) Swiss cheese, shredded
½ pound fresh crabmeat, with cartilage removed
2 green onions, thinly sliced
3 large eggs, beaten
1 cup half-and-half
½ teaspoon salt
½ teaspoon lemon rind, grated
⅛ teaspoon dry mustard
⅛ teaspoon white pepper
⅛ teaspoon mace
¼ cup almonds, sliced

+ Preheat oven to 400°.
+ Sprinkle Swiss cheese in pastry shell.
+ Place crabmeat on top of cheese.
+ Sprinkle green onion over crabmeat.
+ Combine beaten eggs, half-and-half, salt, lemon rind, dry mustard, pepper, and mace in a small bowl. Mix well with a whisk or egg beater.
+ Pour over ingredients in pie shell and flute edge of shell.
+ Sprinkle almonds on top.
+ Bake for 10 minutes.
+ Reduce temperature to 325° and bake about 45 minutes longer, or until set in center.
+ Let stand for 10 minutes before serving.

Serve with marinated fruit and rolls for brunch.

Spinach Quiche

Serves 6

1	large onion, chopped	5	eggs, beaten
1	tablespoon vegetable oil	3	cups (12 ounces) cheese, shredded (white or yellow)
1	10-ounce package frozen chopped spinach, thawed and pressed dry		salt and pepper to taste

- Preheat oven to 350°.
- Sauté onion in oil.
- Add spinach and cook out excess moisture. Cool.
- Combine eggs, cheese, salt, and pepper, and stir into spinach mixture.
- Pour into a greased 9-inch pie plate.
- Bake for 30 minutes, or until set.

Optional: Add sautéed mushrooms or drained can of mushrooms plus chopped parsley and chives, if desired.

Green Onion Tart

Serves 6 to 8

1 cup biscuit baking mix	1 egg
⅓ cup milk	½ cup milk
2 cups green onions, sliced	½ teaspoon salt
1 tablespoon butter	dash of hot pepper sauce
1 8-ounce package cream cheese	

- Preheat oven to 350°.
- Mix biscuit mix with ⅓ cup of milk and pat on bottom and sides of well greased 8-inch pie plate.
- Cook green onions in butter until wilted.
- Beat cream cheese, egg, milk, salt, and hot pepper sauce together until smooth.
- Put onions in biscuit shell and pour cheese mixture over them.
- Bake for 35 minutes or until knife comes out clean.

To ripen tomatoes, put them in a brown paper bag.
Putting an apple in the bag will speed the process.

Breakfast Casserole

Serves 6 to 8

1	pound pork sausage	5	eggs
1	6-ounce box cheese croutons (may use plain)	2	cups milk
		1	teaspoon salt
		1	teaspoon dry mustard
1¼	cups Cheddar cheese, shredded and divided		

- Cook sausage until well done. Drain on paper towels.
- Spread croutons over bottom of 10x10x2-inch pan.
- Sprinkle sausage over croutons.
- Top with ½ cup cheese.
- Beat eggs, milk, salt, and dry mustard together and pour over sausage.
- Sprinkle remaining cheese on top.
- Chill overnight.
- Bake at 350° for 45 minutes or until lightly browned.

Cheese and White Wine Casserole

Serves 6

6	tablespoons butter, softened	½	pound Gruyère cheese, grated
1	clove garlic, crushed	½	cup dry white wine
6	slices white bread	1½	cups chicken bouillon
6	eggs	1	teaspoon paprika
½	cup heavy cream	¼	teaspoon dry mustard

- Preheat oven to 350°.
- Cream together the butter and garlic.
- Trim crust from bread. Spread bread with garlic mixture.
- Arrange in a 9x13-inch casserole dish, butter side down.
- Beat eggs until foamy, then beat in cream.
- Add cheese to egg mixture.
- Stir in wine, bouillon, paprika, and dry mustard.
- Pour over bread. Bake for 40 minutes or until puffed and brown.
- Serve immediately.

Plantation Shortcake

Serves 6 to 8

Shortcake

1 10-ounce package cornbread mix	2 teaspoons prepared mustard
1 8¾-ounce can cream-style corn	1 3-ounce can mushrooms, drained
1½ cups Swiss cheese, shredded and divided	1 14-ounce can artichoke hearts, drained and chopped
2 eggs, slightly beaten	
2 tablespoons milk	

Cream Sauce

2 tablespoons butter or margarine	2 egg yolks, slightly beaten
2 tablespoons flour	1 cup chicken or turkey, cooked and cubed
¾ cup chicken broth, warmed	1 cup ham, cooked and cubed
¾ cup half-and-half	

- Preheat oven to 350°.
- Grease an 8-inch square pan.
- In medium bowl, mix cornbread mix, corn, ½ cup cheese, eggs, milk, and mustard.
- Spread 1 cup batter in baking pan.
- In another bowl, mix artichokes, mushrooms, and remaining cheese. Spoon over batter in baking pan.
- Top with remaining cornbread batter.
- Bake for 35 minutes, or until cornbread is golden brown and has pulled away from sides of dish.
- Let stand for 10 minutes before cutting into squares.
- While cornbread is baking, make cream sauce.
- In medium saucepan, melt butter or margarine.
- Blend in flour.

Continued on next page

- Add chicken broth and half-and-half. Stir constantly over medium-high heat until mixture thickens and bubbles.
- Slowly blend ¾ cup sauce into beaten egg yolks. Mix well.
- Add egg yolk mixture to hot sauce.
- Stir in chicken and ham. Stir constantly over medium-high heat until heated through.
- Keep warm.
- Ladle sauce over cornbread squares.

Cheese Soufflé

Serves 4

2 tablespoons butter	½ cup sharp Cheddar
2 tablespoons flour	cheese, grated
1 cup milk	⅛ teaspoon paprika
½ teaspoon salt, divided	1 teaspoon
⅛ teaspoon pepper	Worcestershire sauce
3 eggs, separated	

- Preheat oven to 350°.
- Melt butter in saucepan over low heat.
- Blend in flour, ¼ teaspoon salt, and pepper.
- Add milk all at once. Cook quickly, stirring constantly, until mixture thickens and bubbles.
- Reduce heat and stir in beaten egg yolks, cheese, ¼ teaspoon salt, paprika, and Worcestershire sauce.
- Cook until well-blended. Cool.
- Whip egg whites until stiff.
- Fold egg whites into cheese mixture.
- Place in an ungreased 7-inch soufflé dish.
- Bake for 40 minutes.

Egg and Sausage Bake

Serves 8 to 10

¼	pound sharp Cheddar cheese, sliced	1	teaspoon salt
¼	pound sharp Cheddar cheese, grated	½	cup sour cream
½	teaspoon dry mustard	1	pound sausage, cooked and drained
½	teaspoon paprika	10	eggs

- Preheat oven to 325°.
- Cover bottom of a 9x13-inch baking dish with the sliced cheese.
- Mix mustard, paprika, and salt with the sour cream.
- Pour half of this mixture over the cheese.
- Spread sausage over top of this mixture.
- Break each egg into a small cup or dish and gently slide on top of sausage.
- Spoon on remaining sour cream mixture.
- Sprinkle grated cheese on top.
- Bake for 20 to 25 minutes.

Four tablespoons equals one fourth cup. There are three teaspoons in a tablespoon.

Blintz Casserole

Serves 12

Batter

2 sticks butter, melted	3 teaspoons baking
½ cup sugar	powder
2 eggs	¼ cup milk
1 cup flour	1 teaspoon vanilla

Filling

1 pound cottage cheese	½ cup sugar
1 pound cream cheese	juice of 1 lemon
2 eggs	rind of 1 lemon,
	grated

◆ Preheat oven to 300°.
◆ Combine batter ingredients and mix well. Set aside.
◆ In another bowl, mix the filling ingredients until blended, but not smooth.
◆ Pour half of the batter into a greased 9x13-inch baking dish.
◆ Spoon on all of the filling.
◆ Cover with the remaining batter.
◆ Bake until golden, 1 to 1½ hours.

Penland Granola

Makes approximately 3 quarts

4 cups old-fashioned oats	½ cup sesame seeds
1 cup wheat germ	½ cup bran
1 cup walnuts, cashews, pecans or almonds	¼ pound flax seed
	⅓ cup ground roasted soy beans
1 cup whole sunflower seeds	⅓ cup hot oil
	⅓ cup hot honey
	½ teaspoon vanilla

- Preheat oven to 350°.
- Pour hot oil and honey over grains. Mix well.
- Pour mixture into large roasting pan.
- Bake approximately 20 minutes, or until light brown. Do not overbake.
- Stir frequently, so it will brown evenly.
- Store in airtight containers.

This is great for breakfast or served over ice cream, yogurt or cottage cheese.

Porridge

1 cup stoneground whole wheat flour	10 large dates, chopped
1 quart water	3 tablespoons almonds, cut
pinch of salt	

- Add salt to water and boil.
- Lower heat and add flour, stir with a whisk until desired thickness.
- Add dates and almonds.
- Cook 20 minutes on low heat, stirring occasionally.
- Serve warm.

This recipe was submitted by Herbert Blomstedt, Music Director of the San Francisco Symphony Orchestra.

Saucy Shrimp Quiche

Serves 6 to 8

1 9-inch deep-dish frozen pie shell	1 cup cream (or half-and-half)
1 4 to 5-ounce can shrimp, drained	3 eggs, beaten
1½ cups Swiss cheese, shredded and divided	1 teaspoon lemon rind, grated
½ cup sour cream	½ teaspoon salt
	paprika

- Preheat oven to 375°.
- Arrange shrimp in bottom of thawed pastry shell.
- Sprinkle with 1 cup of the cheese.
- Combine sour cream with cream and stir with fork until smooth.
- Stir in eggs, lemon rind, and salt.
- Pour into pie shell.
- Sprinkle with remaining cheese and a little paprika.
- Place on cookie sheet on lower oven shelf. Bake 30 to 35 minutes or until knife comes out clean.

When recipe calls for adding raw eggs to a hot mixture, always begin by adding a small amount of hot mixture to the beaten eggs to avoid curdling.

Soups, Sandwiches & Salads

She Crab Soup (see photo)

Shrimp Bisque

Taco Twist Soup

Seafood Chowder

Sassy Black Bean Soup

Chutney Gazpacho

Italian Sausage Broil

Tea Garden Salad

Mango Salad

CSOL Broccoli Slad

and More

Lowcountry Marsh

You know you are in the lowcountry when surrounded by scenes like

this. These wetlands offer a natural beauty that cannot be found

elsewhere. Because these are tidal marshes this beauty changes

continually. Also, the wetlands provide an important food source for

man and wildlife and many recreational opportunities.

A Soup Luncheon for a Winter's Day

Potato Cheese Soup

Taco Twist Soup

Seafood Chowder

Mango Salad

Cornbread From Scratch

Irish Soda Bread

Pecan - Brown Sugar Poundcake

She-Crab Soup

Serves 4

½ stick butter
1 small onion, chopped
1 small stalk celery, chopped
2 tablespoons flour
½ pound claw crabmeat, fresh

1 pint half-and-half and ½ pint milk OR 1 pint milk and ½ pint heavy cream
1 teaspoon Worcestershire sauce
¼ cup dry sherry
salt and pepper to taste

- Sauté onion and celery in butter until clear.
- Add flour and crabmeat. Stir.
- Add milk and stir well.
- Simmer, but do not boil, for 20 to 25 minutes.
- Add Worcestershire sauce, sherry, salt, and pepper.
- Simmer about 5 minutes more.

Crab Stew

Serves 2

2 tablespoons vegetable oil	2 fresh tomatoes, seeded and chopped, or 1 can plum tomatoes
3 tablespoons all-purpose flour	
1 onion, chopped	1 8-ounce bottle clam juice
1 small green pepper, chopped	⅓ cup scallions, thinly sliced
1 carrot, finely chopped or grated	½ pound lump crabmeat
1 stalk celery, finely chopped	salt and pepper to taste

- In large, heavy saucepan, combine oil and flour. Cook over low heat, stirring constantly, for 8 to 10 minutes or until a deep caramel color.
- Add onion, pepper, carrot, and celery. Cook until softened.
- Add clam juice, tomatoes, and 1 cup water.
- Bring to a boil.
- Reduce heat and simmer gently for 15 to 20 minutes or until thickened.
- Stir in crabmeat. Add salt and pepper to taste.
- Stew for 5 minutes.
- Stir in scallions.
- Serve over rice.

Ellen's Oyster Spinach Potage

Serves 8

2 cups milk
2 10¾-ounce cans condensed cream of chicken soup
2 9 or 10-ounce packages frozen creamed spinach or broccoli

2 8-ounce cans oysters, undrained
1 cup dry white wine
¼ teaspoon white pepper
1 lemon, sliced thin

- Stir milk into soup.
- Add vegetables to soup.
- Cook and stir over medium heat, breaking up vegetables with a fork until thawed.
- Simmer, uncovered, for 10 minutes, stirring occasionally.
- Stir in oysters, wine, and pepper.
- Cook and stir until heated through.
- Garnish with lemon slices.

Cabbage and Beef Soup

Makes 3 quarts

1 pound lean ground beef
½ teaspoon garlic salt
¼ teaspoon garlic powder
¼ teaspoon pepper
2 stalks celery, chopped
1 16-ounce can kidney beans, undrained

½ medium head cabbage, chopped
1 28-ounce can tomatoes, chopped (reserve liquid)
1 tomato can of water
4 beef bouillon cubes
parsley, chopped

- In a Dutch oven, brown beef.
- Add all remaining ingredients, except parsley. Bring to a boil.
- Reduce heat and simmer for 1 hour.
- Garnish with parsley.

Can be frozen.

Cioppino (Seafood Stew)

Serves 4 to 6

1 cup green pepper, chopped	1 bay leaf
	sprigs of parsley
1½ cups onion, chopped	2 teaspoons red pepper
⅓ cup olive oil	flakes
3 14-ounce cans Italian-style tomatoes	¾ pound shrimp, peeled and cleaned
2 tablespoons tomato paste	1½ pounds mild fish, cut into 1½-inch pieces
2 cups dry red wine	¾ pound scallops,
1½ teaspoons dried basil	halved if very large
1½ teaspoons dried oregano	24 hard-shell clams (optional)
1½ teaspoons dried thyme	

- In kettle or stock pot, cook pepper and onion in oil until softened.
- Add tomatoes, tomato paste, wine, all seasonings and 1 sprig parsley.
- Bring to a boil, stirring frequently.
- Reduce heat to simmer. Cover and simmer for 1½ hours.
- Discard bay leaf and parsley.
- Stir in clams.
- Boil covered. As clams open, transfer them to a bowl.
- Season mixture with salt, and add shrimp, fish and scallops.
- Bring to a gentle simmer and cook, covered, 5 to 7 minutes.
- Stir in clams gently.
- Sprinkle with parsley and serve with Parmesan toast.

Shrimp Bisque

Serves 4 to 5

¼ cup butter	1 bay leaf
1 cup onion, chopped	2 teaspoons fresh basil,
½ cup celery, chopped	chopped
1 teaspoon garlic,	½ teaspoon hot pepper
minced	sauce
2 tablespoons flour	¼ teaspoon salt
2½ tablespoons tomato	1½ pounds shrimp,
paste	shelled and deveined
3 cups milk	¼ cup scallions, sliced
2 cups clam broth	

- In large pot, melt butter. Sauté onion, celery, and garlic until tender, about 5 minutes.
- Stir in flour and tomato paste. Cook 1 minute.
- Gradually stir in milk, clam broth, bay leaf, basil, hot pepper sauce, and salt.
- Bring to a boil, reduce heat, simmer 10 minutes.
- Add shrimp and scallions. Simmer 5 minutes longer.
- Remove bay leaf and serve.

Wonderful as a main course (for 4 to 5) or as a first course (6 to 8).

One Hour Chicken Soup

Makes 16 Cups

3 10-ounce cans chicken broth
4 broth cans of water
3 chicken bouillon cubes
1½ to 2 pounds boneless chicken breasts
1 15-ounce can carrots, cut (reserve liquid)
1 15-ounce can potatoes, sliced (reserve liquid)
1 10-ounce package frozen spinach

1 10-ounce (or less) package yellow saffron rice mix or 4-ounces small shaped pasta
¼ teaspoon salt
¼ teaspoon pepper
any 2 of the following:
1 teaspoon poultry seasoning
1 teaspoon Greek seasoning
1 bay leaf

- Put broth, water and bouillon cubes in a 6-quart stock pot and place over high heat.
- Cut chicken into bite-size chunks and add to pot.
- Add carrots, potatoes and frozen spinach.
- Reduce heat to maintain a hearty simmer.
- Add rice or pasta.
- Add seasonings.
- Simmer an additional 20 minutes. Add more water if too thick. Serve.

If pasta is used, you may need to reduce simmering time so that pasta is not overcooked. Also, you may need to add liquid on the second day before reheating.

Mimi's Turkey Soup

Serves 6

3 to 4 tablespoons butter
2 onions, chopped
1½ to 2 tablespoons flour
2¼ teaspoons curry powder
3½ cups chicken broth
¾ cup carrots, sliced diagonally
¾ cup celery, chopped
1½ cups potatoes, diced
2½ teaspoons fresh parsley, chopped

¾ teaspoon sage
3 cups turkey, cooked and cut into bite-size pieces
1 pint half-and-half
1 10-ounce package frozen chopped spinach or 1 10-ounce package fresh spinach
salt and pepper to taste

- Sauté onion in butter over medium heat.
- Add flour and curry. Cook and stir for 3 minutes.
- Add broth, carrots, celery, potatoes, parsley, and sage. Bring to a boil.
- Reduce heat. Cover and simmer for 15 minutes.
- Add turkey, half-and-half, spinach, salt, and pepper.
- Cover and simmer another 10 minutes.

May substitute chicken for the turkey.

Smoked Turkey, Broccoli and Black Bean Soup

Serves 8 to 10

¼ cup unsalted butter
1 cup broccoli stems, peeled and diced
2 cups broccoli flowerets
½ cup carrots, chopped
½ cup onion, chopped
½ cup celery, chopped
2 teaspoons dried thyme, crumbled
2 teaspoons dried oregano, crumbled
1 teaspoon dried basil, crumbled
¼ cup dry white wine
4 cups chicken stock

1 16-ounce can black beans, drained
8 ounces smoked turkey or chicken, diced
1 tablespoon Worcestershire sauce
½ teaspoon hot pepper sauce
2 cups heavy cream or half-and-half
2 tablespoons cornstarch
2 tablespoons water
salt and pepper to taste

- Melt butter in heavy, large saucepan over medium-high heat.
- Add broccoli stems, carrots, onion, and celery and sauté for 5 minutes.
- Add thyme, oregano, and basil and sauté 5 minutes.
- Add wine and bring to a boil.
- Add stock and cook until the liquid is reduced by half, stirring occasionally, about 15 minutes.
- Add broccoli flowerets, beans, turkey, Worcestershire sauce, and hot pepper sauce to soup. Simmer 5 minutes, stirring occasionally.
- Add cream and simmer 5 minutes.
- Season to taste with salt and pepper.
- Up to this point, it can be made 2 days ahead. Cover and refrigerate.
- Rewarm over medium heat before continuing.
- Mix the cornstarch with water in a small bowl until smooth.
- Add to soup and cook until it thickens, stirring occasionally, about 3 minutes.

Baked Beef and Vegetable Soup

Makes 6 servings

4 pounds short ribs of beef
1 onion, skin on, studded with 2 whole cloves
3 cloves garlic, peeled and lightly crushed
4 whole black peppercorns
4 cups beef broth
3 small leeks, trim roots, leave on 1 inch of green

3 carrots
3 celery ribs
8 white mushroom caps, sliced thin
2 cups shaped pasta, cooked until just tender
salt and pepper to taste
2 tablespoons fresh parsley, chopped
2 tablespoons fresh dill, chopped

- Preheat oven to 350°.
- Place beef, onion, garlic, peppercorns, and broth into a Dutch oven. Add water to cover by 1½ inches.
- Bring to a boil on top of the stove, then cover and place in oven. Bake about 2 hours, until beef is very tender.
- Remove meat, cool, shred from bones.
- Discard any fat and the bones.
- Pour broth into a gravy separator (or bowl) through a fine mesh strainer. Allow to cool.
- Pour or skim off fat. Return defatted broth to the pot.
- Cut leeks, carrots, and celery into 1x4x2-inch julienne strips. Add to the casserole.
- Bring to a boil, reduce heat and simmer for 3 minutes.
- Add shredded beef and mushrooms to broth, then add pasta, salt and pepper.
- Bake, covered, for 5 minutes.
- Remove from oven, stir in dill and parsley, and serve.

Goulash Soup

Makes 4 servings

3 medium onions, chopped

2 tablespoons margarine

1½ pounds beef, round or sirloin, cut into ½-inch cubes

2 tablespoons paprika

½ teaspoon caraway seeds

1 clove garlic, minced

½ teaspoon lemon rind, grated

4 cups beef bouillon

salt to taste

2 medium potatoes, cut into ½-inch cubes

- Cook onions in margarine until golden.
- Add the beef and paprika. Cook until slightly browned, stirring constantly.
- Add caraway seeds, garlic, lemon rind, and bouillon. Season to taste.
- Simmer, covered, for 1½ hours.
- Add potatoes and cook 30 minutes longer, or until potatoes are done.

Easy Minestrone

Serves 4 to 6

½ pound ground beef
¾ cup onion, chopped
1½ cups spaghetti sauce
  from jar
1 15-ounce can small
  red beans, undrained
1 8½-ounce can lima
  beans, undrained

1 8¼-ounce can
  carrots, sliced,
  undrained
1½ cups water, or more if
  too thick
¼ cup elbow macaroni
  Parmesan cheese,
  grated (optional)

- Cook ground beef and onion. Add spaghetti sauce and rest of ingredients.
- Simmer 15 to 20 minutes, or until macaroni is tender.
- Garnish with Parmesan cheese, if desired.

Can be made one day ahead to meld flavors. Use lean ground beef for an easy, lowfat dish.

Taco Twist Soup

Makes 8 1-cup servings

1	pound lean ground beef	1	14½-ounce can tomatoes, diced in juice
1	medium onion, chopped	1	cup rotini pasta, uncooked
2	cloves garlic, minced	1	small green pepper, chopped
1 to 2	teaspoons chili powder, as desired		Cheddar cheese, shredded
1	teaspoon ground cumin		tortilla chips
3	cups beef broth		
1½	cups Pace Picante Sauce		

- In large saucepan or Dutch oven, brown ground beef with onion and garlic. Drain.
- Sprinkle chili powder and cumin over meat. Cook and stir 30 seconds.
- Add broth, sauce, tomatoes, pasta and green pepper. Mix well.
- Bring to a boil, stirring frequently.
- Reduce heat, cover and simmer 10 to 15 minutes or until pasta is tender, stirring occasionally.
- Ladle into bowls, top with cheese, serve with chips and additional sauce.

This recipe won first prize for Gladys Fulton in the Soups and Stews Division of a contest sponsored by Pace Picante. Also try Gladys's grand prize winning Pennsylvania Dutch Cake and Custard Pie.

Corn Chowder Deluxe

Makes 8 servings

½ stick butter
1 onion, finely chopped
¼ cup flour
2 quarts chicken stock
6 ears corn, cut from cob

3 cups half-and-half
salt and white pepper to taste
¼ teaspoon ground red pepper
red bell pepper strips and dill sprigs for garnish

- Melt butter in a 4-quart saucepan over medium heat.
- Add onion and cook until light brown, stirring occasionally, about 8 minutes.
- Add flour and stir 3 minutes.
- Pour in chicken stock and corn. Boil about 5 minutes, stirring.
- Reduce heat and simmer about 30 minutes to blend flavors.
- Add half-and-half and simmer until slightly thickened, about 30 minutes.
- Puree in food processor, strain through fine sieve (do not if kernels are desired).
- Add red pepper, salt, and white pepper.
- Cool and refrigerate 4 hours.
- Just before serving, bring to a simmer until hot.
- Garnish with thin pepper strips and sprigs of dill.

For a nice change, add 6 slices of bacon, cooked and crumbled. You can also substitute 2 cups whole white milk and 1 cup evaporated milk for the half-and-half.

Corn and Shrimp Chowder

Makes 14 cups

3 tablespoons flour
3 tablespoons vegetable oil
1 medium to large green pepper, chopped
1 medium to large onion, chopped
2 celery stalks, chopped
1 bunch green onions and tops, chopped
3 to 4 cloves garlic, chopped
2 15¼-ounce cans whole kernel corn
4 cans of water, (to start with, add more as needed)
2 15-ounce cans cream-style corn
1 10-ounce can tomatoes with chilies Creole seasoning
2 pounds shrimp, peeled and cleaned

- Make light roux by mixing flour and oil in large pot.
- Cook until lightly browned.
- Add pepper, onion, celery, green onions, and garlic to roux and cook until soft.
- Add both corns, water, and tomatoes. Season to taste with Creole seasoning.
- Cook until thickened for several hours on low heat. Add water as needed while cooking.
- Add shrimp 10 minutes before serving.

This can be made ahead, but do not add shrimp until ready to serve. Can also be made ahead and frozen (without shrimp). After thawing and cooking until hot, add shrimp for 10 minutes and serve.

Seafood Chowder

Makes 12 cups

4	medium onions, chopped	1	teaspoon garlic powder
1	large green pepper, chopped	1	teaspoon sugar
¼	cup vegetable oil	1	teaspoon hot pepper sauce
2	tablespoons all-purpose flour	½	teaspoon pepper
3	14½-ounce cans stewed tomatoes, undrained	2	pounds fresh, medium shrimp, peeled and deveined
1	tablespoon celery salt	½	pound crabmeat
		1	large fish fillet, cut into bite-size pieces.

- Sauté onion and green pepper in oil, in a large saucepan, until tender. Add flour, stirring until smooth.
- Cook 1 minute, stirring constantly.
- Stir in tomatoes, celery salt, garlic powder, sugar, hot pepper sauce, and pepper. Bring to a boil.
- Cover, reduce heat, and simmer 15 minutes.
- Add seafood, cover and simmer an additional 15 minutes.

Curried Asparagus Soup

Serves 6

3 tablespoons unsalted butter	1 pound asparagus
3 teaspoons curry powder	1 medium potato, peeled and diced
1 small onion, minced	salt and pepper to taste
3 tablespoons flour	1 cup sour cream
4 cups chicken broth	

- Melt butter in saucepan. Add curry powder and onion and simmer until soft.
- Blend in flour and cook 1 minute, stirring constantly.
- Slowly stir in chicken broth.
- Cut asparagus into 1-inch lengths, reserving the tips for garnish.
- Add asparagus and potato to broth and simmer until vegetables are tender, about 20 minutes.
- Add salt and pepper.
- Transfer the mixture to a blender or food processor and puree.
- Return mixture to the pan and stir in the sour cream. Heat through.
- Serve garnished with the asparagus tips, which have been cooked in boiling water until just tender.

Sassy Black Bean Soup

Serves 4

1 tablespoon olive oil
1 cup onion, chopped
2 cloves garlic, minced
2 15-ounce cans black
  beans, drained
1 14½-ounce can
  stewed tomatoes,
  undrained and
  chopped

1 10½-ounce can
  chicken broth
½ cup picante sauce
¼ cup water
1 teaspoon ground
  cumin
2 tablespoons fresh lime
  juice

- Heat oil in large saucepan over medium heat until hot.
- Add onion and garlic. Sauté until tender.
- Add beans, tomatoes, chicken broth, sauce, water, and cumin. Stir well.
- Bring to a boil, reduce heat, and simmer, uncovered, for 15 minutes.
- Remove from heat and stir in lime juice. Serve.

Curry Cucumber Tomato Soup

Serves 3 to 4

1 10¾-ounce can cream
  of tomato soup
1 pint buttermilk

½ teaspoon curry
  powder, dissolved in 1
  tablespoon
  Worcestershire sauce
1 or 2 cucumbers, diced

- Place all ingredients in blender or food processor.
- Blend and chill.

Bean and Basil Soup

Makes 4 servings

4	cups chicken stock	2	large garlic cloves
1	28-ounce can plum tomatoes, undrained and chopped	½	cup fresh basil leaves
		2	teaspoons olive oil
1	medium onion, chopped		salt and pepper to taste
1½	teaspoons fresh oregano	4 to 6	ounces elbow macaroni
4	cups navy beans, cooked (rinsed if canned)	4	basil leaves, shredded, for garnish

- In large saucepan, bring chicken stock to a boil over moderately high heat.
- Add tomatoes, onion, and oregano. Lower heat and simmer for 10 minutes.
- Add beans and continue cooking until onion is tender, about 10 minutes.
- In blender or food processor, finely chop garlic and ½ cup basil leaves. Add olive oil and process until combined.
- Add ½ the beans and vegetables to the basil mixture. Process until smooth, then stir the puree back into the soup.
- Bring water to a boil and add salt. Add the pasta and cook until al dente.
- Drain the pasta, reserving about 1 cup of the cooking water.
- Add the pasta to the soup and season with salt and pepper.
- If soup is too thick, add a little of the pasta water.
- Sprinkle with the shredded basil and serve.

Borscht

Serves 6

2 pounds beef chuck
3 stalks celery, sliced
3 5.5-gram packets of instant beef broth
1 large carrot, sliced
1 medium yellow onion, sliced
2 16-ounce cans of beets or 4 large fresh beets

2 medium potatoes, cubed
½ small head cabbage, shredded
1 16-ounce can tomatoes
2 tablespoons tomato paste
pinch of sugar (optional)
salt to taste

- Cut celery and carrot into chunks.
- Put celery, carrots, onion, and meat in large saucepan with the broth.
- Cover with 3 or 4 inches of water.
- Simmer until meat is cooked.
- When meat is cooked, remove from the pot. Strain the broth until it is clear.
- If using fresh beets, cook, peel and cut in strips. (Do this in a second pot, while the meat is cooking).
- Add potatoes and beets to the broth. Simmer. When potatoes are half-cooked, add the cabbage, tomatoes, and tomato paste. Simmer until cabbage is soft.
- Meanwhile, trim fat from meat, then cut meat into ½-inch pieces.
- When potatoes are cooked, return meat to pot and heat through. Add salt and sugar, if needed, and serve.

Healthy Broccoli Soup

Serves 8 to 10

2 tablespoons butter	7 cups broccoli
2 to 3 leeks, sliced (or green onions, sliced)	flowerets and upper stems, coarsely cut
1 small onion, chopped	(discard lower stems)
1 to 2 cloves garlic, minced	small amounts of
3 cups potatoes, peeled and coarsely cut	basil, dill and ginger small amount of fresh
6 cups chicken consommé, fresh, canned or cubes	spinach, shredded grated cheese or sour cream

- In a large pot, sauté leeks, onion, and garlic in butter.
- Add all other ingredients.
- Lightly boil for approximately 1 hour, or until potatoes are well cooked.
- Puree in food processor, small amounts at a time. Return to pot, heat and adjust seasonings.
- Serve with grated cheese or a spoonful of sour cream.

May be served cold. Freezes beautifully.

Ice Cold Carrot Soup

Serves 6 to 8

1 pound carrots, thickly sliced
1 large onion, thickly sliced
4 tablespoons butter
1 tablespoon lemon rind, grated
½ teaspoon curry powder
4 cups chicken broth
salt and pepper to taste
1 cup light cream or whole milk
sour cream for garnish
fresh chives or fresh parsley for garnish

- In soup pan, sauté carrots and onion in butter until onion is transparent.
- Add curry, lemon rind, chicken broth, salt and pepper. Simmer until carrots are tender.
- Puree, 2 cups at a time.
- Stir in cream and chill until very, very cold.
- Before serving, add a spoonful of sour cream and top with chives or parsley.

Chilled Mushroom and Tomato Soup

Serves 6

1 10¾-ounce can cream of mushroom soup
1 10½-ounce can consommé
1 10¾-ounce can tomato bisque
1¼ cups half-and-half
3 tablespoons sherry
1 teaspoon curry

- Combine all ingredients and chill.

For even more flavor, prepare the day before.

Chilled Cucumber Soup

Serves 4

1 cucumber, peeled, seeded and chopped (1 cup)
1 green onion, sliced
1 tablespoon margarine
2 teaspoons cornstarch
¾ cup water
½ cup milk
1 teaspoon instant chicken bouillon granules
¼ teaspoon dried dill weed
⅛ teaspoon salt
½ cup plain yogurt
green onion tops, sliced

- In a saucepan, cook cucumber and onion in margarine for about 5 minutes, or until tender.
- Stir in cornstarch. Add water, milk, bouillon granules, dill weed, and salt.
- Cook on medium-high heat. Stir until slightly thick and bubbly. Cook and stir for 2 more minutes.
- Pour hot mixture into blender or food processor and blend until smooth.
- Place yogurt in a large bowl and stir in hot cucumber mixture.
- Cover and chill.
- Serve cold and garnish with green onion tops.

Madrilene Caviar Sour Cream Soup

Serves 1 to 2

1 10½-ounce can madrilene red consommé, chilled
1 tablespoon sour cream, per serving
1 teaspoon caviar, per serving

- With a fork, break up consommé.
- Place in a cream soup bowl.
- Top with sour cream and caviar.

It is so easy and looks so fancy.

Chunky Gazpacho

Serves 4

½ small onion, sliced
2 large garlic cloves
3 tablespoons olive oil
¼ cup red wine vinegar
2 pounds tomatoes,
  cored, seeded and
  diced
1 large cucumber,
  peeled, seeded and
  diced

1 green bell pepper,
  diced
⅓ cup fresh parsley,
  chopped
2 tablespoons tomato
  paste
  hot pepper sauce
1 5-ounce can tomato
  juice

- Puree onion, garlic, olive oil and vinegar in food processor.
- In a small bowl, combine ½ cup tomatoes, ½ of the cucumber and ½ cup green pepper. Set aside.
- Add parsley, tomato paste, remaining tomatoes, cucumber, and green pepper to processor.
- Blend until chunky puree forms.
- Season to taste with hot pepper sauce, salt and pepper.
- Thin with tomato juice.
- Transfer gazpacho to large bowl.
- Cover soup and reserved vegetables separately.
- Refrigerate until well chilled, about 6 hours.
- Serve with reserved vegetables spooned into each serving.

Very pretty, light and refreshing.

Los Patios Cheese Potato Soup

Makes 10 cups

¼ cup butter or margarine

3 green onions, chopped

3 celery stalks with leaves, chopped

2 carrots, grated

2 10¾-ounce cans chicken broth

3 10¾-ounce cans potato soup

8 ounces Cheddar cheese, grated

parsley, chopped

hot pepper sauce

8 ounces sour cream

3 tablespoons sherry

salt and pepper to taste

- ◆ Melt butter over low heat and sauté onions, celery and carrots.
- ◆ Add chicken broth; cover and simmer 30 minutes.
- ◆ Add potato soup, cheese, parsley, a few drops of hot pepper sauce, salt and pepper.
- ◆ Stir in sour cream. Simmer 15 minutes.
- ◆ Add sherry. Stir.

A raw potato placed in the soup pot will absorb salt if you've added too much.

Pumpkin Soup

Serves 10 to 12

1 medium onion, chopped	1 2-pound fresh or 13-ounce can pumpkin
1 bunch (6 to 8) scallions, chopped	6 cups chicken broth
½ cup plus 3 tablespoons butter or margarine	3 tablespoons flour
	4 cups light cream
	nutmeg for garnish

- In large pan, sauté onions and scallions in ½ cup butter. Do not brown.
- Add pumpkin and cook for 5 minutes.
- Stir in chicken broth and cook for 10 minutes, stirring constantly.
- Blend the flour and remaining butter until smooth.
- Add to broth, stirring with a whisk. Simmer for 10 minutes.
- Add the cream just before serving.
- Garnish with nutmeg.

Cold Sweet Pea Soup

Makes 6 generous servings

2 tablespoons butter or margarine	2 10-ounce packages frozen peas
1 cup onion, chopped	½ cup fresh mint leaves
4 cups chicken broth	½ cup heavy cream or half-and-half

- Melt butter in bottom of medium-sized pan.
- Sauté onion until wilted.
- Add chicken broth, peas, and mint.
- Simmer for 15 minutes.
- Put in blender, then through sieve.
- Stir in cream.
- Season to taste. Chill.
- Garnish with thinly sliced radishes, if desired.

Baked Winter Squash Soup

Makes 12 servings

2 acorn squash (2 pounds each)

2 butternut squash (2 pounds each)

8 tablespoons unsalted butter

8 tablespoons dark brown sugar

3 carrots, peeled and halved

1 large onion, thinly sliced

10 cups chicken stock or canned broth

¾ teaspoon ground ginger

pinch of cayenne pepper

- Preheat oven to 350°.
- Cut the 4 squash in half lengthwise. Scoop out and discard seeds.
- Place squash halves, skin side down, in a shallow roasting pan. Place 1 tablespoon of the butter and 1 tablespoon of the brown sugar in the cavity of each squash half.
- Arrange carrots and onion slices around squash.
- Pour 2 cups of the stock in the pan.
- Cover tightly with aluminum foil and bake for 2 hours.
- Remove pan from oven and allow vegetables to cool slightly.
- Scoop pulp out of skins and place into soup pot.
- Add carrots, onions, and cooking liquid.
- Add remaining 8 cups stock, ginger, and cayenne.
- Stir well and bring to a boil. Reduce heat and simmer, uncovered, for 10 minutes.
- Puree soup in batches in food processor until smooth.
- Return soup to the pot. Adjust seasonings and heat through.
- Garnish with a dollop of sour cream and snipped chives.

Makes 12 very generous portions, however, this recipe halves easily if you want to make less.

Garden Vegetable Soup

Serves 6 to 8

2 tablespoons butter
2 pounds lean stew beef, cut into small pieces
2 tablespoons Worcestershire sauce
1 tablespoon fresh lemon juice
½ tablespoon Greek seasoning
½ teaspoon cinnamon
½ teaspoon allspice
1½ teaspoons garlic salt
1 teaspoon lemon pepper
24 ounces cocktail vegetable juice

3 10½-ounce cans chicken broth
1 16-ounce can red kidney beans
3 stalks celery, diced
1 large onion, diced
1½ cups cabbage, shredded
1 cup carrots, diced
1 cup green beans, cut into small pieces
8 okra pods, thinly sliced
1 16-ounce can tomatoes, diced
1 8-ounce can corn
2 medium potatoes, diced

* In large, heavy pot, brown meat in 2 tablespoons butter, add all spices, and stir.
* Add remaining ingredients and cook slowly for 2 to 2½ hours.

Potato Cheese Soup

Serves 8 to 10

Soup base

1 cup potatoes, shredded
½ cup onion, shredded
½ cup carrots, shredded

⅓ cup green pepper, shredded
3 cups chicken broth

Cheese sauce

4 tablespoons butter
½ cup flour

2 cups milk
3 cups Cheddar cheese, shredded

- Cover shredded potatoes, onion, carrots, and green pepper with water and cook until almost done.
- Add chicken broth. (If desired, small pieces of chicken may be added.)
- To make the cheese sauce, melt the butter in a saucepan.
- Gradually stir in the flour and cook until bubbly, stirring constantly.
- Gradually pour in the milk, stirring constantly, until each addition is smooth.
- Cook over medium heat, stirring constantly, until thickened.
- Remove from heat.
- Add cheese and stir until melted.
- Add cheese sauce to the soup base and heat slowly.

Good reheated.

Cream Cheese Tea Sandwiches

Makes 16 to 24 finger sandwiches

1 8-ounce package cream cheese, softened	½ cup pecans, chopped and toasted slightly
1 ripe banana, mashed	¼ cup crushed pineapple, drained
½ teaspoon fresh lemon juice	16 slices whole wheat or white bread
½ cup raisins	

- Combine cream cheese, banana, lemon juice, raisins, nuts and pineapple.
- Spread on bread to make sandwiches.
- Trim edges and cut into halves or thirds.

Italian Sausage Broils

Serves 4

½ pound bulk Italian sausage	1 8-ounce can tomato sauce with mushrooms (or plain)
½ teaspoon dried basil leaves	1½ cups mozzarella cheese, shredded
½ teaspoon dried oregano leaves	4 English muffins, split, toasted and buttered

- Preheat oven to broil.
- Brown sausage in skillet. Drain fat and add basil, oregano, and tomato sauce.
- Sprinkle 1 tablespoon of the shredded cheese on each half of toasted, buttered English muffin.
- Divide sausage mixture among the muffin halves. Top with remaining cheese.
- Broil about 3 inches from source of heat until cheese melts, about 30 seconds to 1 minute.
- Serve immediately.

These sandwiches can be cut into smaller pieces and served as an appetizer.

Lemon Sandwiches

Makes 80 finger sandwiches

3 egg yolks
½ cup sugar
  juice and grated rind
  of 2 lemons
1 8-ounce package
  cream cheese,
  softened

1 cup pecans, finely
  chopped
20 slices whole wheat
  bread, thinly sliced
  mayonnaise

- Cook egg yolks, sugar, lemon juice and rind until thick, stirring constantly.
- Add cream cheese and pecans, stirring until blended. Refrigerate overnight.
- Remove crusts from bread. Spread with mayonnaise and prepared filling. Cut into fourths.

Delicious and very different.

Apricot Salad

Serves 20 or more

2 4-ounce jars baby
  strained apricots
1 20-ounce can crushed
  pineapple
1 8-ounce package
  cream cheese

1 12-ounce can
  evaporated milk
2 3-ounce packages
  apricot gelatin
½ cup pecans, chopped

- In saucepan, combine apricots and undrained pineapple.
- Bring to rolling boil.
- Pour gradually into cream cheese, beating until very smooth.
- Add dry gelatin and 1 cup of cold water.
- Beat until gelatin is dissolved. Cool.
- Beat evaporated milk until stiff and fold into gelatin mixture.
- Pour into 9x13-inch pan and sprinkle with chopped nuts.
- Refrigerate until set.
- Serve in squares right from pan; do not unmold.

Vegetable Sandwich Spread

Makes 3 cups

1 green pepper, seeded	1 teaspoon lemon juice
2 cups celery (about 5 stalks)	2 cups mayonnaise (may use lowfat mayonnaise)
2 cucumbers, peeled and seeded	¼ cup liquid from vegetables
2 carrots, peeled	1 ¼-ounce envelope gelatin
1 small onion	
1 teaspoon salt	

- Puree all vegetables in food processor.
- Place vegetables in thin dish towel or cheese cloth and squeeze out liquid, reserving ½ cup.
- Add mayonnaise, lemon juice, and salt to vegetable mixture.
- Dissolve gelatin in ¼ cup vegetable juice. Warm to activate and add to vegetable and mayonnaise mixture. Add more vegetable juice if too dry.
- Cover bowl and chill in refrigerator for 3 hours, or until mixture is well set.

Enough spread for sandwiches from 2 loaves of bread. Also good on crackers.

Blueberry Delight

Serves 12

2 3-ounce packages
blueberry or
blackberry gelatin
2 cups boiling water
1 15-ounce can
blueberries
1 8¼-ounce can
crushed pineapple

1 8-ounce package
cream cheese
½ cup sugar
1 cup sour cream
½ teaspoon vanilla
½ cup pecans, chopped

- Dissolve gelatin in 2 cups boiling water.
- Drain fruit, reserve the juice.
- Add enough water to juice to equal 1 cup.
- Add juice to gelatin, stir in fruit, pour into 9x13-inch pan and chill.
- Blend cream cheese, sugar, sour cream, and vanilla. Spread over chilled gelatin.
- Sprinkle with chopped nuts.

An especially good gelatin salad.

Seabie's Orange Mandarin Mold Salad

Serves 8

1 6-ounce package
lemon gelatin
2 11-ounce cans
mandarin oranges

1 12-ounce can frozen
orange juice

- Drain mandarin oranges, reserving juice in measuring cup. Add water to juice to make 2 cups.
- Combine juice and gelatin in 2-quart saucepan. Bring to boil, stirring until gelatin is dissolved.
- Add orange juice, stirring until well blended.
- Cool in refrigerator until soft, then add mandarin oranges.
- Pour into a 5-cup mold; chill until firm.
- Mix a little orange juice with mayonnaise to serve with mold.

Holiday Cranberry Mold

Serves 8

1 20-ounce can crushed pineapple in juice
1 6-ounce package raspberry gelatin
1 cup water
1 1-pound can whole cranberry sauce
3 tablespoons fresh lemon juice
1 teaspoon fresh lemon peel, grated
¼ teaspoon nutmeg
2 cups sour cream (or lowfat sour cream)
⅔ cup pecans, chopped

- Drain pineapple well, saving juice.
- Add juice to gelatin in a 2-quart saucepan. Stir in water.
- Heat to boiling, stirring to dissolve gelatin.
- Remove from heat.
- Stir in cranberry sauce. Add lemon juice, lemon peel, and nutmeg.
- Chill until slightly thickened.
- Blend sour cream into gelatin mixture. Fold in pineapple and pecans.
- Pour into 2-quart mold and chill until firm.

Mango Salad

Serves 12

2 8-ounce packages cream cheese
1 26-ounce jar mango slices, partially drained
3 3-ounce packages lemon gelatin
3 cups boiling water
juice of 1 lemon

- Blend mangos and cream cheese in blender.
- Dissolve gelatin in boiling water. Add lemon juice.
- Combine all ingredients and pour into mold (may use 1 large mold or 12 individual molds).
- Refrigerate until set and serve on lettuce leaves.

Tea Garden Salad and Dressing

Serves 9

Salad

1 3-ounce package
orange gelatin
1 cup hot black tea
1 11-ounce can
mandarin orange
sections

1 9-ounce can
pineapple tidbits or
chunks
1 5-ounce can water
chestnuts, julienne
sliced

Dressing

1 cup heavy cream,
whipped (or frozen
whipped topping)

½ cup mayonnaise
rind of 1 orange,
grated (not dried)
pinch of mace

- Drain mandarin orange sections and pineapple, reserving juice.
- Add enough water to juice to make 1 cup.
- Dissolve gelatin in hot tea and dilute with 1 cup of juice.
- Refrigerate until somewhat thickened; add mandarin oranges, pineapple and water chestnuts.
- Spoon into well-oiled 8x8-inch pan or mold.
- Refrigerate until set, 1 to 2 hours.
- For dressing, mix ingredients in order listed.
- Top chilled salad with dressing.

Old Fashioned Overnight Salad

Serves 8 to 10

Salad

2 15-ounce cans pineapple, drained and cut into small pieces

1 pound seedless grapes, cut in half
½ cup pecans, chopped
5 ounces miniature marshmallows

Dressing

4 egg yolks, beaten
¼ teaspoon salt
juice of 1 lemon

½ cup cream or half-and-half
½ pint heavy cream, whipped

- Mix together pineapple, grapes, pecans, and marshmallows.
- For dressing, combine egg yolks, salt, lemon juice, and ½ cup cream. Cook slowly in double boiler, stirring constantly until thick. (Watch carefully as it tends to lump easily.)
- When cool, blend in whipped cream.
- Mix with fruit and refrigerate for 24 hours.

Tomato Aspic

Makes 8 salads

2 ¼-ounce envelopes unflavored gelatin
½ cup cold water
2 cups boiling water
1 beef bouillon cube

1 10¾-ounce can condensed tomato soup
½ cup vinegar
⅓ cup sugar
½ teaspoon salt

- Dissolve gelatin in cold water.
- Add bouillon cube to boiling water.
- Stir in gelatin. Add vinegar, sugar, salt, and soup.
- Pour into cold, wet molds.

For a nice luncheon salad, add 1 pound of shrimp.

Molded Avocado Ring with Sour Cream Shrimp Dressing

Makes 8 to 10 servings

Avocado Mold

4 cups avocado, mashed	3 tablespoons onion juice
4 tablespoons lemon juice	3 tablespoons unflavored gelatin
2 teaspoons salt	½ cup cold water
⅛ teaspoon cayenne pepper	1¼ cups boiling water
1 teaspoon sugar	few drops green food coloring
	1 cup mayonnaise

Sour Cream Shrimp Dressing

1 clove garlic	1 teaspoon paprika
1 pint heavy sour cream	1 tablespoon lemon juice
1½ cups ketchup	¼ teaspoon dry mustard
2 tablespoons Worcestershire sauce	½ pound shrimp, cooked, shelled and deveined, cut into pieces (or use tiny, frozen, cooked shrimp, thawed)
1½ tablespoons onion, grated	
1 teaspoon salt	
2 tablespoons horseradish	

- To mash avocado, cut in half, peel, and sprinkle with lemon juice. Process in food processor until smooth (or press through ricer, then through sieve.)
- Add salt, pepper, sugar, and onion juice. Mix well
- Soak gelatin in cold water, add boiling water, and stir until dissolved. Chill until gelatin begins to congeal.
- Blend avocado mixture with gelatin. Refrigerate until mixture begins to congeal.
- Add coloring and beat for 3 minutes with rotary beater, then fold in mayonnaise and stir until completely blended.

Continued on next page

- Add more coloring if mixture is too light. Taste to correct seasonings.
- Pour into large greased ring mold and let set overnight in refrigerator.
- To make the dressing, rub mixing bowl with cut garlic and pour in sour cream.
- Add all remaining ingredients except shrimp and stir well (do not beat) until blended.
- Fold in shrimp and refrigerate until ready to serve with avocado mold.

Wonderful with a Mexican meal. Also good with chicken or fish.

Lime Pineapple Salad

Serves 12

1 6-ounce package lime gelatin
2 cups boiling water
1 15-ounce can crushed pineapple

2 cups creamy cottage cheese (lowfat, if desired)
2 teaspoons cream-style horseradish
1 cup (light) mayonnaise

- Drain can of pineapple; reserve juice.
- Dissolve gelatin in 2 cups boiling water.
- Add reserved pineapple juice.
- Chill until slightly thickened, then beat until foamy.
- Fold in pineapple, cottage cheese, horseradish, and mayonnaise.
- Mix well and pour into 9x13-inch pan or individual molds.
- Chill until firm.

Charleston Symphony League's Broccoli Salad

Serves 12

Vegetables

8 cups fresh broccoli flowerets (about 3 pounds)	1 cup raisins
	1 cup pecan pieces, toasted
2 small purple onions, thinly sliced, separated into rings	2 11-ounce cans mandarin oranges, drained

Dressing

1½ cups mayonnaise	3 tablespoons white vinegar
½ cup sugar	

- ◆ Combine broccoli, onions, raisins and pecan pieces in a bowl; set aside.
- ◆ Combine mayonnaise, sugar, and vinegar; add to broccoli mixture, stirring to coat.
- ◆ Gently stir in mandarin oranges.
- ◆ Cover and refrigerate at least 3 hours, preferably overnight.

For a nice change, substitute 1 pound of bacon, cooked and crumbled, and 1 10-ounce package frozen petite peas, thawed, for the mandarin oranges.

Sugar-Free Three Bean Salad

Serves 8

Vegetables

1 15-ounce can cut
   green beans
1 15-ounce can yellow
   wax beans

1 15-ounce can red
   kidney beans
1 medium onion, thinly
   sliced

Marinade

1 cup white vinegar
1 cup cold water
2 tablespoons cooking
   oil
1/8 teaspoon garlic
   powder
1/8 teaspoon paprika

1/2 teaspoon parsley
   flakes
1/2 teaspoon onion flakes
4 packets artificial
   sweetener (more if
   you like)

* Drain and rinse green beans, wax beans, and kidney beans with cold water.
* Combine with onion. Set aside.
* Mix vinegar, water, oil, garlic powder, paprika, parsley, onion flakes, and artificial sweetener. Shake well.
* Pour marinade over vegetables and chill in refrigerator, preferably overnight.
* When ready to serve, pour off excess liquid.

Marinade can be used as a low calorie dressing for salad or coleslaw. This salad can be kept for a week in refrigerator and can also be frozen for future meals.

My Favorite Black Bean Salad

Serves 10

1 pound dried black beans, soaked overnight and drained
1½ cups tomatoes, seeded and chopped
1½ cups fresh cooked corn, scraped from cob, or frozen corn
¾ cup scallions, thinly sliced
½ cup olive oil (may use less)
½ cup fresh lime juice
1 teaspoon salt
⅓ cup fresh cilantro, or to taste

- Cook beans and drain.
- Combine with tomatoes, corn, and scallions.
- Whisk together olive oil, lime juice, salt, and cilantro, and mix with vegetables.
- Refrigerate overnight.

This recipe is very tasty. It also works using 2 cans of black beans and 1 can of shoepeg corn.

Minty Cucumber Salad

Serves 6 to 8

3 large cucumbers, peeled, halved and seeded
½ cup fresh mint leaves
¼ cup fresh parsley, chopped
rind of 1 orange, grated
½ cup olive oil
1 cup red wine vinegar
½ cup sugar

- Cut cucumbers into crescents and toss with mint, parsley, and orange rind.
- Whisk the remaining ingredients together and toss with cucumbers.
- Serve very, very cold.

This has a wonderful and unusual flavor.

Green Bean Salad

Serves 10 to 12

Vegetables

1 15-ounce can whole green beans, drained

1 15-ounce can green peas, drained

1 5-ounce jar stuffed olives, chopped

¼ pound slivered almonds

4 ribs celery, cut to match-stick size

4 carrots, cut to match-stick size

1 bunch green onions, thinly sliced

Marinade

1 cup oil

¾ cup vinegar

1 teaspoon Worcestershire sauce

2 cloves garlic, peeled

1½ teaspoons lemon juice

1½ teaspoons orange juice

1 teaspoon salt

½ teaspoon dry mustard

½ cup powdered sugar

- In large bowl, combine beans, peas, olives, almonds, celery, carrots, and green onions.
- To prepare marinade, combine all remaining ingredients and pour over vegetables.
- Cover and refrigerate.
- Before serving, remove garlic cloves.

This salad will keep in refrigerator for several days.

Marinated Corn Salad

Serves 4 to 6

1 11-ounce can crisp yellow corn
½ cup green pepper, diced
½ cup celery, diced
3 green onions, thinly sliced
1 2-ounce jar pimientos, chopped

2 tablespoons fresh parsley, chopped
4 tablespoons vegetable oil
1½ tablespoons cider vinegar
½ teaspoon salt
½ teaspoon dry mustard
⅛ teaspoon pepper

* Combine corn, pepper, celery, onions, pimientos, and parsley.
* Combine remaining ingredients in jar, shake well and pour over vegetables.
* Cover and chill at least 4 hours or overnight.

Easy and pretty.

Caesar Salad

Serves 6 to 8

1½ cloves garlic (or to taste)
½ cup oil
1 2-ounce can anchovy fillets, drained
2½ tablespoons fresh lemon juice
1 teaspoon Worcestershire sauce

fresh pepper
1 egg
½ cup Parmesan cheese, freshly grated
1 head Romaine lettuce, broken into pieces, large ribs removed
croutons

* Mix garlic, oil, anchovy, lemon juice, Worcestershire sauce, and pepper in blender.
* Add egg and blend.
* Add Parmesan cheese to lettuce and sprinkle with croutons.
* Pour on dressing to taste and toss well.

Gazpacho Aspic

Serves 10 to 12

1 quart tomato juice
2½ ¼-ounce envelopes
   unflavored gelatin
2 tablespoons cumin
2 cloves garlic, peeled
   and chopped
1 tablespoon lemon
   juice
1 tablespoon oil

salt and pepper to
   taste
2 tablespoons almonds
1 cup green pepper,
   chopped
1 cup cucumber,
   chopped
1 cup onion, chopped
1 cup celery, chopped

- Soften gelatin in ½ cup heated tomato juice.
- Cool mixture; add cumin and garlic.
- Slowly add remaining tomato juice, lemon juice, oil, salt, and pepper.
- Stir in almonds.
- Add green pepper, cucumber, onion, and celery.
- Pour into mold and refrigerate.

Spinach Salad with Feta Cheese

Serves 4

3 tablespoons red wine
   vinegar
1½ tablespoons olive oil
½ teaspoon salt
¼ teaspoon freshly
   ground pepper
1 teaspoon sugar
¾ pound spinach, torn
   into bite-size pieces

3 large white
   mushrooms, thinly
   sliced
1 small red onion, sliced
   into rings
¼ pound feta cheese,
   crumbled

- Combine vinegar, oil, salt, pepper, and sugar in large bowl.
- Add spinach, mushrooms, and onions; toss.
- Sprinkle with feta cheese.

Mesclun with Mushrooms

Serves 4

12 ounces mesclun
(young salad greens,
mixed)
1 red or Vidalia onion,
thinly sliced
¼ cup olive oil
3 tablespoons walnuts,
chopped and sautéed
in oil
4 bacon slices
4 large cloves garlic,
chopped

5 ounces portobello
mushrooms (or other
wild mushrooms),
sliced
2 tablespoons raspberry
vinegar
pinch of sugar
½ teaspoon Dijon
mustard
salt and pepper to
taste

- In medium bowl, combine mesclun and onion. Set aside.
- Heat 1 tablespoon oil in skillet, add nuts and cook until golden, stirring constantly. Drain on towels.
- Sauté bacon until crisp. Set aside.
- Heat 1 tablespoon oil in pan, add garlic and mushrooms. Cook 2 to 3 minutes or until tender. (If mushrooms exude a lot of liquid, remove them with a slotted spoon and reduce liquid to 2 tablespoons. This is not a problem with portobellos.)
- Add 2 tablespoons oil, vinegar, sugar, mustard, salt, and pepper to pan. Heat.
- Crumble bacon. Toss bacon and the mushroom mixture with salad greens.
- Sprinkle with toasted nuts and serve immediately.

Good for a ladies' luncheon or served with steak.

Layered Spinach Salad

Makes 8 generous servings

2 quarts fresh spinach leaves, torn into bite-size pieces

1 cup broccoli stems, shredded (sold as broccoli coleslaw)

2 cups fresh mushrooms, sliced

1 cup red or green onion, diced

1 cup yellow or red bell pepper, diced

1 10-ounce package frozen English peas, thawed

2 cups tiny cherry tomatoes

3 slices bacon, crisply cooked and crumbled (optional)

¾ cup mayonnaise-type salad dressing (lowfat)

¾ cup light sour cream

2 teaspoons sugar

4 tablespoons Parmesan cheese, grated

- In a 2½-quart bowl, layer ½ the spinach, all of the broccoli stems, mushroom slices, onion, bell pepper, peas, tomatoes, and bacon, then the remaining ½ of the spinach.
- Combine salad dressing, sour cream, and sugar; mix well.
- Spread evenly over top layer of spinach leaves to seal.
- Sprinkle with Parmesan cheese.
- Cover tightly with plastic wrap and refrigerate until serving (up to 24 hours).
- If desired, toss gently before serving.

A work of art in a bowl.

Frozen Slaw

Serves 4 to 6

1 head cabbage, shredded	1 teaspoon mustard seed
1 teaspoon salt	1 large carrot, grated
1 cup vinegar	1 small green pepper, diced
1½ cups sugar	
½ cup water	1 small red pepper, diced
1 teaspoon celery seed	

- Combine cabbage and salt. Let stand for 1 hour.
- Squeeze out liquid.
- In small pan, combine vinegar, sugar, water, celery seeds, and mustard seeds.
- Boil 1 minute and cool.
- Mix carrot, red pepper, and green pepper with cabbage and cooled vinegar.
- Put into container, juice and all.
- Freeze.
- Remove from freezer 20 minutes before serving.

This really works.

♩MMM♩MMM♩MMM♩MMM♩MMM♩MMM♩MMM♩MMM♩MMM♩MMM♩MMM♩MMM♩MMM♩MMM♩MMM♩MMM♩MMM♩MMM♩MMM♩MMM

Elegant Tarragon Salad

Serves 4

2	tablespoons fresh tarragon, finely chopped	1	small head radicchio, separated into leaves
2	tablespoons fresh lemon juice	1	small bunch watercress (discard stems)
¼	cup olive oil	3	white mushrooms, thinly sliced
½	teaspoon sugar	½	teaspoon salt
1	medium Belgian endive, cored, sliced crosswise (¼- inch thick)	½	teaspoon freshly ground pepper

- In large bowl, combine tarragon and lemon juice; whisk in oil and sugar.
- Add endive, radicchio, watercress, and mushrooms.
- Season with salt and pepper; toss and serve.

Blue Cheese Potato Salad

Serves 12

5	pounds new potatoes	2½	tablespoons Dijon mustard
½	cup dry white wine	2½	tablespoons cider vinegar
	salt and freshly ground pepper to taste	½	pound blue cheese, crumbled
1¼	cups mayonnaise	5	green onions, minced
1¼	cups sour cream	1½	cups celery, chopped

- Cook potatoes; cool slightly; peel and cut into 1-inch pieces.
- Add wine, season with salt and pepper and toss to coat. Cool.
- Combine remaining ingredients; mix with cooled potatoes. Adjust seasoning.
- Cover and refrigerate at least 30 minutes before serving.

May be prepared a day ahead.

Tomatoes Joanne

Serves 6

12 thick tomato slices	½ teaspoon pepper
1 cup olive oil	½ teaspoon dry mustard
⅓ cup wine vinegar	2 cloves garlic, crushed
2 teaspoons crushed	6 lettuce cups
oregano leaves	green onion, minced
1 teaspoon salt	parsley

- Arrange tomato slices in square 8x8-inch baking dish.
- Combine oil, vinegar, oregano, salt, pepper, dry mustard, and garlic; spoon dressing over tomatoes.
- Cover and chill 2 to 3 hours, spooning dressing over tomatoes occasionally.
- To serve, arrange tomato slices in lettuce cups and sprinkle with minced green onion and parsley.
- Drizzle each salad with small amount of the dressing.

This is a tasty, simple, do-ahead salad that goes deliciously with any main course.

Watercress, Endive and Blue Cheese Salad

Makes 4 salads

Dressing

5 tablespoons oil (a little less if desired)

1½ tablespoons red wine vinegar (increase, if oil is decreased)

¼ teaspoon salt

⅛ teaspoon black pepper

Salad

¼ cup walnuts, chopped

3 medium size endive

1 bunch watercress

¼ cup blue cheese, crumbled

- Preheat oven to 350°.
- For dressing, combine oil, vinegar, salt, and pepper in a small bowl.
- Toast walnuts in oven about 6 minutes; cool; set aside.
- Wipe endive with damp towel; cut thin slices from bottom; break off leaves at base.
- Arrange endive on four individual plates.
- Trim stems from watercress; place over endive.
- Sprinkle with toasted walnuts and blue cheese.
- Drizzle with dressing.

Sweet Potato Salad

Serves 6

Salad

2½ pounds yams	½ cup fresh parsley, chopped
1 small onion, minced	½ cup unsalted cashews, chopped
1 rib celery, minced	

Dressing

2 tablespoons olive oil	1 teaspoon marjoram
2 tablespoons lemon juice	salt and pepper to taste
2 teaspoons soy sauce	

- Boil potatoes and drain.
- When cool, peel and cube potatoes and place into medium-sized bowl.
- Add onion, celery, and parsley.
- Prepare dressing by combining oil, lemon juice, soy sauce, marjoram, salt, and pepper. Blend well.
- Pour dressing over salad and toss.
- Top with cashews.

This recipe can be made the day before, except for adding dressing and cashews. It's different, but delicious.

Paradise Potato Salad

Serves 24

Salad

4 pounds red potatoes
1 pound cherry tomatoes, cut in half
6 ounces celery, sliced ¼-inch thick
4 ounces green peppers, seeded, sliced in ¼-inch strips

1 pound ripe papaya, peeled, seeded, cut into ½-inch cubes
1 medium red onion, chopped

Chutney Vinaigrette

½ cup olive oil
¼ cup lime juice
¼ cup white vinegar
4 ounces chutney

¾ ounce jalapeños, seeded and finely chopped
2 tablespoons fresh cilantro, chopped

- Cut potatoes, skin on, into ½-inch cubes; boil until tender; drain and cool.
- In large bowl, combine potatoes, tomatoes, celery, peppers, papaya and onion.
- In jar, combine all vinaigrette ingredients; shake well.
- Pour dressing over salad and toss.
- Chill before serving.

Good with fish or chicken. Unusual flavor for potato salad.

Hot German Potato Salad

Serves 6 to 8

6	medium potatoes	½	teaspoon celery seeds
8	slices bacon		dash of pepper
¾	cup onion, chopped	¾	cup water
2	tablespoons flour	⅓	cup cider vinegar
⅓	cup sugar	2	tablespoons scallion
1½	teaspoons salt		tops, chopped

- Boil potatoes; drain, peel, and slice thin.
- Fry bacon until crisp; drain well; crumble and set aside.
- Sauté onion in bacon fat until golden brown.
- Blend in flour, sugar, salt, celery seeds, and pepper.
- Cook over low heat, stirring until smooth and bubbly.
- Remove from heat; stir in water and vinegar.
- Bring to boil, stirring constantly; boil for 1 minute.
- Carefully stir in potatoes and the crumbled bits of bacon.
- Add chopped scallions for color.
- Remove from heat, cover and let stand until ready to serve.
- Serve warm.

Emily's Chicken Salad

1	chicken, roasted, boned and cubed	1	cup walnuts, chopped
1	cup celery, chopped	1	cup McIntosh apples, thinly sliced
1	cup white grapes, halved		mayonnaise to taste
			dash of ginger

- Prepare chicken.
- Combine chicken with celery, grapes, walnuts and apples.
- Add enough mayonnaise to barely cover.
- Add ginger and toss.
- Serve on bed of lettuce and garnish with fresh mint or parsley.

This recipe was submitted by Emily Remington, Conductor of the Charleston Symphony Orchestra Singers' Guild.

Snow Pea Salad

Serves 4

1 tablespoon vegetable oil	1 teaspoon sugar
1 tablespoon sesame seeds	1 teaspoon soy sauce
1 tablespoon white wine vinegar	1 pound snow peas, stems and strings removed

- In small skillet, heat oil over medium heat; add sesame seeds.
- Cook until light brown (about 3 minutes).
- Remove from heat; add vinegar, sugar, and soy sauce and stir.
- In medium saucepan, bring 2 cups of water to boil. Add snow peas and cook 1 to 2 minutes (pods should be crisp-tender).
- Rinse under cold water and drain.
- In medium bowl, combine snow peas with sesame seed sauce. Toss and chill.

CSOL Best Ever Chicken Salad

Serves 12

4 cups cooked chicken or turkey, cut into bite-size pieces	2 cups celery, chopped
1 20-ounce can water chestnuts, sliced	3 cups mayonnaise
2 pounds seedless grapes, cut in half	2 tablespoons lemon juice
	2 cups sliced almonds, toasted

- Mix chicken, water chestnuts, grapes, and celery together.
- Add mayonnaise and lemon. Toss well.
- Refrigerate overnight.
- Before serving, sprinkle with almonds.

Asparagus and Shrimp Salad

Serves 2 to 4

Salad

¾ to 1 cup white wine
¾ to 1 cup water
  2 teaspoons seafood
     seasoning (optional)

1 pound large shrimp
1 pound asparagus
  watercress

Vinaigrette Dressing

⅔ cup light olive oil
¼ cup fresh lemon juice
1 tablespoon red wine
  vinegar

1 teaspoon salt
  pepper to taste

- Poach shrimp in equal portions of wine and water; add seafood seasoning, if desired.
- Peel, devein and chill shrimp.
- Steam asparagus until crisp-tender.
- Chill in ice water, drain and cut into 3-inch lengths.
- Combine all vinaigrette ingredients.
- Toss shrimp and asparagus with vinaigrette.
- Place on top of large bunch of watercress.

For more color, add tomato wedges as garnish.

Antipasto Salad

Makes 8 appetizers or 4 entrées

½ pound pepperoni, sliced

¼ pound Provolone cheese, cut into ¼-inch cubes

½ 13-ounce jar Italian pepper salad

1 6-ounce jar Italian marinated artichoke hearts

1 small head lettuce (iceberg or Romaine)

2 tomatoes, cut into wedges

1 7-ounce can albacore tuna, drained and flaked

1 2-ounce can flat fillets of anchovies, drained (optional)

¼ cup Italian salad dressing

- In a covered container, combine pepperoni, cheese, pepper salad (including some juice), and artichoke hearts with their marinade.
- Toss, cover and let marinate for at least 3 hours, or overnight, in refrigerator.
- Prepare lettuce as for a regular salad and combine in a salad bowl with tomato wedges. Chill.
- Just before serving, add marinated ingredients, tuna and anchovies to lettuce and tomatoes.
- Toss with salad dressing.

Scallop Salad with Orange Ginger Vinaigrette

Serves 4

1 cup fresh orange juice
1½ teaspoons Dijon mustard
6 tablespoons extra virgin olive oil
2½ teaspoons fresh ginger, peeled and minced
 salt and pepper to taste
4 frozen baby artichoke hearts, thawed (or regular size artichoke hearts)

8 ounces fresh spinach leaves, torn into bite-size pieces
1 tablespoon vegetable oil
12 large sea scallops (may slice in half) white ground pepper
2 oranges, peeled and cut into segments

- Cook orange juice over medium heat until reduced to ½ cup, about 8 minutes.
- Reduce heat to low, whisk mustard into juice, then whisk in olive oil.
- Stir in ginger and season with salt and pepper. Chill.
- Steam artichoke hearts about 6 minutes.
- Divide spinach among 4 serving plates; top with artichokes.
- Heat vegetable oil over medium-high heat, add scallops and sauté until light brown and cooked through, about 1½ to 2 minutes per side.
- Place scallops on top of spinach and artichoke hearts.
- Warm dressing in same skillet and spoon over salad. Season with white pepper and garnish with orange slices.
- Serve warm.

Seafood Salad

Serves 4

1	16-ounce package imitation crabmeat (cooked shrimp or diced chicken optional)	¼	cup mayonnaise juice of 1 lemon salt and pepper to taste pickle, chopped (optional) hard-boiled egg (optional) lettuce
2	ribs celery, sliced		
1	8-ounce can water chestnuts, sliced		
¼	cup onion, minced		
1	8-ounce package cream cheese, softened		

- Combine crabmeat, celery, water chestnuts, onion, and any optional ingredients desired.
- Blend together cream cheese, mayonnaise, and lemon juice until creamy.
- Fold together all ingredients.
- Serve over lettuce.

Salad Dressing

1	10¾-ounce can tomato soup	2	tablespoons onion, chopped
¾	cup oil	½	cup white vinegar
½	cup sugar salt and pepper to taste	3	cloves garlic
2	tablespoons Worcestershire sauce	1	pound Roquefort cheese, crumbled

- Place tomato soup, oil, sugar, salt, pepper, Worcestershire sauce, onion and vinegar in blender and mix.
- Pierce garlic cloves with toothpicks.
- Add garlic and cheese.
- Remove garlic cloves before serving.

Should be prepared 24 hours before serving.

Seafood Salad

Serves 8 to 10

1/4 cup water
1 1/4-ounce package
    unflavored gelatin
1 cup mayonnaise-type
    salad dressing
1 cup sour cream (fat-
    free)
2 tablespoons onion,
    grated
2 tablespoons lemon
    juice

1 teaspoon salt
1/2 cup ripe or green
    olives, chopped
1/2 cup parsley, chopped
2 cups cooked fish,
    flaked (shad, grouper
    or sheepshead)
4 hard-boiled eggs,
    chopped

- Soak gelatin in cold water for 5 minutes, then dissolve over hot water.
- Stir in salad dressing, sour cream, onion, lemon juice, salt, olives, and parsley.
- Add fish and eggs.
- Pour into greased mold and chill until firm, about 2 to 3 hours.
- Unmold and serve on bed of lettuce.

Very good served as spread with saltines.

Curried Tuna Salad

Serves 4

¼ cup mayonnaise
½ teaspoon curry powder
¼ teaspoon garlic salt
dash cayenne pepper
1 tablespoon lemon juice
1 6½-ounce can tuna, drained and mashed

¾ cup apple, chopped
½ cup celery, finely chopped
¼ cup raisins
2 tablespoons green onion, thinly sliced
lettuce
coconut (optional)

- Blend together mayonnaise, curry powder, garlic salt, pepper, and lemon juice.
- Add remaining ingredients and mix well.
- Chill.
- Serve on lettuce cups.
- Sprinkle with coconut (optional).

Patio Peas and Rice Salad

Serves 8 to 10

4 cups cooked white rice
½ cup bottled French salad dressing
2 10-ounce packages frozen tiny peas
½ cup mayonnaise (or more to taste)
2 tablespoons onion, minced

1 teaspoon curry powder, or to taste
salt and pepper to taste
½ teaspoon dry mustard
1½ cups celery, diced
1 4-ounce can water chestnuts, sliced

- Toss warm rice with French dressing and allow to cool.
- Cook peas 1 minute and drain.
- Add remaining ingredients, tossing and mixing well.
- Refrigerate overnight.

A little different and very good.

Salad Niçoise

Serves 6 to 8

Dressing

¾ cup salad oil
¼ cup white wine vinegar
¾ teaspoons salt
1½ teaspoons basil

3 tablespoons fresh parsley, chopped
¼ teaspoon white pepper
2 teaspoons Dijon mustard

Salad

1 small head Romaine, Boston or Bibb lettuce
6 medium red potatoes (peeled or not), boiled, chilled and sliced
1 pound fresh green beans, cooked and sliced, or 1 10-ounce package frozen green beans, cooked, drained and chilled
1 large green pepper, cut in half rings

12 to 20 pitted black olives
1 12¼-ounce can albacore tuna, drained
½ large red onion, cut into thin rings
2 large tomatoes, cut into wedges (12 wedges)
3 eggs, hard-boiled and quartered
12 anchovy fillets (optional)
capers (optional)

- Combine dressing ingredients in a covered jar; shake until well mixed.
- Refrigerate until ready to serve.
- Place bite-size pieces of lettuce on platter or individual salad plates as base of salad.
- Arrange potatoes, beans, green pepper, olives, tuna and onion on leaves.
- Decorate with tomatoes, eggs, anchovies and capers.
- Drizzle dressing over salad just before serving.

Serve with rolls and white wine.

Macaroni Salad

Serves 6 to 8

1 8-ounce box elbow macaroni	1 2-ounce jar pimiento, chopped
½ cup onion, chopped	¾ cup mayonnaise
½ cup green pepper, chopped	¼ cup plus 1 tablespoon sugar
½ cup celery, chopped	2 to 3 tablespoons vinegar
¾ cup cucumber, chopped	

+ Cook macaroni according to package directions.
+ Drain and rinse with cool water and transfer to large bowl.
+ Add onion, green pepper, celery, cucumber, and pimiento to macaroni.
+ Make a paste-like dressing of mayonnaise, sugar, and vinegar.
+ Pour dressing over macaroni and vegetables and toss together.
+ Refrigerate for 1 or more hours before serving.
+ May serve warm, but better cold.

Excellent summer salad. Great with barbecue.

Watercress Salad Dressing

1 bunch watercress	1 tablespoon lemon juice
1 cup mayonnaise (lowfat)	salt and pepper to taste
1 clove garlic, crushed	

+ Remove stems from watercress and place leaves in blender or food processor.
+ Add mayonnaise, garlic, lemon juice, salt and pepper.
+ Blend until smooth.

Very good as salad dressing and also good as spread on sandwiches.

Rice Salad

Serves 6 to 8

Dressing

1 tablespoon Dijon mustard	½ cup olive oil
4 tablespoons red wine vinegar	½ teaspoon pepper
1 teaspoon sugar	parsley or chives, chopped

Salad

4 cups hot cooked rice	½ 10-ounce package frozen peas
½ red pepper, cut into thin strips	¼ cup black olives, finely chopped
½ green pepper, cut into thin strips	⅛ cup fresh parsley, chopped
½ red onion, finely chopped	¼ cup fresh dill, chopped
3 scallions, finely sliced	fresh pepper to taste
½ cup dried currants	

- In blender, mix all dressing ingredients.
- Pour dressing over hot rice, toss well and cool to room temperature.
- Add remaining ingredients; mix well.
- Add additional dressing or seasonings to taste.

Great for a dinner party when serving grilled lamb, steak or even chicken breasts.

Greek Style Pasta Salad

Serves 4

Dressing

½ cup olive or vegetable oil

¼ cup white wine vinegar

1 teaspoon freshly ground pepper

1 teaspoon salt

½ teaspoon sugar

1 clove garlic

Salad

1 pound penne pasta

4 ounces pepperoni, cubed (more, if desired)

4 ounces feta cheese, crumbled

1 bunch scallions, chopped

4 ounces black olives, sliced

¼ cup fresh parsley, chopped

Parmesan cheese, grated

* Prepare salad dressing by combining all dressing ingredients in jar. Toss well. Set aside.
* Cook pasta according to package directions.
* Toss drained pasta with remaining salad ingredients, except Parmesan cheese.
* Remove garlic clove from dressing, pour dressing over salad and toss well.
* Sprinkle with Parmesan cheese.

Shrimp and Pasta Salad

Serves 4

Dressing

1   cup mayonnaise
    juice of 1 lemon

¼   cup fresh basil,
    minced
1   clove garlic

Salad

6   ounces small or
    medium pasta shells,
    cooked and drained
1   pound shrimp,
    cooked, peeled,
    deveined and cut into
    bite-size pieces
¾   10-ounce package
    frozen peas, thawed

¼   cup black olives,
    sliced
½   sweet red pepper,
    diced
¼   cup green onions,
    sliced
    salt and pepper to
    taste
    lettuce
    lemon wedges

◆   Prepare dressing by combining all dressing ingredients. Mix
    well.
◆   Combine all salad ingredients in medium size bowl.
◆   Add dressing, toss and refrigerate.
◆   Serve on bed of lettuce with lemon wedges.

Jeanne Averill's Balsamic Dressing

Makes 16 ounces

½ cup balsamic vinegar
3 tablespoons water
1 cup plus 2
   tablespoons olive oil
2 cloves garlic, minced
2 packets sugar
   substitute (or ½
   teaspoon)

salt to taste (optional)
1 tablespoon lemon
   juice
1½ tablespoons dried
   tomatoes
1 heaping teaspoon
   lemon pepper

+ Place all ingredients in a mixing bowl.
+ Blend with a whisk.
+ Pour into 16-ounce bottle and refrigerate.

Something Special Salad Dressing

Makes about 32 ounces

¼ pound margarine,
   softened
1 quart buttermilk, room
   temperature
1 teaspoon coarse
   ground pepper
2 teaspoons onion salt

2 teaspoons garlic salt
1 teaspoon salt, or less
1 teaspoon seasoned
   salt flavor enhancer
1 teaspoon lemon
   pepper

+ Mix all ingredients in blender or food processor and let stand
  for 12 hours.
+ Store in tightly covered container in refrigerator.
+ Serve on mixed greens.

Pasta, Rice & Grains

Shrimp and Scallop Pasta

Pasta Primavera

Pasta with Chicken and Mushrooms (see photo)

Orange Rice

Pecan Lemon Wild Rice

Cajun Red Beans and Rice

Lowcountry Red Rice (see photo)

Sausage and Macaroni Supper

Jane's Chicken Lasagna with Spinach

Shrimp and Grits

and More

Antebellum Home

Homes along the Battery were built after the seawall was constructed about 1820. Generally, the antebellum homes along East Battery were built by wealthy plantation owners; while the homes along South Battery were built by wealthy shipping merchants. These homes have withstood the ravages of many hurricanes, the earthquake of 1886 and the War Between the States. Fortunately, the original architecture has been preserved.

A Dinner Party

Porgy's Cheese Roll

Mendam Pâté

Scallop Salad

Veal Scalloppini à la Marian

Karl's Rice Pilaf

Tipsy Carrots

Green Salad

Lemon Mousse

Shrimp Marshwinds

Serves 4

1 pound vermicelli
¼ cup olive oil
¼ cup butter
2 tablespoons garlic, minced
½ cup green onion tops, thinly sliced

½ cup celery, finely minced
2 pounds medium size shrimp, peeled and deveined
¼ cup grated Parmesan cheese

- Cook vermicelli according to directions, drain and keep warm.
- Melt olive oil and butter over medium heat.
- Sauté garlic briefly; add green onions and ¼ cup celery and stir 1 minute.
- Add shrimp and stir about 3 minutes or until almost done.
- Add remaining celery and cook 1 more minute.
- Pour over pasta.
- Sprinkle with cheese and toss to combine.

Shrimp and Scallops Pasta

Serves 4

2 tablespoons olive oil	4 tablespoons fresh herb mix (any combination of basil, parsley, oregano and marjoram)
¾ cup onion, finely chopped	
3 medium garlic cloves, minced	
2 28-ounce cans plum tomatoes, slightly drained	½ pound scallops
	½ pound shrimp, peeled and deveined
2 teaspoons fresh thyme	12 ounces spinach fettucini, cooked according to package directions

- Heat oil in large pan over medium-low heat.
- Add onion and sauté until tender; add garlic and stir.
- Add tomatoes, thyme, herb mix, salt and pepper.
- Cook, uncovered, over medium heat for 15 minutes (until slightly thickened).
- Taste and adjust seasoning.
- Add scallops 10 minutes before serving time.
- Add shrimp 5 minutes before serving time, or continue cooking until seafood is done.
- Serve over pasta.

Good with a little freshly grated Parmesan on top of each serving.

Shrimp Pasta

Serves 8

2 sticks butter
2 onions, chopped
1 green pepper,
   chopped
3 stalks celery, chopped
3 cloves garlic, minced
1 tablespoon flour
2 tablespoons fresh
   parsley, finely
   chopped

1 pound Velveeta mild
   Mexican cheese
1 cup half-and-half
2½ pounds shrimp,
   peeled and deveined
1 8-ounce package fine
   egg noodles
   Parmesan cheese

- Preheat oven to 350°.
- In a large pan, melt butter and sauté onions, pepper, celery and garlic.
- Add flour and parsley and heat for 10 minutes.
- Add cheese (can be melted in microwave), cream and shrimp.
- Heat until shrimp is pink.
- Cook noodles and mix with sauce.
- Put into buttered 13x9-inch casserole and sprinkle with Parmesan cheese.
- Bake, covered, for 15 minutes. Remove cover and bake an additional 10 minutes.
- Let stand 10 minutes before serving.

Freezes beautifully.

Linguine with Smoked Salmon Sauce

Serves 4

6 tablespoons butter
1 cup scallions, sliced
1 cup ripe tomatoes,
   peeled, seeded and
   chopped
2 tablespoons lemon
   juice
½ cup dry white wine
4 tablespoons tomato
   paste

2 cups half-and-half
   freshly ground pepper
   to taste
1 to 2 cups smoked salmon,
   coarsely chopped
16 ounces linguine
   fresh dill for garnish
   (optional)

- Heat 4 tablespoons of the butter over medium heat.
- Sauté scallions until limp; add tomatoes and cook briefly.
- Add lemon juice and wine and reduce by ⅓.
- Stir in tomato paste and cream.
- Cook over medium-low heat until slightly reduced and until sauce begins to thicken.
- Add pepper and salmon.
- Cook linguine al dente.
- Drain and toss with 2 tablespoons butter in warm cooking pot.
- Pour hot salmon sauce over linguine and toss gently.
- Serve immediately, topping each serving with fresh dill, if desired.

Pasta with Clam Sauce

Serves 2 to 3

½ cup onions, chopped
1 tablespoon margarine
1 tablespoon olive oil
2 cloves garlic, minced
2 tablespoons flour
⅓ cup dry white wine
1 8-ounce can clam
   juice (or ½ fish-flavor
   bouillon cube
   dissolved in 1 cup
   water)

1 10-ounce can whole
   baby clams, including
   juice
1 7-ounce package thin
   spaghetti, cooked
¼ cup fresh parsley,
   minced
2 teaspoons fresh
   thyme, minced
   freshly grated
   Parmesan cheese
   (optional)

- Sauté onions in margarine and olive oil in 8-inch or larger pan over low heat.
- When onions are golden, add garlic.
- Raise heat to medium and add flour, stirring with wooden spoon for 1 to 2 minutes until blended.
- Stir in wine, clam juice and juice from canned clams. Simmer for 5 minutes.
- Add clams and simmer for 2 minutes.
- Pour sauce over cooked pasta and sprinkle with parsley and thyme.
- Serve with grated Parmesan, if desired.

Pasta Nogales

Serves 4 to 6

½ cup dry sherry
3 teaspoons olive oil
2 tablespoons garlic, minced
½ cup onions, finely chopped
8 sun-dried tomatoes, oil-packed, drained and coarsely chopped
1 tablespoon pickled jalapeño peppers, finely chopped
3 tablespoons canned green chili peppers, chopped

4 cups canned Italian plum tomatoes, coarsely chopped and drained lightly, or the equivalent quantity of fresh tomatoes, or a mixture of both
1 pound fettucine or other long pasta of choice, cooked according to directions
4 tablespoons fresh basil, chopped
4 tablespoons fresh parsley, chopped

- Heat sherry and olive oil to bubbling in a heavy skillet over medium-high heat.
- Add garlic and onions and sauté for 3 minutes.
- Add sun-dried tomatoes, jalapeños and green chilies and tomatoes.
- Reduce heat to low and cook, stirring occasionally, for 20 minutes.
- Add drained pasta to sauce in skillet; sprinkle with basil and parsley.
- Toss well and serve immediately.

A low-cal, lowfat pasta with quite a bit of zing. The level of "zing" can be adjusted to suit individual taste by increasing or decreasing the quantity of jalapeño pepper. Flavor improves overnight.

Rigatoni with Tomatoes and Vodka

Serves 4

2 tablespoons butter
1 small onion, chopped
2 cloves garlic, minced
1 tablespoon dried
   Italian seasonings,
   crumbled
1 16-ounce can Italian
   plum tomatoes,
   chopped, juices
   reserved

3 ounces sliced
   prosciutto, chopped
⅓ cup vodka
¾ cup half-and-half
1 cup Parmesan
   cheese, freshly grated
8 ounces rigatoni,
   cooked according to
   directions

♦ Melt butter in heavy large skillet over medium-high heat.
♦ Add onion, garlic and Italian seasonings and sauté until
   onion is translucent, about 4 minutes.
♦ Add tomatoes, reserved juices and prosciutto and simmer
   10 minutes, stirring occasionally.
♦ Add vodka and simmer 5 minutes.
♦ Add cream and ½ cup of the Parmesan cheese and simmer
   until sauce thickens slightly, about 4 minutes.
♦ Add drained rigatoni and stir until sauce coats pasta.
♦ Season with salt and pepper.
♦ Serve, passing remaining Parmesan cheese separately.

*Evaporated skimmed milk may be substituted for cream
with equally good results.*

Tomato Primavera

Serves 4

2 teaspoons olive oil
1 cup yellow onion, finely chopped
2 cloves garlic, mashed
1 red pepper, cut into 1-inch pieces
8 stalks asparagus, cut into 1-inch pieces
6 cherry tomatoes, halved
1 tablespoon fresh basil, finely chopped

½ teaspoon oregano
¼ teaspoon sage
¼ teaspoon pepper
¼ cup water
1 14 to 16-ounce can tomatoes with juice
4 ounces lowfat cream cheese, softened
12 ounces fettucini, cooked as desired

- Heat oil in non-stick skillet; add onion and sauté 3 to 4 minutes.
- Add garlic and red peppers and cook 1 to 2 minutes more.
- Add asparagus, cherry tomatoes and spices.
- Stir in canned tomatoes and water.
- Reduce heat and simmer gently for 20 minutes.
- Add cream cheese in small slices and stir until melted, about 2 minutes.
- Serve over cooked pasta.

Sauce improves if prepared the day before and refrigerated. If you are making this ahead, hold the cream cheese and add it when sauce is reheated prior to serving.

Pasta Primavera

Serves 6

1 cup zucchini, sliced	salt and pepper to taste
1½ cups broccoli flowerets	¼ cup Italian parsley, chopped
1½ cups snow peas	10 large mushrooms, sliced
1 cup baby peas	⅓ cup pine nuts
6 stalks asparagus, sliced	⅓ cup butter
1 pound spaghetti	½ cup Parmesan cheese
12 cherry tomatoes, cut in halves	1 cup cream
3 tablespoons olive oil	⅓ cup fresh basil, chopped
2 teaspoons garlic, minced	

- Blanch zucchini, broccoli, snow peas, baby peas and asparagus in boiling salted water for 1 to 2 minutes until crisp tender.
- Cook pasta in boiling salted water until al dente, about 8 to 11 minutes, and drain.
- Sauté tomatoes in 1 tablespoon oil with garlic, salt, pepper and parsley; add mushrooms.
- In another pan, sauté pine nuts in 2 tablespoons oil until brown. Add blanched vegetables and sauté until hot.
- In a pan large enough to hold pasta and vegetables, melt butter. Add cheese, cream and basil.
- Stir to melt cheese.
- Add pasta and toss.
- Add ⅓ of the vegetables and toss.
- Top with remaining vegetables and tomatoes.

Sauce can be thinned with consommé.

A wonderful vegetarian meal.

Christopher's Pasta

Serves 6

4	ounces unsalted butter	1	tablespoon garlic, minced
1	cup walnut pieces	1	tablespoon white wine
1	cup pine nuts	2	teaspoons white wine Worcestershire sauce
1	cup raisins, soaked 1 hour or longer in water	1	pound pasta, small shells or other shaped pasta, cooked
½	teaspoon Italian seasoning (or ¼ teaspoon oregano and ¼ teaspoon basil)	1	tablespoon dry sherry
		1	cup Parmesan cheese, grated

- Melt butter in heavy skillet.
- Spin the nuts a few seconds in a blender to reduce them to small pieces, spinning walnuts and pine nuts separately.
- Add nuts, raisins, garlic and Italian seasonings to the skillet.
- When raisins begin to plump up, add wine and Worcestershire sauce.
- Bring sauce to warm temperature, stirring constantly.
- Add drained pasta and toss together.
- Add sherry and ⅓ cup of the cheese.
- Toss briefly and serve immediately.
- Pass the remaining Parmesan.

Any unsalted nuts (pecans, almonds, hazelnuts, etc.) can be substituted. A good vegetarian dish.

Penne Pasta with
Tomato-Bacon Sauce

Serves 6

6 tablespoons olive oil
12 bacon slices, finely chopped
2 large onions, chopped
⅔ cup dry white wine
2 28-ounce cans peeled Italian plum tomatoes, chopped, juices reserved

2 teaspoons dried basil
cayenne pepper to taste
16 ounces penne pasta, freshly cooked
Parmesan cheese, freshly grated

- Heat oil in heavy large skillet over medium-high heat.
- Add bacon and onion and cook until bacon is almost crisp and onions are golden brown, stirring occasionally (about 8 to 10 minutes).
- Add wine, stir and continue cooking 4 minutes.
- Add chopped tomatoes with their juices and dried basil and bring to boil.
- Reduce heat and simmer sauce, uncovered, until thickened, stirring occasionally, about 45 minutes.
- Season to taste with cayenne pepper.
- Place pasta in bowl, add sauce and toss thoroughly.
- Serve pasta hot, passing Parmesan cheese separately.

Pasta with Chicken and Mushrooms

Serves 6

Pasta Dish

3 ounces sun-dried
tomatoes
boiling water
½ clove garlic
olive oil
12 ounces mushrooms

½ cup red or green
pepper, cut into strips
½ cup onion, cut into
strips
2 cups cooked chicken,
cut into strips
spaghetti to serve 6

Pesto

6 tablespoons olive oil
¼ cup Parmesan cheese
3 tablespoons pine nuts
or walnuts, finely
chopped

1 teaspoon fresh
parsley
½ teaspoon fresh basil
⅛ teaspoon pepper
¼ teaspoon salt

- Cover sun-dried tomatoes with boiling water and let stand for 2 minutes.
- Drain and place on paper towel.
- Cook pasta according to package directions.
- Cook garlic in olive oil until golden; discard garlic.
- Sauté mushrooms, peppers and onions in same oil.
- Remove half of the mushrooms and combine in blender with all pesto ingredients.
- Blend until smooth, adding more olive oil if too thick (should be consistency of spaghetti sauce).
- Drain pasta and combine with chicken, tomatoes, mushrooms-pepper-onion mixture and pesto.
- Serve immediately.

Keith's Chicken with Pasta

Serves 4

1 pound chicken breasts, skinned, boned and cut into strips
3 tablespoons oil, divided
3 tablespoons butter, melted (divided)

6 tablespoons fresh parsley, chopped
1 small bunch green onions, chopped
½ cup chicken broth
juice of 2 lemons
4 tablespoons Dijon mustard

- Sauté chicken in 1 tablespoon oil and 1 tablespoon butter until brown.
- Whisk together parsley, onion, broth, lemon juice, mustard and remaining oil and butter.
- Pour over chicken and cook in skillet over medium heat until done (about 5 minutes).
- Serve over pasta

If you like pasta with lots of sauce, double ingredients.

Pesto

Makes about 1½ to 2 cups

3 large cloves garlic, crushed
2 to 3 cups fresh basil leaves
½ cup olive oil

¼ cup pine nuts
⅓ cup Parmesan cheese
1½ teaspoons salt
dash of pepper

- Blend all ingredients in food processor.
- Serve over hot pasta.

Freezes well. Great to have on hand to add to soup, sauces, pizza, etc.

Fox Hollow Red Pepper Sauce for Pasta

Makes approximately 3 cups

¼ cup olive oil
2 medium onions, chopped
3 red peppers, chopped
3 cloves garlic, minced
12 ounces tomato paste
1 tablespoon balsamic vinegar
⅔ cup water
1 teaspoon oregano

1 teaspoon basil, fresh if possible
⅓ cup parsley, chopped
salt and pepper to taste
¼ teaspoon red pepper flakes (or to taste)
hot sauce to taste
grated Parmesan cheese

- Sauté onions until soft, about 10 minutes.
- Add peppers, cover, reduce heat and simmer about 10 minutes, stirring occasionally until peppers are soft.
- Add remaining ingredients and stir until blended.
- Cook, covered, 10 to 15 minutes.
- Cool slightly, then coarsely grind in food processor.
- Serve over hot pasta with Parmesan cheese.

Tomato-Mushroom Sauce

Serves 4

¼ cup olive oil
¼ cup butter
1½ pounds mushrooms, sliced
2 cloves garlic, minced

1 teaspoon salt
pepper, freshly ground, to taste
2½ cups canned Italian tomatoes
½ teaspoon oregano

- Sauté mushrooms, garlic, salt and pepper in combined olive oil and butter for 10 minutes, stirring frequently.
- Add tomatoes and oregano and simmer for 30 minutes.
- Serve over cooked pasta of your choice and pass Parmesan cheese.

A real treat for mushroom lovers. Drain off some of the juice from the tomatoes if you prefer a thicker sauce.

Cindy's Clam Sauce

Makes approximately 2 cups

¼ cup olive oil
2 cloves garlic, minced
¼ cup water
½ teaspoon salt
½ teaspoon oregano
¼ cup fresh parsley, chopped

¼ teaspoon pepper, freshly ground
2 6½-ounce cans minced clams (drain 1 can)

- Heat oil and sauté garlic. Do not let brown. Cool slightly.
- Add water.
- Add remaining ingredients and heat through.
- Serve with freshly grated Parmesan cheese over hot pasta.

Tomato and Zucchini Pasta Sauce

Serves 4 to 6

1 cup onion, chopped
1 cup celery, chopped
1 clove garlic, crushed
2 tablespoons oil
1 teaspoon oregano
1 teaspoon basil
1 small hot pepper, chopped
1 green pepper, chopped

2 medium zucchini, cut into ½-inch cubes
½ medium eggplant, cut into ½-inch cubes
3 8-ounce cans tomato sauce
½ pound mushrooms, fresh, chopped
¼ cup brandy (optional)
cooked pasta
Parmesan cheese

- Sauté onion, celery and garlic in oil until soft.
- Add oregano, basil, hot pepper, green pepper, zucchini, and eggplant.
- Stir in tomato sauce and simmer 25 minutes.
- Add mushrooms and simmer for 25 more minutes.
- Add brandy if desired.
- Serve over pasta; sprinkle with Parmesan cheese.

Eggplant Sauce

Serves 4 to 6

2 large eggplants, cut into small cubes
oil
2 16-ounce cans crushed tomatoes
1 6-ounce can tomato paste
1 cup water

6 to 8 cloves garlic, chopped
1 cup fresh parsley, chopped
1 tablespoon sugar
1 tablespoon basil
freshly ground pepper
½ cup Parmesan cheese, freshly grated

- Stir-fry eggplant in oil until tender; set aside.
- Combine remaining ingredients and simmer, covered, for 1 hour.
- Add eggplant and simmer for another hour.

Sauce is good on chicken, pasta or about anything.

Chris's Hearty Tomato Sauce

Serves 6

2 carrots, finely chopped
2 celery stalks, finely chopped
1 medium to large onion, chopped
2 tablespoons butter
2 tablespoons olive oil

2 large cloves garlic, minced
4 cups fresh tomatoes, peeled, seeded and chopped (may use canned tomatoes)
salt and pepper to taste

- Sauté carrots, onion and celery in butter and oil until tender.
- Add garlic and sauté another minute.
- Add remaining ingredients.
- Simmer sauce over low heat, stirring occasionally, for 30 to 40 minutes.

Freezes beautifully.

Gitche Gu'Mee Wild Rice

Serves 6 to 8

½ cup long grain white rice
½ cup wild rice
1 pound lean ground beef
2 cups celery, chopped
½ medium onion, chopped.

4 teaspoons soy sauce (or more to taste)
1 10½-ounce can cream of mushroom soup, diluted with an equal amount of water
1 pound mushrooms, sliced

- Soak wild rice for 2 hours; drain.
- Preheat oven to 400°.
- Cook beef over medium heat; add onion and celery. Stir and cook about 4 minutes.
- Mix all ingredients and place in greased casserole.
- Bake, covered, for 1½ hours, uncovering the last 15 minutes.

Curried Rice Casserole

Serves 8

½ cup butter
1 teaspoon curry powder
½ pound mushrooms, sliced
2 tablespoons green pepper, chopped

2 tablespoons onion, chopped
½ cup pecans, coarsely chopped
3 cups chicken broth
1½ cups long grain rice

- Preheat oven to 325°.
- Melt butter; stir in curry powder.
- Add mushrooms, green pepper and onion and sauté until onion is limp.
- Add pecans and cook 1 minute, then add broth and rice.
- Place all in a 2-quart casserole.
- May be refrigerated at this point until time to cook.
- Bake for 1 hour.

Herbed Rice Pilaf

Serves 6

2 tablespoons butter	1 bay leaf
¾ cup raw rice	1 10½-ounce can
1 tablespoon oregano	consommé
2 teaspoons brown	¾ cups water
sugar	½ cup dry sherry
½ small onion, chopped	
1 3-ounce can	
mushrooms	

- Preheat oven to 350°.
- Sauté rice, oregano, brown sugar, onion, mushrooms and bay leaf in butter for 20 minutes.
- Combine consommé, water and sherry in a 2-quart casserole.
- Add sautéed ingredients to consommé mixture.
- Bake for 1 to 1¼ hours, covered.
- If too moist, remove cover and cook additional 15 minutes.

Karl's Rice Pilaf

Serves 8

2 cups long grain rice	¾ cup parsley, minced
4 cups chicken broth	½ cup scallions,
6 tablespoons butter	chopped
¾ cup celery, finely	1 cup pine nuts or
chopped	walnuts, chopped
¾ cup carrots, finely	
chopped	

- Preheat oven to 375°.
- Melt butter in an ovenproof casserole.
- Add rice and broth to casserole.
- Stir in rice until coated and bake, covered, for ½ hour.
- Add remaining ingredients and bake an additional ½ hour.

Skillet Mustard Rice with Chicken

Serves 4

1 cup canned low-salt chicken broth
½ cup onions, chopped
¼ cup plus 2 tablespoons Dijon mustard
6 cloves garlic, minced
2 teaspoons Worcestershire sauce
   dash of hot sauce
¼ stick butter

2 tablespoons olive oil
1 whole chicken, cut into pieces
¾ teaspoon dried thyme
½ teaspoon dried parsley
¼ teaspoon dried basil
1 cup rice, cooked parsley, freshly chopped (optional)

- Combine broth, onions, mustard, garlic, Worcestershire sauce and hot sauce in small bowl.
- Melt butter with oil in heavy large skillet over medium-high heat.
- Season chicken with salt and pepper and add to skillet.
- Sprinkle with thyme, parsley and basil.
- Cook until chicken is golden brown, turning occasionally, about 10 minutes.
- Pour mustard mixture over chicken.
- Cover, reduce heat to low and simmer until chicken is just cooked through, about 30 minutes.
- Using slotted spoon, transfer chicken to platter, cover with foil and keep warm.
- Boil liquid remaining in skillet until reduced to sauce consistency, stirring occasionally, about 7 minutes.
- Pour sauce over chicken and sprinkle with fresh parsley, if desired.
- Serve over rice.

Rice doubles when cooked. One cup of raw rice will equal two cups cooked.

Orange Rice

Serves 4

3 tablespoons butter or margarine
2 tablespoons onion, chopped
1½ cups water

1 teaspoon orange rind, grated
1 cup orange juice
1 teaspoon salt
⅛ teaspoon marjoram
1 cup uncooked rice

- Melt butter or margarine in pan.
- Add onion and cook until tender.
- Add water, orange rind, orange juice, salt and marjoram.
- Bring to a boil.
- Slowly stir in rice, cover, reduce heat and cook 20 minutes or until rice is tender.

Goes well with fish or pork.

Pecan Lemon Wild Rice

Serves 4 to 6

1 cup wild rice, uncooked
3½ cups chicken broth
1½ tablespoons lemon rind, divided
1 tablespoon lemon juice

1 tablespoon butter
½ cup pecans, chopped and toasted
3 tablespoons green onions, chopped
¼ cup fresh parsley, chopped

- Wash wild rice in three changes of hot water; drain.
- Combine chicken broth, 2¼ teaspoons lemon rind, lemon juice and butter in a saucepan and bring to boil.
- Stir in rice, cover, reduce heat and simmer 50 to 60 minutes, or until liquid is absorbed and rice is tender.
- Stir in pecans, remaining lemon rind, green onions and parsley.

Wonderfully crunchy and lemony. Goes well with game.

Green and Yellow Rice

Serves 6

3 cups white rice, cooked	1 tablespoon onion, chopped
¼ cup butter	1 tablespoon Worcestershire sauce
4 eggs, beaten	½ teaspoon marjoram
1 cup milk	½ teaspoon thyme
1 pound sharp Cheddar cheese, grated	½ teaspoon rosemary
1 10-ounce package frozen chopped spinach, cooked and drained	½ teaspoon salt

- Preheat oven to 350°.
- Melt butter and add to rice.
- Add milk to eggs, then cheese, then spinach and mix well but gently.
- Add onion, Worcestershire sauce, marjoram, thyme, rosemary and salt.
- Put into a 2-quart casserole dish.
- Set uncovered casserole into a pan of warm water and bake for 45 minutes.

When adding soy sauce to a heated wok, pour against the side of the wok, rather than directly in the center, to give better flavor.

Cajun Red Beans and Rice

Serves 4 to 6

1 pound kielbasa sausage (or pepperoni or ham)	2 15-ounce cans red kidney beans, drained
1 small clove garlic, chopped	½ teaspoon paprika
1 medium onion, chopped	½ teaspoon Cajun seasoning, if desired
½ green pepper, chopped	salt and pepper to taste

- Cut sausage into large bite-size pieces and begin browning.
- As soon as you have some fat in skillet, add garlic, onion and pepper; brown.
- Add beans and seasonings.
- Barely cover all with water and simmer approximately 20 minutes.
- Serve over rice.

A taste of New Orleans.

Orzo and Rice Pilaf

Serves 4

¼ cup butter	2½ cups chicken broth
¼ cup orzo	1 teaspoon salt
1 cup rice	

- Melt butter.
- Sauté orzo in butter until brown.
- Add rice and sauté, stirring frequently.
- Add broth and salt; cook slowly until broth is gone.
- Remove from heat and steam in pot about 20 minutes.

Rice-Sausage Casserole

Serves 6

4 cups water
1 package dry chicken
  noodle soup
2 chicken bouillon
  cubes
1 large onion, chopped
1 green pepper,
  chopped

2 stalks celery, chopped
1 pound sausage,
  cooked and drained
1 cup raw rice
4 ounces slivered
  almonds

- Preheat oven to 350°.
- Bring water to boil and pour over soup, bouillon cubes, onion, pepper and celery.
- When bouillon has dissolved, add sausage, rice, and almonds.
- Bake in covered 2-quart casserole for 1 hour, stirring occasionally.

Kathleen's Spinach-Rice Casserole

Serves 4 to 6

1 6-ounce box long
  grain and wild rice,
  cooked as directed
2 10-ounce packages
  frozen chopped
  spinach, thawed and
  drained

2 cups Monterey Jack
  cheese, grated
¼ cup butter, melted
¼ cup onion, finely
  chopped
¾ teaspoon dry mustard

- Preheat oven to 350°.
- Mix all ingredients.
- Put into a greased 2-quart casserole.
- Bake about 40 minutes, until hot.

Try a different kind of cheese for a totally different taste.

Lowcountry Red Rice

Serves 10

14	bacon slices	¾	cup tomato paste
2	large red bell peppers, chopped	3	cups long grain rice
1	medium onion, chopped	6	cups canned vegetable or chicken broth
4	teaspoons dried thyme	1	tablespoon hot pepper sauce

- Cook bacon in heavy Dutch oven over medium-high heat until brown.
- Transfer bacon to paper towels to drain. Crumble.
- Pour off all but 3 tablespoons bacon drippings.
- Add peppers, onion and thyme and sauté 5 minutes.
- Mix in tomato paste, rice, broth, hot pepper sauce, and bacon.
- Reduce heat, cover and simmer until rice is tender, about 30 minutes.
- Add hot pepper sauce to taste.

For long pasta, use two ounces uncooked (a bunch that is one half inch in diameter) for one cup serving. For short pasta a slightly rounded one half cup dried will make one cup cooked.

Risotto

Serves 4

3 cups chicken stock	1 cup dry white wine
2 to 3 tablespoons olive oil	⅔ cup Parmesan
1 small onion, finely	cheese, freshly grated
chopped	2 to 3 tablespoons butter
1 cup short grain Italian	
rice	

- Heat the stock to a simmer.
- Heat oil in separate saucepan.
- Add onion and sauté until translucent.
- Add rice and stir to coat with the oil until toasted, approximately 5 minutes.
- Stir in the wine. Bring to a simmer.
- With the heat on medium-low, add about ½ cup of the hot stock, or enough that the rice is slightly sloshy.
- When the stock is almost absorbed, add another ½ cup of stock, stirring gently and well.
- Repeat until all stock is used.
- Risotto should cook at a steady simmer without ever drying out. Cooking time will be between 20 and 30 minutes.
- When risotto is creamy, remove from heat and stir in cheese and butter.
- Serve immediately.

For variety, add a 10-ounce package frozen peas, thawed, toward the end of cooking time. Red wine and beef broth can be used instead of the white wine and chicken stock.

Gourmet Noodles

Serves 6

¼ cup butter, melted
1 8-ounce can mushrooms, drained (or fresh mushrooms, sliced)
½ cup onion, chopped
2 cloves garlic, minced

2 tablespoons lemon juice
2 10½-ounce cans beef consommé
1 8-ounce package angel hair pasta

- Put mushrooms, garlic, onions, and lemon juice in large skillet with butter.
- Cook until heated through.
- Add soup and bring to a boil.
- Crumble noodles into mixture, cover and let simmer until liquid is absorbed, stirring frequently.

Macaroni and Cheese Dish

Serves 4 generously

¼ stick butter or margarine
1¼ cups sharp cheese, grated
½ cup (4 ounces) elbow macaroni
¼ cup pimientos, chopped

⅓ cup green bell pepper, chopped
½ teaspoon salt
⅛ teaspoon pepper
1 tablespoon dry or prepared mustard
1 egg
1⅔ cups milk

- Preheat oven to 350°.
- Mix together butter, 1 cup cheese, macaroni, pimientos, green pepper, salt, pepper and mustard.
- Beat egg and milk together and add to first mixture.
- Sprinkle ¼ cup cheese on top.
- Bake for 45 minutes or until browned.

A slightly different twist to the traditional macaroni and cheese.

Sausage and Macaroni Supper

Serves 6

1 pound bulk sausage (hot)	1 teaspoon salt
1 16-ounce can whole tomatoes, undrained and chopped	1/4 teaspoon pepper
	1/2 teaspoon chili powder
	3 cups macaroni, cooked
1 large green pepper, cut into thin strips	1 1/2 cups sour cream
1 large onion, chopped	round buttery cracker crumbs

- Preheat oven to 350°.
- Cook sausage in large skillet until brown and crumbled.
- Remove from heat.
- Stir in tomatoes, green pepper, onion, salt, pepper and chili powder.
- Cover and cook over medium heat 10 minutes, stirring occasionally.
- Add macaroni and sour cream.
- Put in buttered casserole. Top with cracker crumbs.
- Bake until hot, about 15 minutes.

Easy Spinach Lasagna

1 pound lowfat ricotta cheese	3/4 teaspoon oregano
3 cups mozzarella cheese, divided	1/8 teaspoon pepper
1 egg	1 48-ounce jar spaghetti sauce
1 10-ounce package frozen spinach, chopped, thawed and drained well	9 lasagna noodles, uncooked
1/2 teaspoon salt	1/2 cup Parmesan cheese, freshly grated
	1/2 cup water

- Preheat oven to 350°.
- In large bowl, mix ricotta cheese, 2 cups mozzarella cheese, egg, spinach, salt, oregano and pepper.
- Grease 13x9x2-inch pan.
- Layer 1/3 jar spaghetti sauce, 3 noodles and 1/2 of cheese and spinach mixture in casserole.
- Repeat layers.
- Place final 3 noodles over layers.
- Top with remaining 1/3 jar of sauce and reserved cup of mozzarella cheese.
- Sprinkle grated Parmesan cheese over mozzarella and then pour 1/2 cup water around the edges of pan.
- Cover tightly with foil.
- Bake for 1 hour and 10 minutes, until bubbly.
- Uncover and bake an additional 5 minutes.
- Let stand 15 minutes before serving.

The use of bottled spaghetti sauce makes this an easy, last-minute meal.

Jane's Chicken Lasagna with Spinach

Makes 6 to 8 servings

1   10¾-ounce can cream of chicken soup, undiluted

1   10½-ounce can chicken broth, undiluted

1   8-ounce package cream cheese, softened

1   cup cottage cheese, creamed, small curd

½   cup sour cream

½   cup mayonnaise

⅓   cup onion, chopped

1   10-ounce package frozen spinach, chopped, thawed and squeezed

⅓   cup green olives with pimiento, chopped

1   8-ounce package lasagna noodles

3   cups chicken, cooked and chopped

1   tablespoon butter, melted

½   cup breadcrumbs, fine

- Preheat oven to 350°.
- Combine soup and broth, stirring until smooth. Set aside.
- Combine cream cheese, cottage cheese, sour cream and mayonnaise in a large bowl.
- Beat with electric mixer 1 minute or until smooth.
- Add onion, spinach and olives.
- Grease a 13x9x2-inch baking dish.
- Layer half each of noodles, cream cheese mixture, chicken and soup.
- Repeat layers.
- Seal with foil.
- Bake about 45 minutes.
- Remove foil. Let stand for a while if you want.
- Mix butter and crumbs and sprinkle over top of lasagna.
- Bake until hot.
- Let stand about 10 minutes before serving.

Crab Lasagna

Makes 6 servings

¼ pound lasagna noodles
¼ cup onion, chopped
2 tablespoons butter
1½ tablespoons flour
1 teaspoon basil
salt
generous dash pepper
1½ cups milk
1 egg, beaten
½ pound ricotta cheese or small curd cottage cheese

1 cup Swiss cheese, grated
2 medium-sized tomatoes, peeled and sliced
6 ounces crabmeat (can use more)
2 tablespoons parsley, chopped (plus extra for garnish)
2 tablespoons Parmesan cheese, grated

- Preheat oven to 350°.
- Cook lasagna noodles, drain and set aside.
- Lightly sauté onion in butter.
- Add flour, basil, salt, pepper and milk to make a cream sauce.
- Cook on low heat until slightly thick.
- Add beaten egg to sauce.
- Lightly grease 2-quart baking dish.
- Place a little sauce in bottom.
- Layer ⅓ lasagna noodles, ½ of cheeses, tomato, crabmeat and parsley.
- Add a little sauce.
- Repeat with second layer and cover with sauce.
- Place remaining noodles and then remaining sauce on top.
- Sprinkle with Parmesan cheese.
- Garnish with parsley.
- Bake 40 minutes.

Shrimp and Grits

Serves 5

1 pound shrimp, peeled and cleaned	¾ cup extra-sharp Cheddar cheese, cubed
1 cup herb and garlic marinade (or enough to cover shrimp)	5 cups boiling water
	1¼ cups grits
	1½ teaspoons salt
	¼ stick butter

- Place shrimp in a container, cover with commercial herb and garlic marinade and refrigerate for several hours or overnight.
- Mix grits, salt and butter in boiling water and cook mixture until almost serving consistency.
- Stir in ¾ cup cubed extra-sharp Cheddar cheese.
- Cook until cheese is partially melted.
- Add drained shrimp and cook only until the shrimp are heated through.

A lowcountry tradition at its best.

Grits and Cheese

Makes 6 to 8 servings

Grits

1 quart milk	1 teaspoon salt
½ cup butter, cut up	⅛ teaspoon pepper
1 cup grits	

Cheese Mixture

⅓ cup butter, melted	⅓ cup Parmesan
1 cup Gruyère cheese, grated	cheese, grated

- To prepare the grits (do this a day ahead of serving), bring milk to a boil.
- Add butter.
- Gradually stir in grits.
- Resume boiling and cook, stirring, until it looks like cooked farina.
- Remove from heat, add salt and pepper.
- Beat hard with electric mixer for 5 minutes.
- Pour into 11x7-inch glass dish.
- Cool and refrigerate.
- On serving day, cut grits into 8 rectangular pieces and arrange in buttered dish, one piece overlapping the other like rows of dominoes.
- Pour melted butter over grits and sprinkle both cheeses on top.
- Bake at 400° for 35 minutes or until light brown.

If you want to "lighten" it, use skim milk and a little less butter. It still tastes wonderfully creamy.

Cornbread and Grits Poultry Dressing

Serves 10

Cornbread

2 cups self-rising
   cornmeal
1¼ cups milk

1 egg
¼ cup oil

Grits

1 cup grits, regular or
   quick
4 cups boiling water
¼ pound butter
½ teaspoon poultry
   seasoning (more to
   taste)
½ teaspoon dried
   parsley

⅓ cup celery, finely
   chopped
¼ cup onion, finely
   chopped
½ teaspoon salt
2 chicken bouillon
   cubes, dissolved in 2
   cups water

- Preheat oven to 400°.
- Combine cornmeal, milk, egg and oil; and bake in a 7x11-inch pan for 25 to 30 minutes.
- Add grits to boiling water.
- Cook until nearly done.
- Add butter, poultry seasoning and parsley.
- To assemble dressing, crumble baked cornbread in large bowl.
- Add grits mixture, celery, onion, and salt.
- Add dissolved bouillon cubes.
- Pour into greased 13x9-inch pan. Cover with foil.
- Lower oven temperature to 350° and bake for 45 minutes.
- Remove foil and bake until lightly browned.

May add walnuts, chestnuts, or oysters.

Seafood

Shrimp and Rice Surprise (see photo)

Shrimp Creole

Seafood Newburg Casserole

Coquilles St. Jacques

Italian Fillet of Fish

Baked Grouper Fillets

Salmon with Caper Sauce

Poached Salmon with Dill Sauce

Frogmore Stew

Bouillabaisse

and More

Charleston Shrimpers

Historically, shrimp and hominy has been a favorite lowcountry break-

fast. This is reminiscent of the street vendors during the "Porgy and

Bess" era. The first cries of the morning were the vendors calling out

what they were selling. The shrimp vendors also announced the day of

the week, "Comin' on a Saterdey monin'-raw swimps — raw swimps."

Menus

<u>Supper for Four</u>

Fast Fish Bake

Low Country Red Rice

Asparagus Casserole

Frozen Coleslaw

Lazy Lady Lemon Ice Cream

Shrimp Scampi

Serves 6

2 pounds fresh shrimp
   commercial shrimp
   boil seasoning
8 tablespoons butter
6 cloves garlic, minced
4 shallots or scallions,
   minced

½ teaspoon garlic salt
¼ teaspoon salt
   (optional)
⅓ cup white wine
4 green onions, thinly
   cut

- Cook shrimp in boiling water to which commercial shrimp boil seasoning has been added. Do not overcook. It is preferable to undercook.
- Peel and devein shrimp.
- Melt butter in skillet and add garlic and shallots; brown for 3 minutes.
- Add shrimp, garlic salt, salt (if desired), and wine.
- Cook for 5 more minutes.
- Add green onions for color.
- Serve with rice.

Curry and Garlic Shrimp

Serves 4

1 pound fresh shrimp,
   peeled and deveined
4 tablespoons butter
1 teaspoon curry
   powder

2 to 4 cloves garlic, minced
        salt and pepper to
        taste

- Preheat oven to 350°.
- Melt butter.
- Mix in garlic and curry.
- Add salt and pepper, if desired.
- Pour over shrimp in an ovenproof dish.
- Bake for 25 minutes.

Super easy.

Shrimp Curry

Serves 8 to 10

¼ cup butter
1 cup onion, chopped
or grated
1 tart apple, peeled and
chopped
1 clove garlic, crushed
2 to 3 teaspoons curry
powder
¼ cup flour
1 teaspoon salt
¼ teaspoon pepper
ground ginger and
cardamom, to taste

1 10-ounce can chicken
broth, undiluted
2 8-ounce bottles clam
broth
2 tablespoons lime juice
and grated peel of 1
lime
¼ teaspoon thyme
2 pounds shrimp,
cleaned but uncooked

- Sauté onion, apple, garlic, and curry in the butter.
- Blend in flour, salt, pepper, ginger, and cardamom.
- Slowly add chicken and clam broths, lime juice, peel, and thyme.
- Bring to a boil, stirring constantly.
- Simmer uncovered for 20 minutes.
- Add shrimp and cook until pink.

Serve with rice and a green vegetable.

Shrimp Stir-Fry

Serves 4 to 6

1 tablespoon sesame oil	8 large fresh mushrooms, sliced
1 tablespoon peanut oil	
1 pound fresh medium to large shrimp, peeled and deveined	1 10-ounce package frozen snow peas, defrosted
1 8-ounce can sliced water chestnuts, drained	1 clove garlic, pressed
	1 tablespoon ginger root, grated
1 large, sweet red bell pepper, cut into strips	3 tablespoons soy sauce
2 bunches of green onions, sliced	1 to 2 tablespoons Chinese oyster sauce (optional)

- Pour the sesame and peanut oil in a preheated frying pan or wok.
- Add the shrimp and cook until pink, about 2 minutes. Stir constantly.
- Add water chestnuts, red pepper, green onions, mushrooms, snow peas, garlic, ginger root and sauté for 3 minutes. Stir constantly.
- Add the soy sauce and cook for 1 more minute.

Serve with rice or Chinese noodles.

Barbecued Shrimp

Serves 6 to 8

1 cup butter, or less if desired

2 medium onions, finely chopped

2 cups white wine

1 12-ounce can of beer

¾ teaspoon salt

1 teaspoon pepper, freshly ground

¼ teaspoon hot pepper sauce

1 teaspoon Worcestershire sauce

1 teaspoon Dijon mustard

¼ cup lemon juice

1 teaspoon capers

1 clove garlic, minced

2 bay leaves

2 teaspoons fresh parsley, chopped

2 tablespoons fresh thyme, chopped

1½ tablespoons fresh basil, chopped

3 to 4 pounds cooked shrimp, shelled and deveined, with tails left on

- In a 2-quart pan, sauté onions in melted butter for 5 minutes.
- Add remaining ingredients, except shrimp.
- Let simmer for 1 hour over low heat. Remove from heat.
- Add shrimp. Cool and refrigerate 2 to 3 hours, or up to 24 hours.
- Heat just before serving, but do not boil.

Serve with French bread and salad. This is also delicious over rice.

Shrimp Dijon

Serves 6 to 8

2 to 3	pounds raw shrimp, cleaned	1	tablespoon Dijon mustard
4	tablespoons butter, melted	½	teaspoon Worcestershire sauce
2	tablespoons oil	1 to 6	garlic cloves, pressed
	juice of 1 lemon		

- Preheat oven to 450°.
- Place shrimp in ovenproof dish.
- Combine all the other ingredients and whisk or use blender. Pour over shrimp.
- Chill for 2 to 3 hours.
- Just before serving, bake for 5 minutes.

Shrimp and Crab Casserole

Serves 8 to 10

2	cups rice, cooked		salt and pepper to taste
1	cup vegetable cocktail juice	1	2-ounce package slivered almonds (optional)
1	cup mayonnaise		breadcrumbs
2	cups shrimp, cooked		margarine or butter
1	cup crabmeat, fresh or canned		
½	cup green pepper, chopped		

- Preheat oven to 350°.
- Mix all ingredients except almonds and breadcrumbs.
- Place in a greased 10x10-inch casserole.
- Top with breadcrumbs.
- Dot with butter or margarine.
- Sprinkle with almonds.
- Bake for 30 minutes.

You may use extra rice to stretch it. May also be made with only shrimp, but use 3 cups instead of 2.

Shrimp Creole

Serves 6 to 8

1½ tablespoons vegetable oil	¼ teaspoon garlic, minced
1 cup onion, chopped	1 tablespoon flour
1 cup green pepper, chopped	pinch of sugar
¾ cup celery, chopped	2 14-ounce cans tomatoes, chopped
1½ teaspoons seafood seasoning	2 pounds raw shrimp, peeled and deveined
¾ teaspoon thyme leaves	

- Heat oil in saucepan over medium heat.
- Add onion, green pepper, celery, seafood seasoning, thyme, and garlic.
- Cook until onion is transparent, about 5 minutes. Stir often.
- Add flour, stir to blend. Cook and stir another 3 to 4 minutes.
- Add sugar and tomatoes. Cover and cook for 10 minutes over medium-low heat.
- Add shrimp, cover and cook for 5 to 7 minutes or until shrimp are done. Stir occasionally. Do not overcook.
- Serve over rice.

One pound of shrimp, cooked, usually means one pound of raw shrimp. One pound of cooked shrimp means shrimp is weighed after cooking and cleaning (approximately one and one half pounds of raw shrimp.)

Grace Episcopal Church
Shrimp Rémoulade

Serves approximately 60 to 70

48	cups of frozen, cooked shrimp, peeled and deveined	8	cloves garlic, minced
14	cups mayonnaise	1	teaspoon hot pepper sauce
4	cups Dijon mustard	4	cups celery, chopped
4	teaspoons salt	4	cups green bell pepper, chopped
8	tablespoons horseradish	8	teaspoons onion, grated
4	tablespoons lemon juice		

- Prepare shrimp according to directions on bags. If shrimp are too large, cut in half.
- Place shrimp in large containers.
- Mix together all the other ingredients.
- Pour over shrimp and mix well. Refrigerate.

When ready to serve, ladle a cupful over a bed of lettuce. Garnish plates with 3 cherry tomato halves, 3 cucumber slices, and grated carrot. Top shrimp with a sprig of parsley. This recipe halves beautifully.

Bounty of the Sea

Serves 4 to 6

8 tablespoons butter
4 tablespoons all-
purpose flour
1 pint half-and-half
⅛ teaspoon ground
mace
¼ teaspoon salt
⅛ teaspoon white
pepper
4 tablespoons dry
sauterne

1 14-ounce can
artichoke hearts,
halved
½ pound mushrooms,
sliced
½ pound lump crabmeat
or frozen Alaskan king
crab, thawed and
drained
½ pound shrimp, cooked

- Preheat oven to 325°.
- Melt 4 tablespoons of butter in top of double boiler over rapidly boiling water.
- Blend in flour with wire whisk.
- Slowly stir in cream.
- Add mace, salt, white pepper, and wine.
- Cook and stir until sauce is smooth and thick.
- Rinse artichoke hearts in cold water and drain.
- In saucepan, sauté mushrooms in 4 tablespoons butter.
- Turn heat to low, add artichokes, and heat through.
- Arrange artichokes and mushrooms in a 9x13-inch casserole, greased.
- Add crabmeat and shrimp.
- Cover with sauce
- Bake uncovered for 30 minutes.

Wentworth Street Shrimp Casserole

Serves 6

1 14-ounce can artichoke hearts, drained and whole or halved

1½ pounds shrimp, peeled and cooked

3 tablespoons butter

2 cloves garlic, chopped

1 onion, chopped

1 12-ounce box mushrooms, sliced

1 10-ounce can cream of mushroom soup, undiluted

½ cup mayonnaise

1 tablespoon Worcestershire sauce

2 tablespoons dry sherry

½ cup Parmesan cheese, grated

1 10-ounce package frozen spinach, chopped, thawed and drained well

salt and pepper to taste

paprika to taste

- Preheat oven to 375°.
- Sauté garlic, onions, and mushrooms in the butter.
- Mix soup, mayonnaise, Worcestershire sauce, sherry, cheese, salt, and pepper.
- Add to the sautéed mixture.
- Add spinach, then shrimp and artichokes.
- Put in buttered 2-quart casserole.
- Sprinkle with more Parmesan cheese and paprika.
- Bake until hot and bubbly, about 20 minutes.

Coquilles St. Benezet

Serves 12

½ cup margarine
1 cup celery, bite-size pieces
1 cup onion, coarsely chopped
2 cups fresh mushrooms and stems, sliced
1½ teaspoons salt
½ teaspoon pepper, coarsely ground
½ scant cup flour
¾ cup dry sherry

1½ cups plus 3 tablespoons milk
3 eggs
½ teaspoon nutmeg
½ teaspoon basil
2 cups rock shrimp, cooked and cut into chunks (may use lobster, shrimp or crab)
½ cup stuffed olives, sliced
4 ounces Swiss cheese, shredded

- Preheat oven to 375°.
- In large pot, melt margarine over medium-low heat.
- Add celery, onion, salt, and pepper. Stir well.
- Simmer 10 minutes or until tender. Stir frequently. Do not brown.
- Add mushrooms, tossing lightly for 2 minutes.
- Add flour, stirring gently until butter and flour are well-blended. Cook 1 minute. Do not brown.
- Add sherry and stir briskly until thick paste coats vegetables.
- Gradually stir in 1½ cups milk. Bring mixture to low boil, stirring constantly.
- Allow mixture to boil for 1 minute. Remove from heat.
- In a small bowl, whisk together eggs, 3 tablespoons milk, nutmeg, and basil.
- Add 4 tablespoons of the hot mixture, one at a time, to the egg mixture, stirring well.
- Add egg mixture to large pot, stirring carefully.
- Mix in rock shrimp and olives.
- Check seasonings and add more, if desired.

Continued on next page

- Divide mixture evenly among 12 greased baking shells or ramekins.
- May be refrigerated until ready to bake for serving.
- Before baking, top each portion with Swiss cheese.
- Bake 15 to 20 minutes. 30 seconds broiling time may be added for browning, if necessary.

This makes an elegant luncheon treat served with salad and muffins, or alone as an appetizer at dinner.

Shrimp and Rice Surprise

Serves 4

¾ cup rice
1½ cups chicken broth
1 small onion, chopped
1 tablespoon butter
1 teaspoon flour
½ cup dry sherry
½ cup evaporated milk
1 pound shrimp, cooked and cleaned

1 tablespoon mayonnaise
5 small gherkins, chopped
2 tablespoons pimiento, chopped
½ cup green pepper, chopped
¼ teaspoon curry powder

- Cook rice in the chicken broth until done.
- Place in a warm oven to dry and fluff it.
- Cook onion in butter until soft.
- Add flour and stir.
- Add sherry and milk. Stir until thickened.
- Add shrimp.
- Remove from heat.
- Add the rest of the ingredients to the rice and stir well.
- Add shrimp mixture and mix again.

Haydn's "Surprice Shrimphony"

Serves 8

1¾ cups water
¼ teaspoon salt
1 cup long grain and wild rice
2 tablespoons butter
½ cup celery, chopped
½ cup red bell pepper, chopped
½ cup onion, chopped
1 clove garlic, minced
1 cup mushrooms, sliced
1 tablespoon fresh parsley, snipped
¼ teaspoon marjoram, crushed

1 pound small shrimp, cooked and peeled
1 10-ounce package frozen broccoli, chopped, thawed and drained
½ cup slivered almonds
2 tablespoons sherry
2 10-ounce cans cream of chicken soup, undiluted
½ cup breadcrumbs, toasted
1 cup Cheddar cheese, shredded

- Preheat oven to 350°.
- In a medium saucepan, bring water and salt to a boil.
- Stir in rice. Cover and reduce heat to low.
- Simmer 15 minutes.
- Remove from heat and let stand 5 minutes without lifting lid.
- Meanwhile, in a large skillet melt butter.
- Sauté celery, bell pepper, onion, garlic and mushrooms 3 to 5 minutes, or until tender.
- Stir in parsley and marjoram.
- Sauté 1 more minute.
- In a large bowl, mix together shrimp, broccoli, almonds, sherry, and cream of chicken soup.
- Add cooked rice and sautéed vegetables, mixing well.
- Spoon mixture into a 2-quart greased casserole.
- Sprinkle breadcrumbs and shredded cheese over top of mixture.
- Bake for 25 minutes.

Crab Imperial

Serves 4

1 tablespoon margarine	1 tablespoon lemon
1 tablespoon flour	juice
½ cup milk, warmed	1 tablespoon
2 tablespoons green	Worcestershire sauce
pepper, finely	1 tablespoon parsley
chopped	½ cup mayonnaise
2 teaspoons onion,	1 pound crabmeat,
finely chopped	flaked

- Preheat oven to 450°.
- In a medium pan, melt margarine.
- Add flour and stir until margarine is absorbed.
- Slowly pour in heated milk, stirring constantly.
- Add green pepper, onion, lemon juice, Worcestershire sauce, and parsley.
- Remove from heat and add mayonnaise.
- Stir and add crab.
- Bake in a greased 1½ to 2-quart casserole, uncovered, for 20 minutes.

May substitute 1 pound of shrimp for the crabmeat.

Seafood Newburg Casserole

Serves 10

2 pounds shrimp, shelled	¼ cup plus 1 tablespoon sherry
2 pounds scallops	¼ cup mozzarella cheese
2 10-ounce cans cream of shrimp soup, divided	1 cup round buttery crackers, crushed
6 tablespoons flour	3 tablespoons butter, melted
1 5-ounce can evaporated milk	

- Preheat oven to 350°.
- Cook shrimp and scallops in 1-inch boiling water for 2 minutes. Set aside.
- Make paste using ½ can of soup and the flour.
- Place remaining soup in a large skillet.
- Add paste to remaining soup. Stir well.
- Add evaporated milk and sherry; heat but do not boil.
- Add mozzarella cheese and allow to melt.
- Place seafood in greased 13x9-inch casserole.
- Top with sauce.
- When ready to bake, combine cracker crumbs and melted butter. Sprinkle evenly over the top of casserole.
- Bake uncovered for 30 minutes or until hot and bubbly.

♭MMM♭MMM♭MMM♭MMM♭MMM♭MMM♭MMM♭MMM♭MMM♭MMM♭MMM♭MMM♭MMM♭MMM♭MMM♭MMM♭MMM♭MMM

Colonel Gary Hilley's Easy Scallops

Serves 4

40 large scallops
8 tablespoons olive oil
12 tablespoons chunky Italian tomato sauce
8 tablespoons butter

4 tablespoons shallots, chopped
2 tablespoons garlic, finely chopped

- In a large skillet, sear scallops in hot olive oil 4-5 minutes.
- Remove from oil and drain.
- In saucepan, heat tomato sauce.
- Place 3 tablespoons of sauce on each plate as a bed for the scallops.
- In another skillet, sauté shallots and garlic in butter.
- Top scallops with shallots and garlic.

Easy, pretty and delicious.

Grilled Soft-Shell Crabs

Serves 4

8 fresh soft-shell crabs
1 tablespoon curry powder
2 tablespoons lemon juice

2 tablespoons vegetable oil
nutmeg

- Combine curry powder, lemon, and oil.
- Wash crabs and baste with sauce.
- Refrigerate 20 minutes.
- Place on grill and baste again.
- Sprinkle with nutmeg.
- Grill 4 minutes and turn.
- Grill another 4 to 5 minutes, basting again on this side.
- Sprinkle this side with more nutmeg.

Coquilles St. Jacques

Serves 4 as a main course or 6 as a first course

4 tablespoons butter
½ pound mushrooms,
  sliced
4 tablespoons flour
1 pound scallops
1 cup dry vermouth

¼ cup heavy cream or
  evaporated milk
salt and pepper to
taste
lemon juice
breadcrumbs

- Preheat oven to 350°.
- "Plump" up the scallops under barely running cold water for 15 to 20 minutes. Drain.
- Place the scallops and vermouth in a medium saucepan and bring to a boil. Remove from heat.
- Sauté mushrooms in butter for about 5 minutes, stirring constantly.
- Add flour and stir another 3 minutes so that flour is cooked but not brown.
- Add scallops liquid and cream.
- Stir sauce to a thick, smooth consistency.
- Add scallops, salt, pepper, and a squeeze of lemon.
- Place into greased baking shells and sprinkle with breadcrumbs.
- Bake for 25 minutes or until bubbling hot.

Serve with French bread and a cold white Burgundy.

Folly Island Skillet Shrimp and Oysters

Serves 10

¼ cup olive oil	1 cup dry white wine
½ cup shallots, chopped	6 tablespoons fresh
2 pounds large shrimp,	parsley, chopped
uncooked, peeled and	2 tablespoons fresh
deveined	oregano, chopped (or
8 large garlic cloves,	2 teaspoons dried)
minced	1 tablespoon fresh
2 dozen oysters,	rosemary, chopped
shucked	(or 1 teaspoon dried)
1 pound smoked	lemon wedges
kielbasa sausage,	
sliced	

- Heat olive oil in a large skillet over medium heat.
- Add shallots and garlic and sauté for 3 minutes.
- Add shrimp and oysters and sauté until shrimp turn pink, about 3 minutes.
- Using slotted spoon, transfer shrimp and oysters to a bowl.
- Add sausage and wine to skillet and boil until liquid is reduced to ¼ cup, about 8 minutes.
- Add parsley, oregano, and rosemary and cook until heated through, about 2 minutes.
- Add shrimp and oysters.
- Transfer to platter and garnish with lemon wedges.

Crab Cakes

Makes 8 cakes

1 large egg	2 dashes hot pepper
3 tablespoons	sauce
mayonnaise	¼ teaspoon black
1½ teaspoons English-	pepper
style dry mustard	¼ teaspoon salt
¼ cup pimiento, drained	1 pound lump crabmeat
and chopped	1¾ cups saltines, finely
3 tablespoons fresh	crushed and divided
parsley, minced	2 tablespoons vegetable
1 teaspoon dry seafood	oil
seasoning	1 tablespoon unsalted
1 teaspoon	butter
Worcestershire sauce	

- Whisk together egg, mayonnaise, mustard, pimiento, parsley, seafood seasoning, Worcestershire sauce, hot pepper sauce, salt and pepper.
- Add crabmeat and ½ cup saltines.
- Toss gently.
- Spread remaining saltines on a plate.
- Form crab mixture into eight ¾-inch patties.
- Coat top and bottom with saltine crumbs.
- In a large skillet, heat oil and butter; sauté crab cakes until lightly brown.

Catherine's Crab Squares
with Shrimp Sauce

Serves 8 to 10

Crab Squares

3 cups rice, cooked	2 cups milk
1 2-ounce jar pimientos, drained and chopped	¼ cup onion, minced
	¼ cup parsley, chopped
1 teaspoon Worcestershire sauce	1 cup Cheddar cheese, grated
2 6-ounce cans or packages crabmeat	3 eggs, beaten

Shrimp Sauce

1 10-ounce can cream of shrimp soup	1 teaspoon curry powder
½ cup sour cream	1 teaspoon lemon juice

- Preheat oven to 325°.
- Mix all the ingredients for the crab squares together.
- Place in a buttered 9x13-inch baking dish.
- Bake for 45 minutes.
- Combine all ingredients for the shrimp sauce in small pan and heat.
- Cut crab dish in squares.
- Serve with sauce.

Tuna Potato Surprise

Serves 4

2 large baking potatoes,
baked
¼ cup sour cream
butter to taste
milk for consistency
2 eggs, hard-boiled and
chopped
1 6-ounce can tuna,
drained

1 10-ounce package
tiny sweet peas,
thawed
salt and pepper to
taste
sharp Cheddar
cheese, grated

- ◆ Preheat oven to 350°.
- ◆ Cut baked potatoes in halves.
- ◆ Scoop out the shells.
- ◆ Add sour cream and mash.
- ◆ Add a little butter and milk, if needed, for desired consistency.
- ◆ Add eggs, tuna, and peas, and mix well.
- ◆ Stuff mixture into the potato shells.
- ◆ Top lightly with grated cheese.
- ◆ Bake for 20 to 30 minutes.

Seabie Carver's Tuna Casserole

Serves 6 to 8

3 6-ounce cans solid
   white meat tuna, in
   chunks
3 10-ounce cans cream
   of mushroom soup
   seasoned salt to taste

¾ cup onion, chopped
¾ cup celery, chopped
1 6-ounce can Chinese
   noodles, divided
½ cup cashew nuts

- Preheat oven to 350°.
- Mix tuna and soup. Add a little salt.
- Stir-fry onions and celery, but leave crisp.
- Combine with tuna mixture.
- Place ½ of the noodles in the bottom of a greased 2-quart casserole.
- Add the tuna mix.
- Top with the rest of the noodles.
- Bake until hot, about 25 to 30 minutes.
- Sprinkle nuts on top before serving.

Fish and Tomato Bake

Serves 4

4 fresh tomatoes,
  peeled and thickly
  sliced
½ to 1 cup seasoned Italian
  breadcrumbs
  salt and pepper to
  taste
4 flounder fillets

½ cup white wine
4 tablespoons butter
  juice of 1½ to 2
  lemons, divided
  fresh Parmesan
  cheese, grated
  paprika

- Preheat oven to 350°.
- Line a greased 13x9-inch pan with tomatoes.
- Sprinkle tomatoes with breadcrumbs, salt and pepper.
- Place fish on top.
- In a small pan, combine wine, butter, and the juice of 1 lemon.
- Cook on medium-low until heated through.
- Pour over fish.
- Sprinkle cheese, paprika and more lemon juice over all.
- Bake for 20 to 25 minutes. May put under broiler for the last 5 minutes.

The quality of the tomatoes is very important.

Italian Fillet of Fish

Serves 4

4 fillets of mackerel or
   any firm fish
1 8-ounce bottle Italian
   dressing

1 onion, sliced
1 tomato, sliced
1 green pepper, sliced

- Marinate fillets and vegetables in dressing for at least 2 hours.
- Lay fish on broiling pan and top with vegetables.
- Broil until done, about 4 to 6 minutes.

Here's a tip from a fisherman if you don't like "fishy" fish. Use an acid-based marinade, such as wine, vinegar, lemon juice or lime juice, or cook the fish with high-acid vegetables such as onions or tomatoes. This will not only cut the oiliness of the flesh, but will also change its appearance from dark to light.

Baked Grouper Fillets

Serves 6

2 pounds grouper fillets,
   cut into 6 portions
½ cup mayonnaise
3 tablespoons Dijon
   mustard

¼ cup onion, chopped
2 tablespoons parsley,
   chopped
¼ teaspoon thyme

- Preheat oven to 400°.
- Place fish in lightly greased 8x14-inch baking dish and set aside.
- In a bowl, mix mayonnaise, mustard, onion, parsley, and thyme.
- Pour over fish.
- Bake uncovered for 20 to 25 minutes, or until fish flakes easily when tested with a fork.

Shrimp-Stuffed Flounder

Serves 4

¼ cup green pepper
¼ cup sweet red pepper (optional)
¼ cup celery
¼ cup onion
6 tablespoons butter
¾ teaspoon seafood seasoning
1 teaspoon Worcestershire sauce
¼ cup dry sherry

16 medium shrimp, uncooked, peeled and diced
dash of cayenne pepper
1 cup fresh breadcrumbs, divided
4 fillets of flounder
3 tablespoons lemon juice
salt, pepper and paprika to taste
lemon wedges

- Preheat oven to 350°.
- In food processor, chop peppers, onions, and celery.
- Melt 4 tablespoons butter in small pan.
- Add vegetables and sauté until tender.
- Add seafood seasoning, Worcestershire sauce, sherry, cayenne pepper, and shrimp.
- Cook over low heat until shrimp is pink.
- Stir in enough breadcrumbs so that the stuffing sticks together, but is not dry.
- Grease an 8x8-inch baking dish.
- Divide stuffing mixture evenly over each fillet.
- Roll each fillet and secure with toothpicks.
- Sprinkle lemon juice, 2 tablespoons melted butter, salt, and pepper over all.
- Top with remaining breadcrumbs.
- Bake for 25 to 30 minutes, or until fish flakes when tested with a fork.

Cabbage Row Flounder

Serves 4

½ pound mushrooms, finely chopped
2 tablespoons butter, divided
dusting of flour
½ cup white wine
1 tablespoon tomato purée

salt and pepper to taste
4 tablespoons parsley, divided
2 pounds fillet of flounder
⅓ cup fresh breadcrumbs

- Preheat oven to 325°.
- In a small pan, brown mushrooms in 1 tablespoon of butter.
- Add dusting of flour and stir constantly for 3 minutes.
- Add wine, tomato purée, salt, pepper, and ½ of the parsley.
- Simmer over low heat for about 5 minutes.
- Place fillets in a greased 9x13-inch baking dish.
- Pour sauce over fish.
- Sprinkle with breadcrumbs and dot with remaining butter.
- Bake for 15 minutes or until fish flakes when tested with a fork.
- Sprinkle with remaining parsley and serve.

All fish fillets are tasty prepared this way. For a more firmly-textured fish like halibut, however, cooking time increases to at least 20 minutes at a temperature of 350°.

Fast Fish Bake

Serves 4

1	large onion, sliced and divided	2	tablespoons lemon juice
2	pounds flounder fillets	2	teaspoons Worcestershire sauce
½	cup mayonnaise		
1	teaspoon prepared mustard	¼	cup Parmesan cheese, grated

- Preheat oven to 350°.
- Line a greased 13x9-inch baking dish with ½ of the onions.
- Top with fish fillets.
- Place remaining onions on top of fillets.
- Combine mayonnaise, mustard, lemon juice, and Worcestershire sauce, and spread evenly over the onions.
- Sprinkle with cheese.
- Bake for 35 minutes, or until fish flakes easily when tested with a fork.

Fish should be cooked for five minutes per inch of thickness. Its best if not over cooked.

Salmon with Caper Sauce

Serves 2

Salmon

2 4-ounce salmon
steaks
2 tablespoons dry white
wine

lemon slices for
garnish

Caper Sauce

2 tablespoons lowfat
plain yogurt
2 tablespoons lowfat
mayonnaise
1 tablespoon capers,
drained

1 tablespoon lemon
juice
1 tablespoon fresh dill,
chopped, or 1
teaspoon dried

- Preheat oven to 350°.
- Rinse salmon under cold water; pat dry.
- Spray an 8x8-inch baking dish with cooking spray.
- Place salmon in dish and sprinkle with wine.
- Cover and bake for 15 to 20 minutes, or until fish is flaky but not dry.
- Meanwhile, in a small pan, combine all the ingredients for the caper sauce and warm over low heat.
- When ready to serve, pour caper sauce over each steak and garnish with lemon slices.

Poached Fresh Salmon with Dill Sauce

Serves 24 for buffet dinner

Salmon

⅓ cup lemon juice	1 whole salmon
¾ cup onions, sliced	lettuce leaves
1 tablespoon dill weed	watercress

Dill Sauce

1 pint nonfat sour cream	4 teaspoons fresh horseradish
1 pint reduced-fat mayonnaise	2 teaspoons dill weed
3 tablespoons lemon juice	1 3-ounce bottle capers, drained

- Fill a large frying pan ½ full of water.
- Add lemon juice, onions, and one tablespoon dill weed.
- Bring to a boil and simmer for 5 minutes.
- Cut salmon in ½ and place in pan.
- Poach 25 to 30 minutes. Turn at least once.
- Let cool, then remove skin and bones.
- Cut into 3-inch serving pieces.
- Refrigerate until well chilled.
- Mix together all the ingredients for the dill sauce and refrigerate.
- Place salmon on lettuce leaves.
- Pour dill sauce over salmon and garnish with watercress.

Clam Stew

Serves 8 to 10

4 carrots, peeled and sliced
1 cup peas, fresh or frozen
6 small new potatoes, peeled and diced
1 15-ounce can cream-style corn
2 bay leaves
¼ teaspoon dried basil
¼ teaspoon dried rosemary
¼ teaspoon dried thyme
1 10½-ounce can clam juice
6 white onions, peeled
4 celery stalks, sliced
4 6½-ounce cans clams, minced
1 cup margarine
  rounds of French bread, cut ½-inch thick (enough to cover top of Dutch oven)

- Put all the ingredients except clams, margarine, and bread in a Dutch oven.
- Add water to barely cover vegetables.
- Bring to a boil. Cover and simmer until all is tender.
- Add clams and margarine and heat through, about 20 to 25 minutes.
- Top with bread rounds.

Frogmore Stew

Serves 1

seafood seasoning, liberal amount	1 to 1½ ears of corn
	½ pound shrimp
¼ pound kielbasa-type sausage, cut in 2-inch pieces	3 to 4 small red or white potatoes
	small onions

- Bring large quantity of water to a boil.
- Add seafood seasoning.
- Add sausage and boil for 15 minutes.
- Add potatoes and onions and boil for 8 minutes.
- Add corn and boil for 7 minutes.
- Turn off heat and add shrimp. Let stand until shrimp is pink, about 5 minutes.
- Serve immediately with cocktail sauce.

A favorite lowcountry recipe to serve to a crowd. Easy to increase according to the number of guests you'll be serving.

Lowfat Salmon Marinade

Serves 6 to 8

½ cup sherry	¼ cup light soy sauce
3 tablespoons fresh parsley, chopped	½ teaspoon black pepper
2 teaspoons sugar	1 small onion, chopped
2 tablespoons horseradish	

- In a small bowl, combine all ingredients.
- Pour sauce over salmon fillets.
- Marinate 30 to 60 minutes.
- Grill until salmon is cooked but not dry.

This makes enough marinade for 2 pounds of salmon.

Bouillabaisse

Serves 6

2 tablespoons butter	1 teaspoon dried thyme
1 large onion, chopped	1 teaspoon dried chervil
1 clove garlic, chopped	2 pounds fish of your
1 cup celery, sliced	choice, cut into 1-inch
¼ cup parsley, chopped	pieces
2 16-ounce cans	1 pound shrimp,
tomatoes, undrained	shelled, deveined and
1½ cups white wine	raw
3 10-ounce cans	salt and pepper to
condensed chicken	taste
broth	

- Heat butter, then sauté onion, garlic, celery, and parsley for 5 minutes.
- Stir in tomatoes (quartered if whole), wine, broth, thyme, and chervil. Cover and simmer about 20 minutes.
- Add fish and shrimp. Simmer 5 to 6 minutes, or until fish is cooked.
- Season with salt and pepper.
- Serve very hot.

Meats & Poultry

Beef Tenderloin (see photo)

Elegant Beef Stew

Grilled Lamb Kebobs (see photo)

Sweet and Sour Pork Chops

Ham and Brussels Sprout Casserole

Veal Virtuoso

South Carolina Pheasant

Raspberry Chicken

Cajun Chicken Gumbo

and More

Edmondston-Alston House

This splendid home was built around 1825 by Charles Edmondston, a wealthy merchant and wharf owner. About 1838 economic hardship forced him to sell to Charles Alston, a prominent rice planter. Alston remodeled the house. In so doing, it was converted from late-Federal style architecture to the Greek-revival style architecture we know today. From the piazzas one experiences breathtaking views of the Charleston Harbor.

Menus

Sunday Lunch

Chilled Cucumber Soup

Pasta with Chicken and Mushrooms

Tossed Green Salad

Corny Cornbread

Tray of Turtle Brownies,
Pumpkin Bars and Ginger Cookies

Filet Mignon with Peppers and Olives

Serves 2

2 bell peppers (1 red, 1 yellow)

½ tablespoon vegetable oil

2 8 to 9-ounce filet mignon steaks, 1½-inches thick

3 large garlic cloves, minced

⅔ cup chicken broth (low-salt)

⅓ cup Calamata olives

2 teaspoons balsamic or red wine vinegar

1 teaspoon dried oregano, or 1 tablespoon fresh

2 tablespoons unsalted butter

- Roast peppers under broiler until blackened on all sides.
- Put in paper bag for 15 minutes.
- Peel, stem, and seed the peppers, then cut into strips.
- Heat oil in a large, heavy skillet over high heat.
- Season steaks with salt and pepper.
- Sauté about 4 minutes on each side for rare.
- Transfer steaks to a plate and tent with foil to keep them warm.
- Add peppers and garlic to skillet and cook 30 seconds.
- Add broth, olives, oregano, and vinegar; boil about 8 minutes, scraping up browned bits, until liquid is reduced to a glaze.
- Stir in butter.
- Spoon over steaks.

It may be difficult to keep steaks really warm for 8 minutes, so they could be cooked in a separate pan.

MᎱMMMᎱMMMᎱMMMᎱMMMᎱMMMᎱMMMᎱMMMᎱMMMᎱMMMᎱMMMᎱMMMᎱMMMᎱMMMᎱMMMᎱMN

Mother's Whole Tenderloin of Beef

Serves 6 to 8

1 *5 to 7-pound beef*
   tenderloin
¼ *cup olive oil*

1 *¾-ounce package*
   herb salad dressing
   mix
1 *cup red wine*

- Preheat oven to 500°.
- Strip off all the fat and sinew from the meat.
- Rub entire piece of meat with oil and then with the package of seasoning.
- Put the meat in a shallow pan and put into the hot oven.
- Bake for 10 minutes.
- Open oven and pour the wine over meat.
- Reduce oven temperature to 325°.
- Cook an additional 20 minutes. The meat should be medium-rare.
- Remove from oven, slice, and serve on a platter.

Hairspray will usually remove ball point ink stains from hands or clothing.

Beef Tenderloin

beef tenderloin
1 cup good Burgundy

1 cup reduced-sodium
soy sauce
1 cup olive oil

- Place beef in a heavy, zip-lock, plastic bag and add the wine, soy sauce, and olive oil.
- Close the bag securely and rotate to mix the liquids and coat the beef.
- Marinate in the coldest part of the refrigerator for 2 to 3 days, turning the beef once or twice a day.
- Remove from the marinade and bake, uncovered, at 500° for 40 minutes only.
- Serve hot, either as an entrée or as a cocktail dish sliced thin with rye bread and Dijon mustard.

If using this as a cocktail dish, allow 1 pound for 4 people.

Large baking potatoes, wrapped in foil, will bake in the 40 minutes that it takes for the meat to cook, plus the 15 minutes the meat needs to "rest" before serving.

Beer Brisket

Serves 8

5 to 6	pounds lean beef brisket, boned	2	tablespoons brown sugar
	salt and pepper	2	tablespoons chili sauce
1	large onion, sliced		
1	12-ounce can beer	¼	cup flour
		½	cup water

- Preheat oven to 300°.
- Salt and pepper the beef.
- Place beef in shallow roasting pan and cover with sliced onion.
- Make a sauce by combining the beer, brown sugar, and chili sauce.
- Pour the sauce over the roast.
- Cover tightly with a lid or heavy-duty aluminum foil.
- Bake 45 minutes to 1 hour for each pound.
- Uncover the roast for the last ½ hour so it will brown.
- Make gravy from the pan juices combined with flour and water. Stir until thickened.
- Meat should fall apart and be very tender.

Can be doubled for a crowd. Serve with potatoes and a salad.

Barbecued Beef Brisket

Serves 12 to 18

Beef

4 to 6	pounds beef brisket
1 to 2	tablespoons garlic salt
1 to 2	tablespoons onion salt

1 to 2	tablespoons celery salt
2 to 3	tablespoons liquid smoke

Sauce

2	cups ketchup
½	cup sugar
3	teaspoons liquid smoke

½	cup Worcestershire sauce

- Sprinkle brisket with salts and liquid smoke until moderately covered.
- Wrap in heavy aluminum foil; marinate in refrigerator for 24 hours.
- Combine sauce ingredients in a saucepan and simmer until the sugar dissolves.
- Pour half the sauce on the marinated brisket.
- Double-wrap the brisket with heavy foil and place it in the bottom portion of a broiling pan.
- Bake at 250° to 300° for 5 to 7 hours, depending on the size, until tender.
- To serve, cut across the grain.
- Put the remaining sauce in a dish and pass around the table.

May need to double the sauce recipe.

217

London Broil

Serves 4 to 6

Meat
    2½ pounds London broil,
        as lean as possible,
        about 1 inch thick

Marinade

½ cup onion, chopped	2 tablespoons soy sauce
½ cup wine, red or white (or lemon juice)	½ teaspoon celery salt
¼ cup oil	½ teaspoon pepper
½ teaspoon salt	½ teaspoon thyme
4 teaspoons fresh parsley, chopped	1 clove garlic, minced
	½ teaspoon oregano
	½ teaspoon rosemary

◆ Remove excess fat from the steak.

◆ Put the steak in a shallow baking dish or pan.

◆ Mix all marinade ingredients and pour over the steak.

◆ Cover with plastic and marinate for at least 3 hours (can even be done 1 day ahead). Must be turned in marinade frequently.

◆ Preheat the broiler.

◆ Place the meat, uncovered, 4 inches from the heat. Cook for 5 to 8 minutes per side, basting with the marinade every 2 to 3 minutes.

◆ Cut diagonally in thin slices and serve on a heated platter.

Best if served rare. A great party "steak."

Round Steak Sauerbraten

Serves 5 to 6

1½ pounds round steak, ½ inch thick
1 tablespoon fat
1 envelope brown gravy mix (about ¾ ounce)
2 cups water
1 tablespoon instant minced onion
2 tablespoons white wine vinegar

2 tablespoons brown sugar
½ teaspoon salt
¼ teaspoon pepper
½ teaspoon ginger
1 teaspoon Worcestershire sauce
1 bay leaf
hot buttered noodles

* Cut meat into 1-inch squares.
* In a large skillet, brown the meat on all sides, then set aside in another dish.
* Add gravy mix and water to the skillet and bring to a boil, stirring constantly.
* Stir in remaining ingredients, except the noodles.
* Return the meat to the skillet; cover; simmer for 1½ hours, stirring occasionally.
* Remove the bay leaf and serve over the hot buttered noodles.

Elegant Beef Stew

Serves 6 to 8

2	pounds beef stew meat	1	15-ounce jar onions, drained
3 to 4	ribs of celery, cut into large pieces	2	tablespoons instant tapioca
1	green pepper, cut into large pieces	½	cup red wine
4 to 5	carrots, cut into large pieces	10 to 12	ounces tomato juice
5	ounces frozen peas		salt and pepper to taste

- Preheat oven to 325°.
- Place the meat in a 9x13-inch pan, sprayed with cooking spray. Cover with the cut up vegetables.
- Sprinkle salt, pepper, and tapioca over the meat and vegetables.
- Add wine and tomato juice.
- Cover the pan with heavy aluminum foil.
- Bake for 3 hours.
- Check for moisture; add more juice if necessary.
- Loosen the foil the last hour of baking.

May vary the vegetables—potatoes and mushrooms work well, too.

Louisiana Beef Burgundy

Serves 8 to 10

3 *pounds top round steak, cut into 1-inch pieces*	1/4 *cup oil*
1/4 *cup flour*	1 *1-pound can crushed tomatoes*
1 *teaspoon salt*	3 *medium onions, sliced*
1/2 *teaspoon celery salt*	1/2 *cup molasses*
1/4 *teaspoon garlic salt*	1 *cup Burgundy*
1/4 *teaspoon black pepper*	6 *ounces mushrooms, sliced*
1/2 *teaspoon ground ginger*	2/3 *cup raisins*

- Dredge steak in a mixture of flour, salt, celery salt, garlic salt, black pepper, and ginger.
- Brown in oil.
- Add tomatoes, onions, molasses, Burgundy, and mushrooms.
- Heat to boiling.
- Reduce the heat to simmer and cook, covered, for 1½ to 1¾ hours.
- Add raisins and simmer for 15 minutes.
- Serve over rice, egg noodles, or orzo.

Meat Loaf with Sweet-and-Sour Sauce

Serves 4 to 6

Meat loaf

1½	pounds ground chuck or ground round	1½	cups fresh breadcrumbs
1	egg, beaten	1	teaspoon salt
1	medium onion, chopped	¼	teaspoon pepper
		4	ounces tomato sauce

Sauce

4	ounces tomato sauce	1	cup water
2	tablespoons vinegar	2	teaspoons prepared mustard
3	tablespoons brown sugar or molasses		

- Preheat oven to 350°.
- Lightly mix the beef with onion, egg, breadcrumbs, salt, pepper, and tomato sauce.
- Form meat into a loaf and place in a shallow pan.
- Mix the sauce ingredients together.
- Ladle over the meat loaf several times while it is baking.
- Bake 1½ hours.
- Use any extra sauce to serve with the meat loaf.

A new twist to an old favorite.

Mexican Goulash

Serves 4

1 onion, chopped	½ cup water
2 cloves garlic, minced	black olives, chopped
1 pound ground beef	green olives, chopped
1 teaspoon oregano	tomato, chopped
1 teaspoon cumin	lettuce, shredded
1 teaspoon basil	Cheddar cheese,
1 teaspoon chili powder	grated
1 teaspoon salt	salsa
1 6-ounce can tomato	avocado, chopped
paste	sour cream or ranch
1 8-ounce can tomato	dressing
sauce	tortilla chips, plain

- Sauté onion and garlic in a frying pan with a small amount of oil. Add the ground beef; brown, then drain off fat.
- Add the seasonings, tomato paste, tomato sauce, and water.
- Simmer for 30 to 45 minutes.
- Serve over broken tortilla chips.
- Sprinkle individual servings with grated cheese, onion, lettuce, tomato, avocado, olives, and salsa to taste.
- Top with sour cream or ranch dressing.

Packaged taco seasoning mix may be used in place of the spices, tomato sauce and paste. The ranch dressing is tastier than the sour cream.

Inside Out Ravioli

Serves 8 to 10

1   pound ground beef
½ cup onion, chopped
1   clove garlic, minced
¼ cup plus 1 tablespoon
     salad oil
1   10-ounce package
     frozen chopped
     spinach
1   1-pound can
     spaghetti sauce with
     mushrooms
1   8-ounce can tomato
     sauce

1   6-ounce can tomato
     paste
½ teaspoon salt
     dash of pepper
1   7-ounce package shell
     or elbow macaroni,
     cooked
1   cup Parmesan
     cheese, grated
½ cup soft breadcrumbs
2   eggs, well-beaten

+ Preheat oven to 350°.
+ Brown ground beef, onion, and garlic in 1 tablespoon of salad oil.
+ Cook the frozen spinach according to the package instructions.
+ Drain and reserve the liquid, adding water to make 1 cup of liquid.
+ Stir spinach liquid, spaghetti sauce, tomato sauce, tomato paste, salt, and pepper into the meat mixture.
+ Simmer for 10 minutes.
+ Combine the spinach with the cooked macaroni, cheese, breadcrumbs, eggs, and ¼ cup of oil.
+ Spread into 13x9-inch baking dish.
+ Top with meat sauce.
+ Bake for 35 minutes.
+ Let stand for 10 minutes before serving.

Great for an informal dinner party, or when you've been asked to bring a covered dish.

Noodle Stroganoff

Serves 6

¼ cup butter or margarine

¼ cup scallions, sliced, or onions, chopped

1 clove garlic, minced

½ pound mushrooms, sliced, or 2 3-ounce cans sliced mushrooms, drained

1 pound ground chuck

3 tablespoons Burgundy or other red wine

3 tablespoons lemon juice

1 10-ounce can condensed consommé, undiluted

1 teaspoon salt

¼ teaspoon pepper

¼ pound medium noodles

1 cup sour cream

parsley, snipped

◆ Sauté scallions, garlic, and mushrooms in hot butter, until lightly browned.

◆ Add meat and stir until the red color disappears.

◆ Stir in the red wine, lemon juice, consommé, salt, and pepper.

◆ Simmer, uncovered, for 15 minutes.

◆ Stir in uncooked noodles.

◆ Cook, covered, for 5 minutes, or until the noodles are tender.

◆ Mix in the sour cream.

◆ Heat quickly, but do not boil. Serve at once, sprinkled with parsley.

Moussaka

Serves 8

Meat Mixture
- 2 eggplants, sliced lengthwise
- ½ cup shortening
- 2 tablespoons butter
- 4 medium onions, sliced
- 3 cloves garlic, finely chopped
- 1 pound ground beef, lamb, or veal
- 1 teaspoon salt
- ½ teaspoon thyme
- ½ teaspoon oregano
- ½ cup canned tomatoes
- ½ cup white wine
- 2 egg whites (reserve yolks for sauce)
- ½ cup breadcrumbs, divided

Sauce
- 2 tablespoons flour
- 2 tablespoons butter, melted
- 1½ cups milk, warmed
- ½ teaspoon salt
- 2 egg yolks
- ¼ teaspoon nutmeg
- 4 teaspoons Parmesan cheese, grated

- ◆ Fry eggplant in shortening until brown on both sides. (Or you may brush both sides of the eggplant with oil or spray with cooking spray and place on a cookie sheet in 400° oven to brown. Watch carefully.)
- ◆ Transfer to a platter until needed.
- ◆ Add butter to the skillet; toss in sliced onions and garlic.
- ◆ Cook until limp.
- ◆ Stir in the ground meat, salt, thyme, oregano, tomatoes, and wine.
- ◆ Cover and cook slowly for 30 minutes.
- ◆ Cool; mix in the unbeaten egg whites and half the breadcrumbs.
- ◆ For the sauce, stir the flour into the melted butter in a saucepan.
- ◆ Add the milk and salt.
- ◆ Cook over low heat, stirring constantly, until the sauce is smooth and thick.

Continued on next page

- Beat the egg yolks slightly. Gradually add a little of the heated sauce to the egg yolks.
- Stir the egg mixture into the remaining sauce.
- Season with nutmeg.
- Grease a 9x13-inch baking dish.
- Cover the bottom of the dish with the remaining breadcrumbs.
- Arrange a layer of eggplant and a layer of meat mixture on the breadcrumbs.
- Repeat with layers of eggplant and meat.
- Pour the sauce on top.
- Sprinkle with cheese.
- Bake at 350° for 1 hour.

Tasty Lamb Curry

Serves 4

½ to ¾ cup celery, chopped
½ cup onion, chopped
¼ cup green pepper, chopped
1 clove garlic, minced drippings left from roast lamb
1 cup cooked lamb, chopped

2 tablespoons flour
1 beef bouillon cube, dissolved in 1 cup hot water
1 tablespoon Worcestershire sauce
2 teaspoons curry powder
½ teaspoon ginger powder

- Sauté the celery, onion, green pepper, and garlic in the lamb drippings.
- Add the meat, and stir in the flour.
- Gradually stir in the bouillon, Worcestershire sauce, and the curry and ginger powders.
- Simmer for 1 hour, adding water if needed.
- Serve over rice.

Maestro's Lamb Kebobs

Serves 4 to 6

2	tablespoons rosemary	1	tablespoon Worcestershire sauce
2	large cloves garlic, crushed	½	cup red wine vinegar
2	shallots, minced	1	cup olive oil
1½	tablespoons Dijon mustard	2	pounds boned leg of lamb, cut into 2-inch cubes
2	teaspoons salt		
1	teaspoon pepper		

- ◆ Combine all ingredients except meat.
- ◆ Coat lamb with marinade.
- ◆ Cover and refrigerate at least 8 hours or overnight.
- ◆ Preheat grill or broiler.
- ◆ Drain and reserve marinade.
- ◆ Skewer meat, leaving small space between cubes to ensure cooking.
- ◆ Grill or broil 10 to 15 minutes, turning and basting frequently with reserved marinade.

This recipe was submitted by David Stahl, Conductor of the Charleston Symphony Orchestra.

Lamb Pilaf

Serves 4

2 cups chicken broth, or
3 chicken bouillon
cubes, dissolved in 2
cups boiling water
5 tablespoons butter
2 teaspoons lemon juice
1 teaspoon salt
1 bay leaf
1 cup white rice

1 medium onion, finely
chopped
1 small green pepper,
diced
1 to 1½ cups cooked lamb,
cut into small cubes
salt and pepper to
taste
¼ teaspoon thyme

- Preheat oven, if not using the microwave, to 350°.
- Combine the chicken broth, 3 tablespoons of butter, lemon juice, salt, and bay leaf in a large saucepan and bring to a boil.
- Add the rice, cover, lower the heat, and cook about 20 minutes, or until rice is tender and liquid is absorbed.
- While the rice is cooking, melt remaining 2 tablespoons butter in a large skillet, add the onion and green pepper, and sauté until tender.
- Add the cooked lamb and seasonings, and cook 5 minutes longer.
- Turn ⅓ of the rice into a buttered 1½-quart casserole dish, cover with ½ of the lamb mixture, add ⅓ of the rice on top, the remaining lamb mixture, and then the last of the rice.
- Cover the casserole and bake in a conventional oven for 15 minutes, or in a microwave on high for 5 minutes.

Braised Lamb Shanks

Serves 4 to 6

4 to 6 lamb shanks, (4 to 6 pounds)
¼ teaspoon black pepper
1 teaspoon salt
3 tablespoons oil
1 cup onion, chopped
1 cup mushrooms, quartered (about ¼ pound)
¾ cup celery, sliced
1 cup turnips, diced
⅓ cup all-purpose flour
3 tablespoons tomato paste

¼ teaspoon fresh rosemary, finely chopped, or ⅛ teaspoon dried rosemary, crushed
¼ teaspoon fresh thyme leaves, or ⅛ teaspoon dried thyme leaves
1 large bay leaf
2 cloves garlic, minced
½ cup Burgundy
3 cups lamb or beef stock

+ Preheat oven to 350°.
+ Season lamb shanks with salt and pepper.
+ Heat the oil in a large Dutch oven or heavy roaster.
+ Brown the lamb shanks on all sides in the hot oil.
+ Remove from pan.
+ Add onions, mushrooms, celery, and turnips to the pan, cooking and stirring until brown.
+ Add the flour, stirring to brown slightly.
+ Stir in the tomato paste, seasonings, wine, and stock.
+ Return the shanks to the pan and bring to a boil.
+ Cover and bake for 2 hours, or until tender.
+ Remove lamb shanks to a hot platter and keep warm.
+ Skim fat from the sauce.
+ Spoon over the lamb shanks.

Delicious as is, or over rice.

Sullivan's Island Hot Pot

Serves 6

2 tablespoons butter
6 medium potatoes, peeled and sliced into rounds
6 lean shoulder lamb chops, about 1-inch thick
1 teaspoon salt

black pepper, freshly ground
6 oysters, shucked (optional)
3 medium onions, thinly sliced
2 cups water
1 tablespoon parsley, finely chopped

- Preheat oven to 350°.
- Coat a 4 to 5-quart casserole with 1 tablespoon of the butter.
- Spread ⅓ of the potato slices evenly on the bottom of the casserole.
- Add 3 of the lamb chops, side by side, on top.
- Sprinkle with some salt and ground black pepper.
- Add 3 of the oysters (if using), and half the onions.
- Cover the onions with another ⅓ of the sliced potatoes.
- Place the remaining 3 chops, plus the oysters, and the last third of the sliced potatoes on top again.
- Sprinkle with salt and pepper.
- Pour on the water.
- Dot with the remaining butter.
- Bake on the middle rack of oven, covered, for 1½ hours.
- Remove the cover and bake another ½ hour to brown the top.
- Sprinkle with parsley and serve very hot.

If serving 4 people, use 4 lamb chops and decrease other proportions slightly. This is a wonderful hearty dish, which will wait for the diners. A crock pot could be used.

Danish Pork Chops

Serves 3 to 6

1 tablespoon grated orange peel	1 teaspoon butter, melted
2 teaspoons salt	1 12-ounce package pitted prunes
¼ teaspoon pepper	½ cup dry white wine
¼ teaspoon nutmeg	½ cup apple juice
6 loin pork chops, ¾ inch thick	½ cup heavy cream

- Preheat oven to 350°.
- Combine the spices and rub onto both sides of chops.
- Brown the chops on both sides in a large skillet, using the melted butter.
- Place the wine, prunes, and apple juice in the bottom of a large, flat, ovenproof casserole dish.
- Place the chops on top.
- Bake for 1 hour and 20 minutes.
- Put the chops and prunes on a serving platter.
- Skim excess fat from the casserole dish and blend in the cream.
- Spoon some of the sauce over the chops, putting the remaining sauce in a sauce boat.

Pork Chops and Sweet Potatoes

Serves 4

4 loin pork chops, thick-
 cut
3 medium sweet
 potatoes
2 tablespoons butter,
 melted
½ cup currant jelly

½ cup fresh orange juice
1½ tablespoons lemon
 juice
1 teaspoon dry mustard
½ teaspoon ginger
½ teaspoon paprika

- Preheat oven to 350°.
- Boil, then peel and slice the sweet potatoes and arrange in the bottom of a 13x9-inch baking dish.
- Place the pork chops on top and add salt and pepper.
- In a saucepan, melt the butter and add the other ingredients. Simmer until the jelly has dissolved.
- Pour ¾ of the sauce over the chops and bake, uncovered, for 45 minutes.
- Baste with the remaining sauce.
- Cover if the chops begin to look dry.

A raw potato placed in the soup pot will absorb salt if you've added too much.

Sweet-and-Sour Pork Chops

Serves 4

4 pork chops
1 10-ounce can beef broth
1 8-ounce can pineapple chunks
¼ cup green pepper, diced

¼ cup catsup
2 tablespoons wine vinegar
1 tablespoon brown sugar
1 teaspoon soy sauce
½ teaspoon dry mustard

- Brown the pork chops in a medium skillet.
- Drain.
- Combine remaining ingredients and pour over chops.
- Cook, uncovered, for 45 minutes, spooning sauce over the chops often.
- Remove the chops, cook down the sauce until it thickens, or thicken with 2 teaspoons of water added to 1 teaspoon of corn starch.
- Serve over the chops.
- Serve with rice.

Stove Top Pork

Serves 4 to 6

2½ pounds boneless pork roast, center cut or lean butt
1 cup apple juice
1 cup pitted prunes, chopped

1 cup Granny Smith apples, peeled, cored, chopped coarsely
salt and pepper to taste

- Combine in a Dutch oven on top of the stove.
- Bring to a boil and then simmer, covered, for 1½ hours, or until tender.
- Purée the liquid in a blender.
- Slice the pork and pour the juices over it.
- Serve with mashed potatoes.

Ham and Brussels Sprouts Casserole

Serves 8

½ cup mayonnaise
1 teaspoon lemon juice
½ teaspoon vinegar
1 10½-ounce can cream of celery soup (chicken or mushroom)

2 8-ounce packages frozen Brussels sprouts, cooked as directed on package
3 to 4 cups slivered ham
1 cup buttered breadcrumbs
½ cup Parmesan cheese, grated

- Preheat oven to 350°.
- Mix the soup, mayonnaise, lemon juice, and vinegar together.
- In a 3-quart ovenproof casserole, place the Brussels sprouts and the ham.
- Pour the soup mixture over the top.
- Cover with breadcrumbs.
- Top this with grated cheese.
- Bake, uncovered, for 25 minutes.

Veal Virtuoso

Serves 4

3 tablespoons butter or margarine	4 tablespoons heavy cream (room temperature)
4 veal chops or 1 pound veal stew meat	2 tablespoons olive oil
2 tablespoons wine vinegar	½ teaspoon salt
1 teaspoon Dijon mustard	¼ teaspoon black pepper
2 teaspoons butter, softened	¼ cup parsley, finely chopped

- Melt 3 tablespoons butter in a skillet. Cook the chops over medium heat, 10 minutes each side, or until tender and golden.
- Blend the vinegar, mustard, soft butter, cream, oil, salt, and pepper together in a saucepan.
- Heat gently but do not boil.
- Remove cooked veal from pan and arrange on a hot platter.
- Add mustard mixture to pan in which the veal was cooked and heat, stirring in the pan juices and glaze.
- Pour over veal and sprinkle with parsley.

It can be made without the butter and oil.

Veal Scallopini à la Marian

Serves 3 to 4

1 pound veal, thinly sliced	¼ teaspoon nutmeg
¼ cup salad oil	3 tablespoons flour
¼ cup lemon juice	¼ pound mushrooms, sliced
1 teaspoon salt	1 medium onion, sliced
1 teaspoon paprika	⅔ cup chicken bouillon
1 clove garlic, minced	6 green stuffed olives, sliced
1 teaspoon dry mustard	
½ teaspoon sugar	

- Cut veal into serving pieces.
- Make a marinade of oil, lemon juice, salt, paprika, garlic, mustard, sugar, and nutmeg.
- Marinate meat at least 2 hours, turning occasionally.
- Brown floured meat in skillet with some oil.
- Add the mushrooms and onions.
- Combine marinade with bouillon and pour over meat.
- Cook slowly, covered, for 1 hour.
- Garnish with olives and serve over rice.

Baked Doves

Serves 4

8 to 12 dove breasts	½ teaspoon salt
bacon	2 cups milk
4 tablespoons butter	1 cup white wine
4 tablespoons flour	

- Preheat oven to 350°.
- Wrap each dove breast with a strip of bacon and secure with a toothpick.
- Place in a baking dish.
- Make a white sauce by combining the butter, flour, salt and milk.
- Cover the doves with the sauce.
- Bake, covered, for 45 minutes.
- Add the wine and bake, uncovered, for another 45 minutes.
- Serve over rice.

Baked Quail

Serves 4

12 quail	1 yellow or green
4 ounces butter	pepper, cut into strips
1 cup celery, chopped	1 cup white wine
1 large onion, chopped	3 tablespoons lemon
1 cup mushrooms,	juice
sliced	3 tablespoons water

- Preheat oven to 325°.
- Brown the quail in the butter. Salt to taste.
- Place in a baking dish.
- In the same skillet, sauté celery, onion, mushrooms, and pepper.
- Pour the sautéed vegetables over the quail.
- Combine wine, lemon juice, and water, and pour over quail and vegetables.
- Cover with foil and bake for 2 hours.
- Serve with wild rice.

Quail or Dove Bake

Serves 4 to 6

8	whole quail or dove breasts	½	cup sherry
¼	pound butter		salt and pepper to taste
4	tablespoons flour		cooked rice
2	cups chicken broth		

- ◆ Preheat oven to 350°.
- ◆ Brown quail in the butter in a heavy skillet.
- ◆ Remove the birds to a casserole dish.
- ◆ Add flour to butter in skillet and stir well. Scrape any browned bits in skillet. Add chicken broth and sherry.
- ◆ Salt and pepper to taste.
- ◆ Cook until slightly thickened.
- ◆ Pour over birds.
- ◆ Cover with foil and bake for 1 hour.
- ◆ Serve with rice

Baked Duck

Serves 4

4	small ducks	1	onion, quartered
1	8-ounce bottle Italian salad dressing	1	celery rib, quartered
1¼	cups white wine	1	green pepper, quartered
½	cup wine vinegar	4	strips bacon
1	apple, quartered		salt and pepper

- ◆ Preheat oven to 275°.
- ◆ Marinate ducks in salad dressing, wine and vinegar mixture for at least 2 hours.
- ◆ Drain ducks and reserve marinade.
- ◆ Stuff cavity of each duck with ¼ apple, ¼ onion, ¼ celery rib, and ¼ green pepper.
- ◆ Spoon 2 tablespoons of marinade into each cavity.
- ◆ Salt and pepper each duck and place strip of bacon over.
- ◆ Wrap each duck in foil. Bake for 4 hours.

South Carolina Pheasant

Serves 2

1 whole pheasant, split	8 ounces mushrooms, sliced
¼ pound butter	1 small onion, sliced
¼ pound bacon, chopped	1 to 2 cloves garlic, minced
	¼ cup white wine

- Brown pheasant in butter.
- Remove from skillet.
- Brown bacon pieces.
- Add sliced mushrooms, onion, garlic, and sauté.
- Return pheasant pieces to skillet.
- Add wine and cook slowly.
- If boned, cook approximately 1 hour.
- If on the bone, cook for 1½ hours.

Crockpot Venison Roast

Serves 6 to 8

1 roast of venison	2 to 3 celery ribs, coarsely chopped
1 package beef stew seasoning mix (about 1½ ounces)	2 onions, cut into wedges
2 to 3 carrots, thickly sliced	1 cup water

- Wash and dry roast.
- Place roast in crockpot.
- Sprinkle with beef stew seasoning mix.
- Place carrots, onions, and celery around roast.
- Add water.
- Cook on high for 2 hours.
- Switch crockpot to low and cook for another 3 to 4 hours, until fork tender.
- Remove roast and slice.
- Discard the vegetables.

Two Hour Venison Stew

Serves 6

½ pound bacon, minced
2 pounds venison, cut
   into 1-inch cubes
¼ cup flour
1 quart water
½ teaspoon black
   pepper
2 teaspoons salt
⅛ teaspoon cayenne
   pepper

3 onions, chopped
1 16-ounce can
   tomatoes, diced
1 cup raw potatoes,
   diced
1 cup frozen butter
   beans
1 cup chopped frozen
   okra
1 cup frozen whole
   kernel corn

- Fry the bacon in Dutch oven.
- Remove the bacon.
- Dredge the meat in flour and brown it well in bacon fat.
- Add water, black pepper, salt, cayenne and onions.
- Bring to a boil, then reduce to a simmer and cook for 1 hour.
- Add the cooked bacon, tomatoes (including juice), potato, and butter beans.
- Simmer for 40 minutes.
- Add okra and simmer for 10 minutes.
- Add corn and simmer for 10 minutes.

Ham Venison

Serves 6 to 8

1 whole venison ham	fresh ground pepper,
½ gallon milk,	liberal amount
approximately	Madeira wine, high
cloves garlic	quality
rosemary, liberal	
amount	

- Take the venison ham and remove all the connective tissue on the outer surface of the meat. This step is vital as the connective tissue impedes marination as well as contributes to the gamey flavor.
- Put ham in a large plastic bag, such as a clean garbage bag, and marinate in the milk, in the refrigerator, overnight.
- Next morning, rinse and dry the ham.
- Make a few small incisions in the meat and insert garlic clove into each incision.
- Sprinkle the ham with rosemary and pepper.
- Marinate the ham in another plastic bag with the high quality Madeira wine, at room temperature, for approximately 6 to 8 hours. (It is very important to use a high-quality Madeira wine).
- If the dish is to be prepared in the oven, do so for 25 minutes at 500°, then reduce the heat and proceed at 325° for approximately 12 minutes per pound.
- If you wish to grill the ham, sear with high heat for 20 minutes, then cook approximately 2 hours on low indirect heat, using the same 12-minutes-per-pound guideline. The best way to heat indirectly is to have the fire on one side of the grill and the meat on the other. Place a pan of water over the fire. Those of you with a commercially-available smoker can use this recipe for that device.

Continued on next page

Due to the fact that venison is exceptionally lean, cooking times will vary and doneness should be monitored closely. Also, venison has essentially no fat and is therefore quite a healthy dish. The down-side to venison being so lean is that it is so easy to overcook and it also cools down quickly. When the ham is removed from the oven or grill it will continue to cook, so take this into account when determining the time allowed for cooking. If you are not going to serve the ham immediately, place several pats of butter on the ham and cover with foil and towels. This will ensure that the ham is warm and succulent at the time of serving. Serve as you would any other roast.

Barbecued Chicken with Orange Marinade

Serves 4

1 2-pound frying chicken, cut into 4 parts	hot pepper sauce or cayenne pepper to taste (optional)
8 fresh squeezed oranges or 2½ to 3 cups orange juice	1 clove garlic, minced
	1 bunch green onions (scallions), diced
1 tablespoon fresh lemon juice	¼ cup olive oil
1 tablespoon red or white vinegar	salt and pepper to taste

- Mix all ingredients, except chicken, in large mixing bowl.
- Place chicken in marinade and cover for several hours.
- Place chicken on hot barbecue grill, cover and cook until tender, turning every 15 minutes.
- About 10 minutes before the chicken is done, baste generously with extra marinade.

Australian Chicken

Serves 6 to 8

2 chickens, cooked and cubed	3 tablespoons butter salt and pepper
2 sweet red peppers, chopped	3 tablespoons prepared mustard
2 green peppers, chopped	3 tablespoons Worcestershire sauce
1 large onion, chopped	3 cups heavy cream paprika
2½ cups mushrooms, chopped	

- Preheat oven to 350°.
- Place chicken cubes in a greased casserole.
- Lightly fry peppers, onion and mushrooms in butter.
- Add to chicken. Season to taste.
- Add mustard and Worcestershire sauce to cream and whip until cream is quite stiff.
- Spoon over vegetables, spreading gently with a knife.
- Sprinkle with paprika.
- Bake for 20 to 25 minutes, or until sauce is melted and top is slightly brown.
- Serve with rice, salad and French bread.

Recipe submitted David Zinman, Music Director of the Baltimore Symphony Orchestra.

Opening Night Chicken

Serves 4

4 chicken breast-halves, boned and skinned	½ stick margarine
½ cup flour	¼ cup white wine
1 teaspoon salt	½ pound fresh mushrooms, sliced
¼ teaspoon pepper	4 slices provolone cheese
½ teaspoon tarragon leaves	

- Pound chicken to ¼-inch thickness between 2 pieces of wax paper.
- Mix together flour, ½ teaspoon salt, ⅛ teaspoon pepper, and tarragon in small bowl.
- Add chicken, 1 piece at a time, turning to lightly coat.
- Melt butter in shallow fry pan over medium heat.
- Add chicken. Cook, turning once, about 6 minutes, or until brown.
- Add wine and increase heat to high. Baste with wine while turning chicken.
- Remove chicken, place in 9x13-inch baking pan and keep warm.
- In the same fry pan, over medium heat, add mushrooms; sauté about 3 minutes or until tender; add remaining salt and pepper.
- Top each serving with 2 tablespoons mushrooms and 1 slice provolone.
- Broil in oven, about 6 inches from heat, until cheese melts.

Pot Roasted Chicken

Serves 4

8 tablespoons butter, softened	salt and pepper to taste
2 tablespoons parsley, chopped	1 egg, beaten
2 tablespoons breadcrumbs	1 3 to 3½-pound roasting chicken
1 tablespoon tarragon	1 slice bread
	1 tablespoon oil
	1½ tablespoons flour

- Combine 4 tablespoons softened butter, parsley, breadcrumbs, tarragon, salt, and pepper.
- Add egg and mix well.
- Carefully slit some of the skin of the chicken around the breast and the legs.
- Place some of the butter mixture under the skin.
- Place the rest of the butter mixture inside the cavity of the chicken, sealing with a piece of bread.
- Tie chicken legs together.
- In a heavy Dutch oven, melt the remaining 4 tablespoons of butter with the oil on low heat.
- Place chicken in Dutch oven and brown on each side for about 4 minutes, or until all is golden brown.
- Turn burner to very lowest point and let chicken "roast" in covered Dutch oven for about 1½ hours.
- Turn chicken occasionally during roasting period.
- Gravy can be made from the pan drippings by thickening with about 1½ tablespoons flour.

Serve with roasted potatoes, and a green vegetable or salad.

Raspberry Chicken

Serves 2 to 4

2 whole chicken breasts, boneless and skinless	4 tablespoons raspberry vinegar
2 tablespoons sweet butter	¼ cup chicken broth
¼ cup yellow onions, chopped very fine	⅓ cup heavy cream
	1 tablespoon canned crushed tomatoes
	2 or 3 dozen fresh raspberries

- Cut each chicken breast in half and flatten by pressing between palms of hands or pressing on cutting board.
- Melt butter in large skillet. Add chicken pieces; raise heat and cook about 3 minutes on each side, or until lightly browned. Remove chicken from skillet and set aside.
- Cook chopped onion in skillet juices on slow heat, covered, until tender, about 10 or 15 minutes.
- Add raspberry vinegar and cook over medium heat until it is reduced to a spoonful of syrupy sauce.
- Whisk in chicken stock, heavy cream and crushed tomatoes, and simmer for 1 minute.
- Return chicken to skillet and simmer in sauce until sauce is slightly reduced and thickened, about 5 minutes. Baste often. Do not overcook.
- Remove chicken with tongs and arrange on platter.
- Add raspberries to sauce and cook over low heat for 1 minute. Swirl or shake raspberries in skillet but do not stir them, as stirring can crush the delicate berries.
- Pour sauce over chicken and serve.

Wonderful with wild rice and green beans.

Chicken Sadie

Serves 4

Chicken

4	pieces of split chicken breast with skin and bone	1	teaspoon thyme
6	large white potatoes	2	bay leaves
1	large onion	4	ounces butter
½	pound mushrooms (or 1 large can)		oil
			salt and pepper to taste

Shallot Sauce

2	shallots, chopped	1	ounce butter
6	ounces dry white wine		oil

- Preheat oven to 400°.
- Thinly slice potatoes and fry until dark brown.
- Sprinkle with salt and pepper.
- Drain and set aside.
- Cut onion into thin rings and cook in a little butter until translucent; set aside.
- Meanwhile, in a Dutch oven or large skillet, melt 2 ounces butter and oil; brown chicken pieces with the thyme and bay leaves.
- For the last 5 minutes of cooking, add mushrooms; set aside.
- In an ovenproof casserole dish, melt 2 ounces butter. Place 1 or 2 layers of the cooked potatoes in the casserole, overlapping the layers.
- Add the chicken pieces and mushrooms, then cover with the rest of the potato slices.
- Drizzle with cooking juices.
- Place the covered casserole in the oven and bake for 25 minutes.
- Reduce oven heat to 250° and bake for another 20 minutes.
- Meanwhile, to prepare shallot sauce, melt 1 ounce butter with a small amount of oil.

Continued on next page

- Add chopped shallots and cook until golden brown.
- Deglaze all pots and casseroles with white wine and add to shallots.
- Simmer gently for 5 minutes.
- Remove chicken casserole dish from oven, tip onto serving dish and sprinkle with onions.
- Serve with shallot sauce and green vegetable.

Carver's Pecan Chicken

Serves 4

4 chicken breast halves, skinned and boned
6 tablespoons butter
3 rounded tablespoons Dijon mustard
6 ounces pecans, coarsely ground

⅔ cup sour cream (may use lowfat)
¼ teaspoon pepper
salt and pepper to taste
oil

- Preheat oven to 400°.
- Sprinkle chicken with salt and pepper.
- Melt butter in small pan. Remove from heat and stir in 2 tablespoons mustard.
- Dip each piece of chicken into butter mixture, then heavily coat with pecans, patting with hands.
- Place chicken in oiled baking dish and bake for about 15 to 20 minutes. The cooking time will depend on how thick the breasts are.
- In a small pan, mix the sour cream, 1 tablespoon mustard, and ¼ teaspoon fresh pepper.
- Bring quickly to boil and remove from the heat.
- Pour the sauce on the plate and place the chicken on top

This is an elegant party dish, and yet so easy.

249

Sautéed Chicken with Basil and Mint

Serves 2

2 chicken breast-halves, boneless and skinless
1 tablespoon virgin olive oil
4 cloves garlic, minced
1 tablespoon fresh basil, minced
1 tablespoon fresh mint, minced
¼ teaspoon freshly ground pepper (may use peppercorns blended with allspice)
1 cup chicken broth generous dash cayenne pepper

- Heat oil in medium skillet.
- Add garlic and chicken.
- Brown chicken over medium heat, being careful not to burn garlic.
- Add basil, mint, pepper, cayenne, and broth.
- Reduce heat to low, cover and simmer until chicken is done (10 to 15 minutes).
- Remove chicken to plate and keep warm.
- Increase heat to high and reduce liquid by half. Remove sauce from heat.
- Serve over rice or angel-hair pasta and pour sauce on top.

Curry Chicken

Serves 6

6 chicken breasts,
   skinless
4 tablespoons
   margarine
½ cup honey

¼ cup Dijon mustard
1 teaspoon salt
1 teaspoon curry
   powder

- Preheat oven to 350°.
- Melt margarine and stir in honey, mustard, salt and curry powder.
- Place chicken in shallow baking dish making a single layer.
- Pour honey-mustard mixture over chicken.
- Cover with foil. Bake for 1 hour.
- Serve over rice.

To lower fat content, reduce margarine as required.
Makes excellent sauce for rice dishes.

Easy Chicken Pot Pie

Serves 6

1 12½-ounce can
   chicken
2 cans refrigerator
   crescent rolls
1 15-ounce can small
   peas
1 15-ounce can carrots,
   sliced

3 potatoes, diced and
   boiled
1 10¾-ounce can cream
   soup (chicken,
   mushroom, celery,
   etc.)

- Preheat oven to 400°.
- Roll out 1 can of rolls in greased 9x12-inch pan
- Mix chicken, vegetables, potatoes and soup together.
- Pour over rolls.
- Roll out second can of rolls to make top crust.
- Bake until golden brown, about 35 to 40 minutes.

An easy way to make an old-fashioned favorite.

Curry Chicken with Apples and Raisins

Serves 6 to 8

8 chicken breast halves, boneless and skinless
½ cup raisins
2 medium apples, peeled, cored, and chopped finely

½ cup slivered almonds
⅓ cup brown sugar
½ cup butter, melted
½ teaspoon cinnamon
2½ teaspoons curry powder

- Preheat oven to 350°.
- Mix all ingredients, except chicken, together.
- Place chicken in a well-oiled 9x13-inch baking pan.
- Pour mixture on top. Cover lightly with foil. (This can all be done the day before).
- Bake for about 30 minutes (longer if chilled).
- Remove foil and bake for another 10 minutes.
- Serve with rice and green beans.

Mandarin oranges and chutney may be substituted for apples and raisins. An easy, inexpensive and tasty dish.

Chinese Stir-Fry (Chicken or Pork)

Serves 4 to 6

Sauce

2 tablespoons cornstarch

1¼ cups water

⅓ cup soy sauce

⅓ cup corn syrup (either light or dark)

¼ teaspoon crushed red pepper

Stir-Fry

1 pound chicken (or pork), cut into thin strips

2 cloves garlic, minced

2 cups broccoli flowerets

2 onions, cut into wedges

1 large carrot, cut into julienne strips

½ pound mushrooms, sliced

4 tablespoons oil

- Combine all sauce ingredients; set aside.
- Heat 2 tablespoons of the oil.
- Add chicken (or pork) and garlic.
- Stir-fry for 5 minutes, or until tender.
- Remove from skillet.
- Heat 2 more tablespoons of oil and add broccoli, onions, and carrot strips.
- Stir-fry 2 minutes, then add mushrooms.
- Stir-fry until vegetables are tender-crisp.
- Return chicken (or pork) to skillet.
- Stir sauce mixture again and add to skillet.
- Bring to boil over medium heat, stirring constantly. Boil for 1 minute.
- Serve over rice.

Better than take-out.

Cajun Chicken Gumbo

Serves 4 to 6

1 to 2 chickens, cut in large
pieces (may be
boneless and skinless,
if desired)
1 large onion, sliced
1 large green pepper,
sliced
3 tops of celery stalks

3½ tablespoons butter or
margarine
5 tablespoons flour
4 to 5 cups water
salt and pepper to
taste
Cajun seasoning to
taste

- Brown chicken in a heavy skillet using ½ tablespoon shortening.
- Remove chicken.
- Over low heat, make a roux by melting 3 tablespoons of butter or margarine and mixing in the flour, a little at a time. Stir continuously until the flour browns (very dark brown) DO NOT BURN.
- Chop ½ of the onion slices and ⅔ of the green pepper slices. Add to the roux and sauté until softened.
- Add water all at once.
- Put chicken into mixture and simmer about 20 minutes.
- Add remaining sliced onions, sliced green peppers, and celery tops.
- Season to taste.
- Continue to simmer until chicken is cooked. Large vegetables should be al dente.
- Remove from heat and add Cajun seasoning powder. (If Cajun seasoning powder is allowed to boil it will become stringy.)

In Cajun country, the chicken (with bones and skin) is served in a soup bowl with lots of gumbo and rice.

Broccoli and Chicken Crêpes

Serves 8

Crêpes

1 tablespoon olive oil

1 pound skinless and boneless chicken breasts, slivered

3 cups broccoli flowerets and stems, thickly sliced

¾ cup scallions, thinly sliced

2 cups mushrooms, sliced

1½ cups chicken broth

1½ tablespoons cornstarch

3 tablespoons soy sauce

¾ cup roasted unsalted cashews, coarsely chopped

16 crêpes

white pepper to taste

Crêpe Sauce

1 tablespoon cornstarch

1 cup chicken broth

- Heat olive oil in large skillet.
- Stir-fry chicken until it loses its pink color.
- Add broccoli, scallions, and mushrooms. Stir-fry 1 minute longer.
- Add broth and pepper. Cook 5 minutes at medium-low.
- In a small bowl, mix cornstarch and soy sauce well.
- Add to skillet and cook, stirring until thick. Add cashews.
- Fill crêpes with mixture and place, seam side down, in a lightly greased 9x12-inch baking pan. (Can be refrigerated or frozen at this point).
- At serving time, preheat oven to 300°. Bake for 15 to 20 minutes, until warmed through.
- Prepare crêpe sauce by combining 1 tablespoon cornstarch and 1 cup chicken broth. Cook until thick and pour over crêpes before serving.

This is a great dish to make ahead of time.

Cheese Stuffed Chicken Wraps

Serves 12

6 whole chicken
breasts, halved,
skinned and boned
⅓ cup lemon juice
1 8-ounce package
cream cheese
⅓ cup green onions

½ teaspoon dried
tarragon
½ teaspoon salt
12 slices bacon
toothpicks or small
skewers

- Preheat oven to 350°.
- Flatten chicken pieces by pounding between slices of wax paper.
- Dip in lemon juice.
- Combine cheese, onions, tarragon, and salt.
- Place about 2 tablespoons of this mixture on each piece of chicken.
- Roll like a jelly roll and wrap with a slice of bacon. Secure with toothpick or skewer.
- Place in a shallow 9x12-inch buttered baking dish and bake, uncovered, for about 30 to 40 minutes.

Light Chicken Enchiladas

Serves 6

1   16-ounce container
    light sour cream
1   7-ounce can diced
    green chilies
4   large green onions,
    chopped
½   cup fresh parsley,
    chopped
1½ teaspoons ground
    cumin
2   cups chicken, cooked
    and diced
2   cups lowfat sharp
    Cheddar cheese,
    grated

salt and pepper to
taste
6   8-inch diameter flour
    tortillas
1   8-ounce package light
    cream cheese, cut
    lengthwise into 6 long
    strips
2   16-ounce bottles mild
    picante sauce or salsa
    additional fresh
    parsley, chopped
    (optional)

- Butter 13x9x2-inch glass baking pan.
- Mix 1¾ cups sour cream, chilies, green onions, parsley, and cumin in large bowl.
- Mix in chicken and 1 cup Cheddar cheese.
- Season filling to taste with salt and pepper
- Spoon generous ½ cup filling down center of each tortilla.
- Top filling with cream cheese strip.
- Roll up tortilla, enclosing filling.
- Arrange enchiladas, seam side down, in prepared dish. (Can be made ½ day ahead. Cover and chill).
- Pour picante sauce over enchiladas.
- Cover and bake at 350° until sauce bubbles and enchiladas are heated through, about 45 minutes.
- Uncover, sprinkle with remaining 1 cup Cheddar cheese and bake until cheese melts, about 5 minutes.
- Top with remaining sour cream and garnish with additional parsley, if desired.

Chicken Alberghetti

Serves 6 to 8

4 whole chicken breasts, halved, skinned and boned	8 slices Swiss cheese, paper-thin
2 eggs, beaten	8 slices mozzarella cheese, paper-thin
16 ounces marinara sauce	½ cup freshly grated Parmesan cheese
½ cup milk or half-and-half	fresh breadcrumbs
	butter as needed
	olive oil as needed

- Preheat oven to 300°.
- Dip chicken breasts in beaten egg mix.
- Roll in breadcrumbs to coat evenly.
- Sauté chicken in mixture of butter and olive oil until lightly golden.
- Combine marinara sauce and milk. Cover bottom of shallow baking dish with sauce.
- Layer chicken in sauce and top with slices of Swiss and mozzarella cheese.
- Sprinkle Parmesan over all and dot with butter, if desired.
- Bake, covered, for 30 minutes.
- Uncover and bake 10 to 15 minutes more. (Oven may be turned up to slightly brown cheese).
- Serve hot.

This dish can be cooked ahead and reheated before serving. Nice with linguine and salad.

Poppy Seed Chicken

Serves 6 to 8

6 to 8 chicken breasts or 1 whole chicken

2 10½-ounce cans cream of chicken soup

1 8-ounce container sour cream

1 cup round buttery cracker crumbs

2 ounces margarine

2 tablespoons poppy seed

- Preheat oven to 350°.
- Boil chicken and cut up.
- Grease casserole dish.
- Place chicken in dish.
- Mix soup and sour cream.
- Pour mix over chicken.
- Sprinkle cracker crumbs on top of casserole.
- Pour melted butter on top.
- Sprinkle with poppy seed.
- Bake for 35 minutes.
- Serve over rice or noodles.

Chicken Sausage Patties

Serves 8 small or 6 large portions

1 pound ground chicken (or turkey) breast, cooked

⅓ cup fresh sage leaves, chopped

1 tablespoon olive oil

1 small onion, minced

2 Granny Smith apples, peeled, cored and coarsely chopped

salt and pepper to taste

pinch of nutmeg

pinch of cinnamon

- Preheat oven to 350°.
- Combine ground chicken, sage, cinnamon, nutmeg, salt and pepper. Mix well.
- Sauté onion for 2 minutes in oil. Add apples and cook until soft. Let cool.
- Combine with ground chicken mixture.
- Form into patties.
- Brown 4 at a time in skillet with a little oil, then bake for 10 minutes.
- Serve immediately.

Patties can be made a day ahead and refrigerated.

Caribbean Stew

Serves 6 to 8

6 chicken breast halves, boned and cut into 1-inch pieces
1 pound smoked pork, cut into 1-inch cubes
1 large onion, sliced
2 tablespoons olive oil
2 cups water
8 ounces tomato sauce
½ cup coconut, shredded
1½ teaspoons salt

1½ teaspoons crushed red pepper
5 whole cloves
1 bay leaf
¼ teaspoon leaf thyme
2 pounds sweet potatoes
2 bananas, peeled and sliced ¾-inch thick
¼ cup green onions, sliced

- Sauté onion until golden in oil in Dutch oven, about 5 minutes.
- Remove with slotted spoon.
- Brown chicken in same kettle, adding more oil as needed. Return onion to Dutch oven.
- Add pork.
- Stir in water, tomato sauce, coconut, and salt.
- Tie pepper, cloves, bay leaf, and thyme in a small square of cheesecloth; add to stew.
- Bring to boil then lower heat; cover and simmer 15 minutes.
- Pare sweet potatoes and cut into ½-inch slices.
- Add to stew, pushing them into liquid.
- Simmer 35 to 40 minutes longer until meats and potatoes are tender.
- Taste and add more salt as needed.
- Stir bananas and green onion into stew, cover and simmer 5 minutes longer.
- Arrange in serving dish and garnish with additional coconut and green onion.

A very unusual dish!

Greek Chicken with Feta Cheese

Serves 4

2 tablespoons olive oil
1 medium onion, chopped
2 garlic cloves, minced
1 4-ounce jar pimiento
½ cup red wine
1 16-ounce can tomatoes, sliced
½ 6-ounce can tomato paste
1 teaspoon basil, dried
1 teaspoon marjoram, dried

1 to 2 drops hot pepper sauce
2 whole chicken breasts, skinless, boneless and divided in half
1 tablespoon paprika
salt and pepper to taste
⅓ pound feta cheese, crumbled

+ Heat olive oil in 8-inch fry pan over medium heat.
+ Add onions; sauté for 3 minutes. Add garlic; sauté 2 minutes more.
+ Add pimiento (and juice), red wine, tomatoes, tomato paste, basil, marjoram, and hot pepper sauce.
+ Stir with wooden spoon; simmer for 15 to 20 minutes.
+ Preheat oven to broil.
+ Spray 8x8-inch baking dish with oil.
+ Cover each piece of chicken with oil and rub with salt, pepper, and paprika. Place in baking dish.
+ Broil each side of chicken for 2 minutes or slightly more.
+ Reduce oven to 350°.
+ Cover chicken with sauce.
+ Sprinkle with crumbled feta cheese and bake, uncovered, for 20 to 25 minutes.
+ Serve with rice or couscous.

Recipe may be doubled.

Savory Glazed Cornish Hens
Stuffed with Wild Rice

Serves 2

¼ cup celery, minced
¼ cup shallots, minced
¼ cup green pepper,
  finely chopped
¼ cup plus 2
  tablespoons butter or
  margarine

1 6-ounce box long
  grain and wild rice
  (regular, not quick-
  cooking)
2 1 to 1¼-pound
  Cornish hens
  salt and pepper to
  taste
¾ cup red currant jelly
¼ cup brandy

- Preheat oven to 375°.
- Sauté celery, shallots, and green pepper in 2 tablespoons butter or margarine in a medium saucepan.
- Cook rice according to package directions.
- Combine cooked rice with sautéed vegetables.
- Remove giblets from hens. Rinse hens with cold water and pat dry; sprinkle cavities with salt and pepper.
- Stuff hens lightly with rice mixture.
- Close cavities and secure with wooden picks; truss. (Keep extra rice warm to serve on plates with hens.)
- Place hens, breast side up, in a shallow baking pan.
- Melt ¼ cup butter in saucepan; brush hens with butter. Reserve remaining butter in saucepan.
- Bake hens for 30 minutes.
- Combine jelly and brandy in saucepan with remaining butter.
- Cook over low heat, stirring often, until jelly melts.
- Brush hens with jelly mixture.
- Bake 30 to 40 additional minutes, depending on size of hens, basting every 10 minutes with jelly mixture.

Vegetables & Condiments

Asparagus Casserole

Green Beans with Tomatoes and Garlic (see photo)

Tipsy Carrots

Vidalia Onion Casserole

Tomatoes Stuffed with Vermicelli (see photo)

Cold Spiced Fruit

Baked Curried Fruit

Great Mustard Sauce

Cranberry Citrus Relish

Pear and Apple Conserve

and More

Rainbow Row

Rainbow row overlooks the Cooper River, which historically has been the site of the shipping industry. Busy merchants had offices on the first floor, lived above and owned wharves across the street. In the early 1900's a number of these homes were slated for demolition. A Charlestonian purchased and restored several of these homes. This concept marked the beginning of the preservation movement in America. The first Preservation Society was founded here in 1920.

Menus

Saturday Evening Supper

Chunky Gazpacho

Noodle Stroganoff

Broccoli Elegant

Sweet Potato Muffins

Elegant Dessert

Asparagus Casserole

Serves 8

round buttery cracker
crumbs
1 19-ounce can
asparagus, drained
(reserve juice)
1 10¾-ounce can cream
of mushroom soup

1 8-ounce can water
chestnuts, sliced
sharp Cheddar
cheese, grated
1 2.8-ounce can
French-fried onions
butter or margarine

- Preheat oven to 350°.
- Grease 12x7-inch baking dish.
- Line bottom of dish with round buttery cracker crumbs.
- Spread asparagus on crumbs.
- Pour mushroom soup over asparagus.
- Add ¼ cup reserved juice and water chestnuts.
- Cover with grated sharp cheese.
- Add a layer of cracker crumbs and dot with butter.
- Bake for 15 minutes or until bubbly.
- Add French-fried onions and bake for 5 more minutes.

Sesame Broccoli

Serves 4

1 large bunch broccoli,
broken into flowerets,
stems peeled
½ cup sesame seed,
toasted
¼ cup dry sherry

1½ tablespoons soy
sauce
2 teaspoons vegetable
oil (or sesame oil)
2 teaspoons honey

- Cook broccoli in boiling salted water just until crisp-tender.
  Drain.
- Combine remaining ingredients in large bowl.
- Toss broccoli with sauce, just before serving.
- Serve at room temperature.

*Good with other Oriental dishes. Also nice with lamb or
pork roast.*

Broccoli Elegant

Serves 6 to 8

1½ cups water
¼ cup plus 2
   tablespoons butter
1 6-ounce package
   cornbread stuffing mix
2 10-ounce packages
   frozen broccoli
   spears, thawed
2 tablespoons all-
   purpose flour

1½ teaspoons chicken-
   flavored bouillon
¾ cup milk
¼ teaspoon salt
1 3-ounce package
   cream cheese,
   softened
6 green onions, sliced
1 cup Cheddar cheese,
   shredded
   paprika

- Preheat oven to 350°.
- Combine water and ¼ cup butter in a saucepan (if stuffing mix has a separate seasoning packet, add it to the water and butter). Bring to a boil.
- Remove from heat; stir in stuffing and let stand 5 minutes.
- Spoon around inside edge of lightly buttered 13x9x2-inch baking dish.
- Leave a well in the center.
- Place broccoli in well and set aside.
- Melt 2 tablespoons butter in heavy saucepan, over low heat; add flour, stirring until smooth.
- Cook 1 minute, stirring constantly; stir in bouillon.
- Gradually add milk; cook over medium heat, stirring constantly until thickened and bubbly.
- Add cream cheese and salt, stirring until smooth.
- Stir in green onions.
- Spoon mixture over broccoli in center of dish.
- Sprinkle with cheese and paprika.
- Cover with foil and bake 35 minutes.
- Remove foil and bake additional 10 minutes.

Spicy Green Beans

Serves 6

½ cup butter
1 cup onion, sliced
1 cup celery, sliced
½ cup pimientos, cut in strips
¼ cup snipped fresh dill weed or 2 teaspoons dried dill weed

1 tablespoon lemon juice
1 teaspoon salt
¼ teaspoon pepper
1 pound green beans, cooked and drained

- Melt butter in 10-inch skillet.
- Add onion and celery. Cook 5 minutes or until tender.
- Add pimiento strips, dill weed, lemon juice, salt and pepper. Cook 3 minutes longer.
- Toss with cooked and drained green beans.

Kielbasa Cabbage Casserole

Serves 4

4 cups cabbage, thinly sliced
1 medium onion, sliced
1 pound kielbasa sausage, cut into ½-inch slices
¾ cup sour cream

2 tablespoons prepared brown mustard
¼ teaspoon salt
⅛ teaspoon pepper
1 teaspoon caraway seeds
3 tablespoons water

- Combine cabbage, onion and kielbasa sausage in a large skillet.
- Cover and cook over medium heat 15 to 20 minutes, until onion and cabbage are soft and translucent.
- Stir in sour cream, mustard, salt, pepper, water and caraway seeds. Heat through.

Green Beans with Tomatoes and Garlic

Serves 6

1½ to 2 pounds green beans,
ends removed, halved
2 tablespoons olive oil
1 medium onion, halved
and thinly sliced
3 garlic cloves, minced

1 29-ounce and 1 14-
ounce can Italian plum
tomatoes, drained and
chopped
1 teaspoon sugar
salt and freshly
ground pepper to
taste

- Add beans to a large saucepan of boiling water, and boil, uncovered, for 8 to 10 minutes, until crisp-tender.
- Drain and rinse under cold running water until cool.
- Drain thoroughly.
- Heat 2 tablespoons olive oil in a large sauté pan.
- Add sliced onion and sauté for 5 minutes.
- Add garlic and sauté 1 minute.
- Add beans and toss to coat.
- Add tomatoes (do not add liquid from tomatoes), salt, pepper and sugar.
- Bring to a boil.
- Cover and cook on low heat for 10 minutes.
- Remove cover and cook a minute or two to thicken slightly.

May add 3 to 4 strips bacon, crumbled. May be made ahead and reheated.

Cuban Black Beans

Serves 8

2 tablespoons olive oil
2 to 4 cloves garlic, chopped
2 medium carrots, cut in half-moons
1 medium onion, chopped
1 teaspoon to 2 tablespoons curry powder, to taste

1 8-ounce can chopped or whole tomatoes, drained (reserve liquid)
1/2 cup frozen corn (optional)
2 15-ounce cans black beans, drained
1 teaspoon salt

- Heat olive oil in a saucepan.
- Add carrots, onions, garlic, curry and salt. Sauté for 3 to 4 minutes.
- Add some liquid from the tomatoes if mixture becomes dry.
- Add tomatoes. Continue to sauté approximately 2 minutes.
- Add corn and black beans. Heat through.

Serve as a side or with brown rice for an excellent vegetarian entrée.

Tipsy Carrots

Serves 4

1 1/2 pounds carrots, sliced thin and diagonally
3 medium stalks of celery, finely diced

1 small onion, minced
1 tablespoon sugar
2 tablespoons butter
1/2 to 3/4 cup dry vermouth

- Mix all ingredients in a saucepan.
- Cook over low heat for 20 minutes or until tender.

German Red Cabbage

Serves 4 to 6

1 to 2½ *pounds red cabbage*	1 *medium onion,*
⅔ *cup red wine vinegar*	*pierced with 2 cloves*
2 *tablespoons sugar*	⅔ *cup onion, finely*
2 *teaspoons salt*	*chopped*
2 *tablespoons bacon fat*	5 *cups boiling water*
2 *medium size cooking*	¼ *cup dry red wine*
apples, chopped	3 *tablespoons red*
	currant jelly

- Cut up and core cabbage, discarding tough outer leaves. Wash under cold running water and shred very fine.
- Place into a bowl and sprinkle with vinegar, sugar and salt.
- Melt bacon fat in large pan over moderate heat; add apples and chopped onion and stir 5 minutes.
- Add the chopped cabbage, the clove-pierced onion and the boiling water.
- Bring to a brisk boil, then cover pan and let cabbage simmer for 1½ hours or until tender.
- Check liquid occasionally, adding a little more water if necessary.
- Before serving, remove the onion with cloves. Add the red wine and the currant jelly, and stir to dissolve.
- Excellent reheated!

If you have your oven on, the cabbage can cook in it very happily.

Carrot Ring with Lima Beans

Serves 4 to 6

Carrots

2 pounds carrots, diced	¼ pound butter
½ to 1 cup brown sugar, packed	salt and pepper to taste

Lima Beans

2 10-ounce packages frozen lima beans (baby size)	1 pimiento, minced
	4 tablespoons butter
4 tablespoons onions or shallots, chopped	½ cup thick sour cream

- Preheat oven to 375°.
- Cook carrots until soft, then mash.
- Add sugar, butter, salt and pepper.
- Place in small greased ring mold.
- Bake 20 minutes, or until very hot.
- Cook lima beans according to package directions.
- Sauté onion and pimiento in butter.
- Mix with sour cream.
- Stir mixture into lima beans, tossing several times to blend thoroughly.
- Keep hot until ready to assemble with carrots just before serving time.
- Unmold carrot-ring onto deep dish platter.
- Spoon lima beans into center of mold.
- Garnish with parsley.

This may be prepared a day ahead and refrigerated until time to bake.

Marci's Whipped Carrots with Dill

Serves 4

Mock Crème Fraîche
   1½ cups Neufchâtel
      cheese

   6 tablespoons plain
      lowfat yogurt

Whipped Carrots with Dill
   1 pound carrots, sliced
      chicken broth to cover
  ½ cup Mock Crème
      Fraîche

   1 tablespoon dried dill
   1 teaspoon salt

- Make Mock Crème Fraîche first.
- Mix cheese and yogurt in food processor until smooth. Place in small jars.
- Cover tightly.
- Set jars in a warm place (100°) for 2 hours.
- Stir before using.
- Can be refrigerated up to 3 weeks.
- Simmer carrots in 1-inch of broth for 15 minutes. Drain.
- Puree in food processor with crème fraîche, dill and salt.
- Return to saucepan. Heat thoroughly.

Irish Zucchini Potatoes

Serves 6 to 8

   5 large potatoes, peeled
  ½ cup milk
   2 medium zucchini,
      grated

  ½ onion, chopped fine
   3 tablespoons butter
      salt and pepper to
      taste

- Boil potatoes until tender and mash them with the milk.
- Add zucchini and onions to mashed potatoes and beat well.
- Heat and stir, over very low flame, until mixture is hot.
- Add butter, salt, and pepper.

Virginia Style Corn Pudding

Serves 4 to 6

4 ears fresh corn	2 eggs, beaten
3 tablespoons sugar	1½ tablespoons butter,
2 tablespoons flour	melted
½ teaspoon salt	1 cup milk
pepper	

- Preheat oven to 325°.
- Cut corn off cob, scraping ears.
- Add sugar, flour, salt and pepper.
- Blend in beaten eggs, butter and milk.
- Bake in a greased 9-inch square casserole dish for about 1 hour.

1 teaspoon vanilla and a dash of nutmeg may be added, if desired.

Potato Side Dish

Serves 6 to 8

4 potatoes, peeled and sliced	salt and pepper to taste
8 carrots, peeled and sliced	1 10¾-ounce can cream of mushroom soup
2 onions, peeled and sliced	½ can water
	margarine

- Preheat oven to 350°.
- Grease a 9x13-inch baking dish.
- Layer vegetables alternately in dish. Salt and pepper each layer and dot with margarine.
- Mix soup and water. Pour over vegetables.
- Cover and bake for about 1 hour.

Mushroom Dinner Pie

Serves 8 to 10

4 cups mushrooms, sliced	1 pint (or more) half-and-half
¼ cup onion, finely chopped	1 teaspoon salt
6 tablespoons butter, divided	⅛ teaspoon pepper pastry for 2-crust 10-inch pie, unbaked
4 tablespoons flour	1 tablespoon milk

* Preheat oven to 350°.
* Sauté the mushrooms and onions in 2 tablespoons butter, then drain, reserving the liquid.
* Combine the reserved liquid and enough half-and-half to make 3 cups.
* In a saucepan, combine the cream mixture, flour, and 4 tablespoons butter. Cook over low heat until slightly thickened.
* Add salt, pepper, onion and mushrooms. Blend well, then pour into prepared pie shell.
* Cover the filling with the second crust. Make several slits in the top crust to vent.
* Brush top with a little milk to aid browning.
* Bake for 1 hour, or until crust is golden brown.
* Let pie cool for about 1 hour before serving so it is easier to cut and serve.

Marvelous as a substitute for potatoes or starch when serving steak, roast beef or poultry. For easy entertaining, make this pie days ahead of serving and freeze it.

Mushroom Casserole

Serves 6

1 egg yolk
1 cup light cream
¼ pound butter
1½ pounds mushrooms
  and stems, sliced
3 tablespoons flour

1 tablespoon parsley,
  chopped
juice of ½ lemon
dash paprika
½ large box of round
  buttery crackers,
  crushed

- Preheat oven to 325°.
- Beat together egg yolk and 1 tablespoon cream. Set aside.
- Melt ½ stick butter in a large fry pan and sauté mushrooms until golden.
- Stir in flour and parsley.
- Reduce heat to low and add remaining cream, lemon juice, and paprika; stir.
- Add egg yolk and cream mixture; stir thoroughly.
- Place in greased, flat, 1-quart casserole.
- Melt remaining butter and mix into cracker crumbs.
- Top casserole with cracker crumbs.
- Bake for ½ hour, until top browns slightly.

Will serve 6 as a main dish, or 12 to 14 as an appetizer with crackers.

Stuffed Mushrooms

Serves 6

12 large mushrooms	4 tablespoons butter
2 tablespoons parsley, chopped	½ teaspoon seasoned salt
1 tablespoon onion, chopped	½ cup white wine
½ small garlic clove, chopped	2 tablespoons Parmesan cheese, grated
4 tablespoons fine breadcrumbs	

- Preheat oven to 400°.
- Rinse mushrooms and remove stems. Put a pinch of salt in each cap.
- Place hollow side up in baking dish.
- Chop stems fine.
- Sauté stems in skillet with parsley, onion, garlic, breadcrumbs, butter and salt.
- When golden, add 3 tablespoons of wine
- Fill each cap with mixture and top with cheese.
- Pour remaining wine and a little water in bottom of baking dish and bake for ½ hour.

Vidalia Onion Casserole

Serves 4

3 to 4 large onions, sliced
(red, sweet or Vidalia)
2 tablespoons olive oil
1 clove garlic, minced
1 10¾-ounce can cream
of mushroom or
cream of chicken
soup

¼ cup milk
8 ounces Swiss cheese,
grated
1 small loaf French
bread
melted butter

- Preheat oven to 350°.
- Sauté sliced onions and garlic in olive oil until golden.
- Layer onions in a buttered 3-quart casserole dish.
- Mix the soup with the milk and pour over the onions.
- Spread the cheese over this mixture.
- Cut the French bread into ½-inch thick slices, dip into melted butter, and place on top of the cheese, buttered side up.
- Bake, uncovered, for 30 to 40 minutes or until golden brown.

Sweet Potatoes with
Brown Sugar and Rosemary

Serves 2

1 to 1½ pounds sweet
potatoes
1 teaspoon dried
rosemary
1½ tablespoons brown
sugar, packed

3 tablespoons light sour
cream
⅛ teaspoon salt
freshly ground pepper
to taste

- Peel potatoes, cover with water and cook in covered pot for 12 to 15 minutes or until tender.
- Drain potatoes and place in food processor with crumbled rosemary, brown sugar, sour cream, salt and pepper.
- Puree the mixture.

Jane's Onion Pie

Serves 4 to 6

1 9-inch pie crust	2 tablespoons flour
4 medium onions, thinly sliced	1 teaspoon salt
	1/8 teaspoon fresh pepper
1 tablespoon olive oil	3 ounces Swiss cheese, grated
3 tablespoons butter	
2 eggs	pinch of nutmeg
1 cup half-and-half	

- Preheat oven to 375°.
- Partially bake the pie crust, about 10 minutes.
- Sauté onions in oil and butter over low heat until golden.
- Beat eggs, half-and-half, flour, salt, pepper and nutmeg, then add onions and ½ of the cheese.
- Pour into crust; sprinkle with remaining cheese.
- Bake for 25 to 30 minutes or until brown.

For a nice change, add 2 cups of thinly-sliced baking potatoes. After sautéing the onions for 5 minutes, add potatoes and continue with recipe.

Sautéed Italian Vegetables

Serves 6

3 tablespoons olive oil	3/4 teaspoon dried oregano leaves
3 zucchini, sliced julienne	1/2 teaspoon seasoned salt
1 large onion, sliced	
2 large firm tomatoes, cut in chunks	1/4 teaspoon pepper
fresh mushrooms, sliced (optional)	1/4 teaspoon garlic powder

- In large skillet, heat the oil; sauté zucchini and onion on high until almost tender.
- Add tomatoes, mushrooms and seasonings.
- Stir until heated.

Quick and easy.

Stuffed Baked Potatoes with Horseradish Cream

Serves 6

Stuffed Potatoes

6 large baking potatoes, rinsed and dried

6 tablespoons sour cream

6 tablespoons butter

2 tablespoons prepared white horseradish, drained

salt and pepper to taste

Topping

½ cup sour cream

2 tablespoons prepared white horseradish, drained

2 tablespoons fresh dill, chopped

- Preheat oven to 400°.
- Pierce potatoes with fork and bake for 1 hour.
- Remove from oven, place on baking sheet, and cool for 5 minutes.
- Slice skin away from top of each potato.
- Carefully scoop out pulp, leaving ¼ of pulp in shell. Be careful to leave shells intact.
- Spoon pulp into mixing bowl. Mash with 6 tablespoons sour cream, 6 tablespoons butter, 2 tablespoons horseradish, salt and pepper.
- Spoon mixture into potato shells.
- Return to oven and bake for 50 minutes.
- To make topping, combine all topping ingredients. Cover and chill until potatoes are done. (Can be prepared a day ahead).
- When potatoes are done, remove from oven, spoon topping on each and serve.

Potatoes can also be prepared a day ahead. Cover and chill. Bake for the last 50 minutes before serving.

Yum-Yum Sweet Potatoes

Serves 6 to 8

Potato Mixture

5 cups sweet potatoes, cooked (not canned)	1 5-ounce can evaporated milk
¾ cup sugar	2 teaspoons vanilla
2 eggs	3 teaspoons cinnamon
4 tablespoons butter (not margarine)	3 teaspoons lemon juice
	½ cup raisins

Topping

½ cup light brown sugar	½ cup butter, softened
½ cup flour	1 cup pecans, chopped

- Preheat oven to 325°.
- Beat all ingredients for potato mixture together until light and fluffy.
- Pour into casserole dish.
- Combine all topping ingredients.
- Spoon topping over mixture and bake until light brown, about 45 minutes.

Eggplant Casserole

Serves 4

1 quart tomatoes, stewed	½ teaspoon sugar
½ bell pepper, chopped	1 eggplant, peeled and cubed
1 onion, chopped	grated sharp Cheddar cheese to cover top
salt and pepper to taste	

- Preheat oven to 350°.
- Cook tomatoes, bell pepper, onion, salt, pepper, sugar and eggplant together for about 20 minutes, or until done.
- Put in ovenproof casserole and sprinkle with grated sharp Cheddar cheese.
- Heat in oven until cheese melts.

Spinach Soufflé

Serves 6 to 8

1 pound fresh spinach or 1 10-ounce package frozen spinach	½ cup milk
	3 tablespoons margarine
2 large eggs or 3 small eggs	2 tablespoons flour
	½ teaspoon salt

- Preheat oven to 350°.
- Wash fresh spinach and parboil in about ½ inch of water in covered saucepan for a few minutes.
- Lift spinach from water, drain and place in blender.
- If using frozen spinach, thaw and drain well.
- Add eggs, milk, margarine, flour and salt to blender.
- Blend at high speed for 10 seconds.
- Pour into greased 1½-quart casserole.
- Place casserole in pan of hot water and bake for 45 minutes.
- Can also be baked in custard cups and unmolded.

Baked Spinach

Serves 12

1 onion, grated	1 pint half-and-half
2 cloves garlic, minced	½ cup grated Parmesan cheese, plus more for the top
2 tablespoons butter	
5 10-ounce packages chopped frozen spinach, thawed and squeezed dry	¼ cup breadcrumbs

- Preheat oven to 350°.
- Sauté onion and garlic in butter.
- Combine onion, garlic, spinach, half-and-half, ½ cup Parmesan cheese, and breadcrumbs in 9x12-inch baking dish.
- Sprinkle additional Parmesan cheese on top.
- Bake until top browns, approximately 30 minutes.

Cheesy Eggplant Pie

Serves 6

1 eggplant, pared and
  cubed (about 4 cups)
½ cup onion, chopped
¼ cup green pepper,
  chopped
2 tablespoons butter
1 tablespoon all-
  purpose flour
1 10¾-ounce can
  condensed cream of
  chicken soup

1 teaspoon sugar
¼ teaspoon salt
½ teaspoon oregano
3 eggs, beaten
1 tomato, chopped
4 ounces sharp
  Cheddar cheese,
  shredded
  pastry for 2-crust 9-
  inch pie

- If using frozen pie crusts, defrost both crusts and use one for decorative cut-outs.
- Bake crust and cut-outs in a 450° oven for 8 minutes.
- Cook eggplant in salted, boiling water until tender; drain well; set aside.
- Sauté onion and pepper in butter until tender.
- Blend in flour; add soup and seasonings.
- Stir until bubbly, then remove from heat.
- Stir ½ of mixture into eggs and return it all to saucepan.
- Fold in tomato, cheese and eggplant.
- Pour into partially-baked pie crust. Top with cut-outs.
- Bake at 350° for 30 minutes.

To ripen tomatoes, put them in a brown paper bag.
Putting an apple in the bag will speed the process.

Ratatouille

One large bowl

3 tablespoons olive oil	1 medium zucchini, sliced
2 cloves garlic	8 ounces mushrooms, sliced
2 large onions, diced	1 28-ounce can crushed tomatoes
1 medium or large eggplant, cubed	salt and coarsely ground pepper to taste
2 large peppers, green or red, diced	
2 to 3 ribs of celery or fresh fennel, diced	

- Heat 3 tablespoons olive oil in 4-quart heavy saucepan.
- Sauté garlic and diced onions until golden.
- Add eggplant and peppers and cook for 10 to 15 minutes.
- Add celery, zucchini, mushrooms, tomatoes, salt, and pepper.
- Simmer for 45 minutes to 1 hour.

Serve this dish cold, as a cocktail dip with toasted pita wedges, or serve it hot as a vegetable side dish for lunch or dinner.

Baked Tomatoes

Serves 8

4 tomatoes olive oil	4 ounces fresh breadcrumbs
4 ounces sharp Cheddar cheese, grated	1 tablespoon basil
	4 tablespoons butter or margarine, melted

- Preheat oven to 350°.
- Wash tomatoes and cut in half.
- Rub with olive oil and sprinkle with salt.
- Combine cheese, breadcrumbs, basil and butter. Divide equally on top of tomatoes.
- Bake in shallow dish for 20 minutes.

Squash Casserole

Serves 8

2 pounds yellow squash
½ cup margarine
2 cups herb stuffing mix
1 cup cream of chicken soup
1 onion, chopped

1 8-ounce carton sour cream
1 8-ounce can water chestnuts, sliced
salt and pepper to taste

- Preheat oven to 350°.
- Steam squash until partially cooked.
- Mix margarine and stuffing mix together and put ½ of mixture in buttered 2-quart casserole.
- Mix squash, soup, onion, sour cream and water chestnuts together and add to casserole.
- Top with remaining stuffing mix.
- Bake, uncovered, for about 30 minutes.

Artichoke Hearts and Tomatoes

Serves 6

1 14-ounce can artichoke hearts, drained
½ cup onion, chopped
4 tablespoons butter
2 14-ounce cans whole tomatoes, drained

½ teaspoon basil
1 tablespoon sugar (optional)
salt and pepper to taste

- Preheat oven to 325°.
- Quarter artichokes.
- Sauté onion in butter.
- Add tomatoes, basil, sugar, salt and pepper. Heat for 5 minutes.
- Put in greased, uncovered, 2-quart casserole dish.
- Bake for 15 minutes.

Tomatoes Stuffed with Vermicelli

Makes 15 tomatoes

Pesto Sauce

1 cup fresh basil leaves
3 cloves garlic
⅓ cup grated Parmesan
   cheese

⅓ cup grated Romano
   cheese
¼ cup olive oil

Stuffed Tomatoes

1 pound vermicelli,
   cooked
1 cup pesto sauce
¼ pound pine nuts
   salt and pepper to
   taste

   grated Parmesan
   cheese
15 tomatoes
   fresh basil leaves,
   chopped

- Combine all pesto ingredients in blender and mix until smooth.
- Place cooked vermicelli in large bowl and toss with 1 cup pesto sauce and pine nuts.
- Season with salt, pepper, and Parmesan cheese.
- Carefully scoop pulp out of tomatoes.
- Fill tomatoes with vermicelli mixture and top with basil.

Pesto can be made ahead and frozen in small plastic bags.

Leann's Vegetable Casserole

Serves 8

Vegetable Mixture

1 16-ounce can French-
   style green beans,
   drained
1 11-ounce can white
   shoepeg corn, drained
1 cup celery, chopped
1 cup green pepper,
   chopped

1 cup onion, chopped
1 cup sour cream
1 10¾-ounce can cream
   of celery soup
1 2-ounce package
   slivered almonds

Topping

½ cup butter, melted
1 cup Cheddar cheese,
   shredded

1 cup cheese crackers,
   crushed

- Preheat oven to 350°.
- Combine all ingredients for the vegetable mixture and blend well.
- Pour into 13x9-inch baking dish.
- Mix topping ingredients together and sprinkle over vegetable mixture.
- Bake, uncovered, for 45 minutes.

Anything that grows underground---potatoes, beets, carrots, etc.---should be put on to cook in cold water. Anything that grows above ground---peas, beans, etc.---should be started in boiling water.

Vegetable Casserole

Serves 4 to 6

1½ cups green beans, cut
     up
1   medium green
     pepper, chopped
3   medium tomatoes,
     chopped
6   ounces Cheddar
     cheese, shredded

½   cup buttermilk biscuit
     mix
1   teaspoon salt
½   teaspoon cayenne red
     pepper
½   cup milk
3   eggs

- Preheat oven to 350°.
- Cook and drain beans.
- Spread beans and peppers into greased 9-inch square baking pan.
- Sprinkle with tomatoes and cheese.
- Beat remaining ingredients until smooth.
- Pour over vegetables and cheese.
- Bake, uncovered, until golden brown, about 45 minutes.
- Let stand 5 minutes before serving.

Pineapple Casserole

Serves 6 to 8

5   slices white bread
1   stick butter (¼ pound)
1   20-ounce can crushed
     pineapple, drained

2   beaten eggs
3   tablespoons flour
1   cup sugar

- Preheat oven to 350°.
- Cube bread and brown in butter in a skillet. Set aside.
- Combine pineapple, eggs, flour and sugar in a 1½-quart casserole.
- Put toasted bread cubes on top.
- Bake for 30 to 40 minutes.

Quick, easy and foolproof. Especially good as a side dish with ham or pork.

Cold Spiced Fruit

Serves 15

2 unpeeled oranges, sliced and seeded	1 29-ounce can pear halves
1 20-ounce can pineapple chunks	1 cup sugar
1 16-ounce can peaches, sliced	½ cup cider vinegar
1 16-ounce can apricot halves	3 cinnamon sticks
	5 whole cloves
	1 3-ounce package cherry flavored gelatin

◆ Cut orange slices in half; place in a saucepan; cover with water.
◆ Simmer until orange rind is tender.
◆ Drain well and set aside.
◆ Drain canned fruits VERY WELL, reserving all the pineapple juice and half of peach and apricot juices.
◆ Combine reserved juices, sugar, vinegar, cinnamon, cloves and gelatin; simmer 30 minutes.
◆ Combine drained fruits in a 9-cup container.
◆ Pour hot juice mixture over fruit. Refrigerate at least 24 hours.

May add 16-ounce can dark pitted cherries (drained) during holiday season.

Hot Mustard

Makes about 2½ cups

1 cup white vinegar	1 cup sugar
1 cup dry mustard	1 pinch salt
2 eggs	

◆ Mix vinegar with dry mustard and let stand overnight.
◆ Next day, stir in 2 well-beaten eggs.
◆ Cook, stirring constantly, until the spoon is coated.
◆ Cool and refrigerate.

Baked Curried Fruit

Serves 24

3 tablespoons flour
3 teaspoons curry powder
1 cup brown sugar
½ teaspoon ground ginger
2 16-ounce cans red sour cherries
2 16-ounce cans sliced peaches

2 16-ounce cans pears, sliced in squares
2 16-ounce cans pineapple chunks
2 16-ounce cans apricots, cut in pieces
2 16-ounce cans white grapes
½ pound butter

- Preheat oven to 350°.
- Mix dry ingredients together and set aside.
- Butter a 12x14-inch ovenproof dish.
- Drain fruit and mix together.
- Pour into baking dish.
- Sprinkle dry ingredients on top.
- Dot with 2 sticks of butter.
- Bake for 45 minutes.

Great Mustard Sauce

Makes about 1 cup

¼ cup prepared yellow mustard
1 cup sour cream
1 teaspoon sugar

1 teaspoon Worcestershire sauce
2 teaspoons horseradish, drained

- Combine all ingredients in small saucepan.
- Heat mixture, but do not boil.

Excellent condiment with ham.

Macaroon Stuffed Peaches

Serves 6

6 peaches, blanched
6 macaroons, crushed
½ cup sugar

½ stick butter, softened
2 egg yolks
   amaretto (optional)

- Preheat oven to 375°.
- Blanch peaches in boiling water for 1 minute; lift them out with a slotted spoon and slide off the skin.
- Cut peaches in half and remove stone.
- Scoop out the middle of each peach to make a deeper cavity. Reserve pulp.
- Crush macaroons with a rolling pin.
- Add sugar, butter, egg yolks, and a little peach pulp to macaroon mixture.
- Stuff each peach half with the well-mixed macaroon mixture and arrange halves side-by-side in a buttered 8x8-inch ovenproof dish.
- Bake for about 25 minutes, basting occasionally with the juices that develop.
- Sprinkle with a little amaretto, if desired.

May use canned peaches (rinsed and drained). Could easily be used for brunch buffet as well as dinner dessert with whipped cream in a side dish.

Sauce for Green Beans

Enough for 32-ounce can of green beans

⅛	teaspoon white pepper	2	teaspoons lemon juice
¼	cup green pepper, finely chopped	3	tablespoons onion, grated, including juice
¼	cup pimiento, finely chopped	¾	cup mayonnaise

- Mix white pepper, green pepper, pimiento, lemon juice and onion together well, then add mayonnaise.
- Heat, stirring constantly. Pour over cooked green beans.

If using canned whole green beans, rinse well with cold water, then heat and pour sauce over all to serve.

Barbecue Sauce

Makes 2½ cups

1	medium onion, finely chopped	⅛	teaspoon cayenne pepper
2	tablespoons butter	1	cup water
2	tablespoons vinegar	1	cup ketchup
2	tablespoons brown sugar	3	teaspoons Worcestershire sauce
4	tablespoons lemon juice	½	teaspoon ground mustard
		1	teaspoon celery salt

- Mix all ingredients together in saucepan.
- Bring to a boil and simmer for 5 to 10 minutes.
- Spoon over meat periodically while cooking.

Wonderful barbecue sauce for pork chops, spare ribs and chicken.

Orange Sauce

Makes approximately 1½ cups

1	6-ounce can frozen orange juice	3	tablespoons brown sugar
4	tablespoons Triple Sec	3	heaping tablespoons orange marmalade
2	tablespoons Dijon mustard	1	11-ounce can mandarin oranges, drained

- Combine all ingredients, except mandarin oranges, in a small saucepan.
- Cook over medium-low heat until thickened.
- Stir in mandarin oranges.

Great for pork or ham.

Kaki's Marinade

Makes 1½ cups

½	cup soy sauce	⅓	teaspoon hot pepper sauce
½	cup water	2	large garlic cloves, minced
2½	tablespoons fresh lemon juice	¼	teaspoon fresh ground pepper
2	tablespoons brown sugar		
2	tablespoons oil		

- Mix all ingredients together in a heavy zip-lock bag.
- Marinate beef (flank steak, round steak, etc.) overnight.
- Marinate chicken 4 to 6 hours.

Great for grilling. This marinade makes flank steak taste better than filet. Buy prime flank and have it scored on one side to prevent excessive shrinking. Also good with pork loin.

Raw Ripe Tomato Relish

Makes 13 pints

1 peck (15 pounds) ripe
   tomatoes
2 cups celery, chopped
6 large onions, chopped
4 large green peppers,
   chopped

2½ cups cider vinegar
2   cups sugar
½   cup salt
2   ounces blanched
    mustard seed

- Peel, chop, and drain tomatoes.
- Combine all ingredients.
- Seal in jars.
- Keep in cool dry place.
- Refrigerate after opening.

Cranberry Citrus Relish

Makes about 4 cups

1 12-ounce package
   cranberries
1 orange
1 lemon
1 lime

1 cup sugar or ½ cup
   sugar and ½ cup
   granulated sugar
   substitute

- Pick over and rinse cranberries.
- Chop fine in food processor and pour into bowl.
- Chop lemon, lime, and orange fine in food processor and add to cranberries.
- Stir in sugar and let stand several hours in refrigerator to mix flavors.
- Serve as a relish with poultry or meat.

Apple Chutney

Makes 3 cups

3 cups apples, chopped	1½ teaspoons garlic, chopped
1 cup onions, chopped	½ teaspoon crushed red pepper
1 cup brown sugar	
1 cup water	¼ teaspoon ground nutmeg
¾ cup cider vinegar	
½ cup red pepper, chopped	¼ teaspoon ground allspice
½ cup dried currants	pinch of cloves
1 tablespoon fresh ginger, chopped	

- Combine all ingredients and bring to a boil, stirring until sugar dissolves.
- Simmer until liquid is syrupy, stirring occasionally.
- Cool.

Cranberry Chutney

Makes about 3 cups

1 pound cranberries	1 cup water
1 cup raisins	½ cup onion, chopped
1⅔ cups sugar	1 medium apple, peeled, cored and chopped
1 tablespoon cinnamon	
1½ teaspoons ginger	
¼ teaspoon cloves	½ cup celery, chopped

- Cook cranberries, raisins, sugar, cinnamon, ginger, cloves, and water in a large, covered saucepan for 15 minutes, or until berries pop and the sauce thickens.
- Stir in the rest of the ingredients and simmer 10 to 15 minutes longer, uncovered.
- Cool and refrigerate.
- Will keep for weeks.

Fresh cranberries are best, but if using whole canned cranberries, eliminate sugar and water.

Pear and Apple Conserve

Makes 7 to 8 12-ounce jelly jars

1 quart pears, diced	2 cups seedless raisins
1 quart apples, diced	1½ cups English walnuts,
2 lemons, juice and rind,	broken
grated	7 cups sugar, or less

- In large heavy pan combine all ingredients except nuts.
- Cook until thick and clear (45 minutes to 1 hour, approximately).
- Add nuts about 5 minutes before removing from fire.
- Pack and seal in sterilized jars. Do not add water.
- Store in refrigerator if not packed in sealed jars.

Zucchini Apricot Jam

Makes 6 half-pint jars

6 cups zucchini, grated	1 20-ounce can crushed
½ cup water	pineapple
6 cups sugar	2 3-ounce packages
2 tablespoons lemon	apricot gelatin
juice	

- Place the zucchini and the water in a large kettle.
- Bring to a boil and continue boiling for 6 minutes.
- Drain, then add sugar, lemon juice and pineapple.
- Boil for 6 minutes.
- Add the apricot gelatin and boil 2 minutes.
- Pour into canning jars and process in boiling water bath for 5 minutes.
- Store jars. For best results, let stand for 4 to 6 weeks.

Serve with cream cheese and ginger wafer cookies.

Wendover Farm
Blueberry Marmalade

Makes 9 half-pints

1 medium orange	3 cups blueberries,
1 medium lemon	fresh or frozen
¾ cup water	5 cups sugar
	6 ounces liquid pectin

- Remove peel from orange and lemon.
- Scrape excess white membrane from peel and discard.
- Cut peel into very fine shreds.
- Place in a large saucepan; add ¾ cup water, bring to a boil and simmer, covered, for 10 minutes.
- Scrape any white membrane from the fruit.
- Finely chop pulp, removing seeds.
- Add pulp to peel with crushed blueberries.
- Add sugar.
- Bring to a full rolling boil. Boil for 1 minute, stirring constantly.
- Remove from heat and quickly stir in liquid pectin.
- Skim foam.
- Stir and skim for 7 minutes.
- Ladle into scalded jars.

Microwave Pickles

Makes 2 pints

½ cup vinegar (or less to taste)
½ cup sugar
½ to ¾ teaspoon salt
½ teaspoon mustard seed
½ teaspoon celery seed
1 teaspoon turmeric
2 large cucumbers, thinly sliced
1 medium onion, thinly sliced

- Mix vinegar, sugar and spices in a microwaveable glass dish.
- Add cucumbers and onions; stir.
- Cover with glass cover.
- Microwave on high for 7 minutes.
- Put in jars.
- Refrigerate.

One pound of coffee makes forty five cups. Two pounds of butter will butter one hundred rolls. One bushel of potatoes, mashed or boiled, will serve one hundred twenty five to one hundred and forty people.

Desserts

Shoo-Fly Pie

Lemon Chess Pie

Pecan-Brown Sugar Pound Cake

Chocolate Mousse Cake

Carrot Cake

Kiwi Dessert Tart (see cover)

Almond Crusted Chocolate Torte

Tacy's Torte

White Chocolate Crunch

Lazy Lady Lemon Ice Cream (see photo)

and More

Magnolia Plantation

This plantation has been home to the Drayton family for over 300 years.

Although originally a rice plantation, today it is internationally known for

its beautiful gardens. Many of these gardens were designed by the

Rev. John Grimke-Drayton. He began by importing Camellia Japonica

and Azalea Indica in the 1840's. Upon retirement he devoted his

life to gardening.

Menus

A Bridal Shower

CSOL Tea Party Punch

Sherry Cheese

Spinach Rolls

Spiced Nuts

Hot Crab Dip

Marinated Fruit

Turtle Brownies

Pam's Crisp Little Lemon Cookies

Party Cheese Cakes

Blueberry Banana Pie

Serves 6 to 8

1 9-inch fresh-baked pie shell	½ cup sugar
1 15-ounce can blueberries in heavy syrup (drain berries, reserving liquid)	2 tablespoons butter
	2 tablespoons fresh lemon juice
	2 to 3 bananas (depending on size)
2½ tablespoons cornstarch	1 cup heavy cream, whipped

- Mix cornstarch and sugar in saucepan.
- Add the liquid ONLY from the blueberries. Stir.
- Cook on medium heat until thickened, stirring constantly.
- Remove from heat.
- Add butter, lemon juice, and berries.
- Cool.
- Line bottom and sides of baked pie shell with banana rounds (¼ to ⅓-inch thick).
- Pour over blueberries.
- Top with whipped cream.

Cut a meringue pie cleanly by buttering both sides of the knife.

Pennsylvania Dutch Cake and Custard Pie

Serves 8 to 10

1   15-ounce package
    Pillsbury All Ready Pie
    Crusts

Filling

⅓ cup sugar
2 tablespoons flour
1 teaspoon apple pie
   spice

1 cup applesauce
⅔ cup dairy sour cream
⅓ cup molasses
1 egg beaten

Cake

½ cup sugar
¼ cup margarine or
   butter, softened
½ cup sour milk
1 egg
1 teaspoon vanilla

1¼ cups Pillsbury BEST
    All Purpose or
    Unbleached Flour
1 teaspoon baking
   powder
½ teaspoon salt
¼ teaspoon baking soda

Glaze

½ cup powdered sugar

2 tablespoons coffee

- Preheat oven to 350°.
- Prepare pie crust according to package directions for filled one-crust pie using 9-inch pie pan or 9-inch deep dish pie pan. (Refrigerate remaining crust for later use.)
- In medium bowl, combine ⅓ cup sugar, 2 tablespoons flour and apple pie spice; mix well.
- Stir in remaining filling ingredients; blend well.
- Set aside.
- In small bowl, combine ½ cup sugar and margarine; beat until well blended.
- Add sour milk, 1 egg and vanilla; beat until smooth.
- Lightly spoon flour into measuring cup; level off.
- Add flour, baking powder, salt and baking soda; mix well.
- Spoon into crust-lined pan.

Continued on next page

- Carefully pour filling mixture over batter.
- Bake for 45 to 60 minutes or until center springs back when touched lightly and top is deep golden brown.
- Meanwhile, in small bowl combine glaze ingredients; blend well.
- Drizzle over hot pie.
- Serve slightly warm.

This dessert won the grand prize ($50,000.00) in the 35th Pillsbury Bake-off contest. The creator of this wonderful dessert is Gladys Fulton, who is one of our CSOL members. Also, try Gladys' award winning Taco Twist Soup. It's great!

Maple Pecan Chess Pie

Serves 6 to 8

1 cup brown sugar	1½ cups pecans, coarsely chopped
2 tablespoons butter	1 9-inch unbaked pie shell
2 eggs, beaten	
2 tablespoons flour	whipped cream
dash of salt	
1 cup maple syrup	

- Preheat oven to 400°.
- Cream butter and sugar.
- Add eggs, beating well.
- Add flour, a dash of salt, and syrup.
- Add pecans and mix well.
- Pour into unbaked pie shell.
- Bake for 5 minutes.
- Reduce heat to 375° and bake until mixture sets, about 35 to 40 minutes.

Serve plain or topped with whipped cream flavored with vanilla.

Frozen Chocolate Velvet Pie

Serves 16

Crust

3 egg whites
¼ teaspoon salt
6 tablespoons sugar

3 cups walnuts, finely chopped

Filling

6 tablespoons white corn syrup
4 teaspoons water
5 teaspoons vanilla
1½ cups semi-sweet chocolate pieces

1 cup sweetened condensed milk, chilled
2 cups heavy cream

* Preheat oven to 400°.
* To make crust, beat egg whites with salt to soft peaks.
* Gradually beat in sugar.
* Beat until stiff, then add walnuts.
* Spread crust mixture over bottom and sides of a greased 10-inch pie plate, making a ¾-inch rim.
* Bake 12 minutes. Cool.
* To make filling, bring corn syrup and water just to a boil, stirring constantly.
* Remove from heat, then stir in vanilla and chocolate until melted. Cool.
* Pour filling mixture into a large bowl with milk and cream.
* Blend on low speed, then beat until it stands in stiff peaks.
* Pour filling into pie shell and freeze until firm.
* Remove from freezer 25 minutes before serving.
* Garnish with chocolate curls and additional whipped cream.

For Christmas, arrange candy canes on top in "spoke" fashion.

Buttermilk Lemon Chiffon Pie

Serves 6

1 ¼-ounce envelope
   unflavored gelatin
½ cup sugar and ⅓ cup
   sugar
¼ teaspoon salt
3 eggs, separated

1 cup buttermilk
1 teaspoon lemon rind,
   grated
¼ cup lemon juice
1 9-inch baked pastry
   shell

- Combine gelatin, ½ cup sugar, and salt.
- Beat together egg yolks and buttermilk.
- Stir in gelatin mixture.
- Cook on low heat, stirring constantly, until gelatin dissolves and mixture thickens (about 5 minutes).
- Remove from heat. Cool.
- Stir in lemon rind and lemon juice.
- Stir occasionally until mixture mounds slightly when dropped from spoon. (May put in refrigerator. Check frequently.)
- Beat egg whites until foamy.
- Gradually add ⅓ cup sugar and beat until stiff.
- Fold into gelatin mixture.
- Pour into baked pie shell.
- Chill until set.
- Garnish with lemon slices and whipped cream, if desired.

A light dessert for a heavy meal.

Lemon Chess Pie

Serves 6 to 8

2 cups sugar	¾ tablespoon lemon
1 tablespoon flour	rind, grated
1 tablespoon cornmeal	¼ cup lemon juice
4 eggs	1 9-inch unbaked pie
¼ cup butter, melted	shell
¼ cup milk	

- Preheat oven to 350°.
- Toss sugar, flour, and cornmeal lightly with a fork.
- Add eggs, melted butter, milk, grated lemon rind, and lemon juice and beat until smooth.
- Pour into pie shell and bake for 35 to 40 minutes, until top is brown.

Shoo-Fly Pie

Serves 14

2 8-inch unbaked pie crusts	1 tablespoon cinnamon (optional)
4 cups flour	1 cup boiling water
2 cups brown sugar	1 teaspoon baking soda
1 cup butter or margarine	¾ cup molasses

- Preheat oven to 350°.
- Mix flour, brown sugar, butter, and cinnamon together to form crumbs.
- In separate bowl, mix boiling water, baking soda, and molasses.
- Alternate layers in prepared pie pans, ending with crumbs on top.
- Bake for 45 minutes.

This traditional Pennsylvania Dutch pie gets its name because it is so good you constantly have to keep shooing the flies away.

Apple Cake Supreme

Serves 16

Cake

1½	cups oil	½	teaspoon salt
1½	cups granulated sugar	1	teaspoon baking soda
½	cup brown sugar	3½	cups tart apples,
3	eggs		peeled
3	cups flour	1	cup walnuts, coarsely
1½	teaspoons cinnamon		chopped
1	teaspoon nutmeg	2	teaspoons vanilla

Glaze

3	tablespoons butter	3	tablespoons heavy
3	tablespoons		cream
	granulated sugar	¼	teaspoon vanilla
3	tablespoons light		
	brown sugar		

- Preheat oven to 325°.
- Dice apples into large pieces and place in bowl of lightly salted water until ready to use. (Do not drain—lift them out with hands into mixture).
- Generously grease and flour 10-inch tube pan, shaking out excess flour.
- Combine oil and sugars in large bowl, blending well.
- Add eggs, 1 at a time, beating thoroughly with each addition.
- Sift dry ingredients together and add to first mixture, blending well.
- Fold in apples, nuts, and vanilla.
- Spread evenly in prepared pan and bake until cake tests done, about 1¾ hours.
- Let cool in pan about 30 minutes before turning out onto wire rack.
- Combine glaze ingredients in saucepan and bring to a boil for 1 minute.
- Spoon over warm cake.

Cranberry Cake

Cake

1 cup unsalted butter	½ teaspoon baking soda
2 cups sugar	½ teaspoon salt
4 eggs	2 tablespoons ginger
2½ cups all-purpose flour	⅓ cup buttermilk
1 teaspoon baking powder	2½ to 3 cups cranberries

Glaze

1½ cups sugar	1½ cups cranberries
1½ cups water	

- Preheat oven to 350°.
- To make cake, gradually add sugar to butter and beat until light and fluffy.
- Add eggs, 1 at a time, beating well after each addition.
- Sift together all dry ingredients.
- Add to butter mixture, alternating with the buttermilk. Begin and end with the flour.
- Fold in cranberries.
- Pour into buttered and floured Bundt pan and bake for 1 hour, 15 minutes.
- Cool 10 minutes and remove from pan.
- To make glaze, dissolve sugar in water, add cranberries and bring to a boil (do not stir).
- Cook until syrupy.
- Strain and press the juice from the cranberries.
- Cool and pour over cake.

2 tablespoons of ginger may sound like a lot, but it's just the right amount for this cake.

Excellent Fruit Cake

Makes approximately 24 slices

3 8-ounce packages
pitted dates
1 pound candied
pineapple
1 pound whole cherries
(mix red and green)
2 cups all-purpose flour,
sifted

2 teaspoons baking
powder
½ teaspoon salt
4 eggs
1 cup sugar
8 cups pecan halves

- Preheat oven to 275°.
- Grease 2 9x5x3-inch pans with margarine and line with brown paper—then grease paper.
- Cut up dates and pineapple.
- Add whole cherries.
- Put flour in sifter with baking powder and salt.
- Sift over fruit mixture.
- Mix well with fingers, separating pieces of fruit so all are well coated.
- Beat eggs until frothy, then gradually beat in sugar.
- Add to fruit mixture using a large spoon.
- Add pecan halves.
- Mix with hands until nuts are evenly distributed.
- Pack into 2 pans, pressing with palms of hands. Fill in all empty spaces.
- Bake for 1½ hours.

Freezes well. Thaw only slightly before serving.

Crumb Crust Lemon Cake

Serves 8 to 10

Cake

1 cup light brown sugar	1/2 cup butter or
yellow peel from 1/4	margarine
lemon, chopped	1/2 teaspoon baking soda
1 cup all-purpose flour	1 egg
1/3 cup whole wheat flour	1/2 cup plain yogurt
1/2 teaspoon salt	1 tablespoon lemon
1/2 teaspoon allspice	juice

Frosting

1/2 cup 4X powdered	1 tablespoon lemon
sugar, sifted	juice
	1/2 cup pecans, chopped

- Preheat oven to 350°.
- Mix sugar, peel, flours, salt, allspice, and butter until mixture forms coarse crumbs.
- Remove 1 cup.
- Press into 8x8-inch square pan or pie pan to form crust.
- Add baking soda, egg, yogurt, and lemon juice to remaining mixture.
- Spoon into crust.
- Bake for 30 to 35 minutes or until cake tests done (or microwave for 7 minutes in covered glass or ceramic plate).
- Cool.
- To frost cake, combine sifted powdered sugar and lemon juice and spread over cake.
- Sprinkle with pecans.

Boater's special. Carries and keeps well.

Carrot Cake

Serves 12

Cake

2 cups sugar	1½ cups vegetable oil
2 cups all-purpose flour	4 eggs, beaten
2 teaspoons salt	2 to 3 cups carrots, grated
2 teaspoons cinnamon	pecans, chopped
1 teaspoon baking soda	(optional)

Frosting

8 ounces cream cheese	1 pound powdered
¼ cup butter or	sugar, sifted
margarine	pecans, chopped
2 teaspoons vanilla	(optional)

- Preheat oven to 350°.
- To make cake, mix all dry ingredients.
- Add oil, eggs, and carrots and mix until moist.
- Bake in 3 greased and floured 9-inch layer cake pans for 30 to 40 minutes.
- Mix all frosting ingredients.
- Spread between layers and on top of cooled cake.

Chopped pecans (½ to 1 cup) may be added to either the cake or to the frosting.

Party Cheesecakes

Makes 4 to 5 dozen

Crust

2½ cups graham cracker
     crumbs
6 teaspoons sugar

⅔ cup butter or
     margarine, melted

Filling

24 ounces cream cheese
1½ cups sugar
4 eggs
4 teaspoons vanilla

16 ounces sour cream
     strawberries and/or
     kiwi slices for garnish

- Preheat oven to 350°.
- To make crust, combine graham cracker crumbs and sugar.
- Stir in melted butter until thoroughly blended.
- Pack mixture into 13x9x2-inch pan and press firmly.
- Bake for 8 minutes.
- Cool.
- To make filling, mix cream cheese, sugar, eggs, and vanilla.
- Fill crust with filling mixture.
- Bake for 30 minutes.
- Cool about 3 minutes, then spread with sour cream.
- Cool overnight in refrigerator.
- Cut in about 1¼-inch squares and top with strawberries, kiwi slices or both.

Easy Chocolate Almond Cake

Serves 12 to 16

Cake

½ cup butter or margarine, softened
1 cup sugar
4 eggs
1 cup all-purpose flour
1 teaspoon almond extract
1 teaspoon baking powder
¼ teaspoon salt
1 16-ounce can chocolate syrup

Icing

1 cup sugar
½ cup butter or margarine
⅓ cup evaporated milk
6 ounces semi-sweet chocolate chips

- Preheat oven to 350°.
- To make cake, mix together butter, sugar, eggs, flour, almond extract, baking powder, and salt.
- Add chocolate syrup and mix well.
- Pour into a greased 9x13-inch pan and bake for 30 minutes.
- For icing, heat sugar, butter, and evaporated milk over medium heat, stirring constantly, until it comes to a rapid boil.
- Boil 1 minute.
- Remove from heat.
- Add chocolate chips, stirring until well mixed.
- Pour over warm cake.

Four tablespoons equals one fourth cup. There are three teaspoons in a tablespoon.

Pecan-Brown Sugar Pound Cake

Serves 12 to 16

1 pound butter
1 cup granulated sugar
1 pound light brown
  sugar
5 eggs
3 cups flour, sifted

1 teaspoon baking
  powder
1 cup milk
1 teaspoon vanilla
1 cup pecans, chopped

- Preheat oven to 300°.
- Cream butter, and add sugars, 1 cup at a time.
- Add eggs, 1 at a time, beating after each addition.
- Sift together the sifted flour and baking powder. Add to flour mixture, alternately with milk, beating well. (Start and end with flour.)
- Mix in vanilla.
- Add nuts and mix well.
- Pour into greased and floured tube pan.
- Bake for 1 hour and 30 minutes, or until cake tests done with a toothpick.
- Cool about an hour in pan before removing.

Cold Oven Cake

Serves 12 to 16

½ cup shortening
2 sticks margarine
3 cups sugar
4 eggs
3 cups flour

1 cup milk
1 teaspoon vanilla
1 teaspoon lemon
  extract

- Cream shortening, margarine, and sugar.
- Beat in eggs, 1 at a time.
- Put vanilla and lemon extract in milk and add to creamed mixture alternately with flour.
- Beat until well mixed.
- Pour into tube pan and put in COLD OVEN.
- Bake at 325° for 1½ hours.

Delicious Lemon Cake or "Poke & Pour" Cake

Makes 15 generous servings

1 18¼-ounce package
   lemon cake mix
1 3-ounce package
   lemon gelatin

1 3½-ounce package
   lemon instant pudding
   mix
   whipped topping

- Prepare cake mix, following directions.
- Pour into 13x9-inch pan.
- Bake and cool.
- Poke holes at 1-inch intervals.
- Prepare lemon gelatin mix.
- Cool and pour over cake.
- Chill several hours or overnight.
- Prepare instant pudding and pour over cake.
- Chill again.
- Top with whipped topping.

Served at a Symphony League card party, to rave reviews!

Estonian Pepparkakor Cookies

Makes about 9 dozen cookies

3⅓ cups flour	½ teaspoon salt
1 tablespoon ginger	1 cup butter
1 teaspoon baking soda	1 cup sugar
2 teaspoons cinnamon	½ cup light molasses
2 teaspoons ground cloves	1 cup almonds, chopped

- Sift flour with ginger, baking soda, cinnamon, cloves, and salt.
- Cream butter. Gradually add sugar, creaming well.
- Blend in molasses.
- Add dry ingredients gradually, mixing well.
- Stir in almonds.
- Shape into rolls.
- Wrap in plastic wrap.
- Chill well.
- Preheat oven to 350°.
- Cut rolls into ¼-inch to ⅛-inch slices.
- Bake on ungreased cookie sheets about 10 minutes.

Potato Chip Cookies

Makes 2 dozen

2 sticks margarine,
softened to room
temperature

½ cup sugar

2 cups flour

2 teaspoons vanilla

1 cup potato chips,
crushed

½ cup pecans, crushed

sugar

- Preheat oven to 350°.
- Cream margarine and sugar.
- Add flour and mix.
- Add vanilla and mix.
- Add potato chips and mix.
- Add pecans and mix.
- Continue mixing until well blended.
- Drop by teaspoonsful on greased cookie sheet.
- Flatten dough with bottom of a glass. Dip bottom of glass in water, then in sugar, and then press down dough.
- Bake 15 to 18 minutes until lightly browned.

Sounds strange—tastes good!

Jodi's Ginger Crinkles

Makes 4 dozen cookies

2½	cups flour	½	teaspoon salt
2	teaspoons baking soda	1	cup brown sugar, packed
1	teaspoon ground ginger	¾	cup shortening
1	teaspoon ground cinnamon	¼	cup molasses
½	teaspoon ground cloves	1	egg granulated sugar

- Preheat oven to 375°.
- Combine flour, baking soda, ginger, cinnamon, cloves, and salt and stir together.
- Combine brown sugar, shortening, molasses, and egg.
- Add to flour mixture and beat well.
- Form 1-inch balls and roll in granulated sugar.
- Place 2 inches apart on a greased cookie sheet.
- Bake 10 minutes.

Easy Chocolate Cookies

Makes 2 dozen

1 12-ounce package semi-sweet chocolate chips	2 tablespoons butter
	1 teaspoon vanilla
	1 cup flour, sifted
1 14-ounce can condensed milk	¼ teaspoon salt
	walnuts or pecans

- Preheat oven to 350°.
- Melt chocolate chips, condensed milk, and butter in top of double boiler.
- Remove from heat and mix in vanilla, flour, and salt.
- Drop by teaspoonsful on greased cookie sheet.
- Top with nuts.
- Bake 10 to 15 minutes.

This is a soft cookie that needs to be stored in an airtight container.

Pam's Crisp Little Lemon Cookies

Makes about 5 dozen cookies

1 18¼-ounce package lemon cake mix with pudding	½ cup butter or margarine, melted
	1 egg, slightly beaten
1 cup crisp rice cereal	ground nutmeg (optional)

- Preheat oven to 350°.
- Combine all ingredients except nutmeg, blending well.
- Form into 1-inch balls and place 2 inches apart on ungreased cookie sheets, pressing to flatten.
- Bake 9 to 12 minutes or until light golden brown around the edges.
- Cool 1 minute and remove from cookie sheet.
- Sprinkle with fresh ground nutmeg, if desired.

Other cake mix flavors may be used instead of lemon.
Add 3 tablespoons water to chocolate mix flavors.

Peanut Butter Cup Cookies

Makes 80 cookies

1 cup granulated sugar	1/2 teaspoon salt
1/2 cup brown sugar	1 teaspoon baking soda
1/2 cup plus 1 tablespoon shortening	1 teaspoon cream of tartar
1/2 cup butter or margarine	2 1/2 cups flour
4 tablespoons cocoa	80 miniature chocolate peanut butter cup candies, unwrapped
1 egg	
1 teaspoon vanilla	

- Preheat oven to 350°.
- Cream together sugars, shortening, butter, and cocoa.
- Add egg and vanilla.
- Add dry ingredients which have been mixed together.
- Spray miniature muffin cups with cooking spray.
- Roll dough into small balls and place 1 in each muffin cup.
- Bake for 8 to 10 minutes.
- Remove from oven and IMMEDIATELY press an unwrapped peanut butter cup candy into the center of each cookie.
- Allow to cool for a few minutes before removing from pan.

For reasons unknown, these cookies don't keep for a long period of time. However, the dough can be made into balls and placed in the freezer on a cookie sheet until firm, and then stored in the freezer in plastic bags. Place the frozen balls in the muffin cups and proceed as above.

Spanish Peanut Cookies

Makes about 10 dozen cookies

1 cup shortening	2 cups salted peanuts
2 cups brown sugar	1 cup corn flakes
2 eggs, beaten	1 cup toasted whole
1 teaspoon vanilla	wheat flakes cereal
2 cups flour, sifted	1 cup oatmeal,
1 teaspoon baking soda	uncooked
1 teaspoon baking powder	

- Preheat oven to 375°.
- Cream shortening, brown sugar, and eggs.
- Add vanilla.
- Sift together flour, baking soda, and baking powder.
- Add sifted ingredients to creamed mixture.
- Combine peanuts, wheat flakes, corn flakes, and oatmeal and add to mixture.
- Drop on cookie sheet.
- Bake 8 to 10 minutes.

Ultimate Brownies

Makes about 15 brownies

1 cup butter, melted	1¼ cups sugar
5 1-ounce squares semi-sweet chocolate, melted	1½ teaspoons baking powder
2 1-ounce squares unsweetened chocolate, melted	½ cup flour
	½ teaspoon salt
3 eggs	1 cup semi-sweet chocolate chips
1 tablespoon vanilla	1 cup pecans, chopped (optional)

- Preheat oven to 350°.
- In a large bowl, combine all of the ingredients and mix well.
- Pour into a greased and floured 13x9x2-inch baking pan.
- Bake for 30 minutes.

Date Nut Balls

Makes about 3 dozen ¾-inch balls

2 eggs	1 cup nuts, chopped
1 cup sugar	(walnuts or sesame
1 teaspoon baking	seeds)
powder	1 cup dates, chopped
¼ cup flour	powdered sugar
½ teaspoon salt	

- Preheat oven to 350°.
- Beat eggs and sugar gradually.
- Stir in remaining ingredients.
- Pour into greased 9x9x2-inch pan.
- Bake for 20 minutes.
- Spoon out by teaspoonsful and roll into balls.
- Drop into bag with powdered sugar and shake well to coat evenly.

Keeps well in freezer.

Macadamia Nut Bars

Makes about 40 bars

1 cup granulated sugar	2 cups all-purpose flour
1 cup butter	1½ cups macadamia nuts,
1 egg	chopped
1½ teaspoons vanilla	

- Preheat oven to 350°.
- Cream together sugar and butter.
- Beat in egg and vanilla.
- Blend in flour.
- Stir in half of the nuts.
- Spread thick batter evenly in 9x13-inch greased pan.
- Sprinkle remaining nuts over batter.
- Bake 20 to 30 minutes.
- Cut into bars while hot and remove from pan while warm.

Pumpkin Bars

Makes about 60 bars

Basic Bars
1 cup oil	½ teaspoon salt
2 cups sugar	2 cups flour
4 eggs	2 teaspoons baking powder
2 cups pumpkin	
2 teaspoons cinnamon	1 teaspoon baking soda

Cream Cheese Frosting
3 ounces cream cheese	6 tablespoons butter, softened
1 tablespoon milk	
1¾ cups powdered sugar	1 teaspoon vanilla

- Preheat oven to 350°.
- Combine oil, sugar, eggs, and pumpkin. Beat about 5 minutes.
- Add mixture of cinnamon, salt, flour, baking powder, and baking soda. Beat about 3 minutes.
- Pour into large (at least 10x15-inch) greased pan.
- Bake for 25 minutes.
- Cool.
- Combine frosting ingredients, beat until smooth and spread on cooled bars.

Turtle Brownies

Makes 24 to 30 brownies

14 ounces caramel candy squares (about 44 candies)

⅔ cup evaporated milk

1 18½-ounce box German chocolate cake mix

1 cup walnuts or pecans, chopped

¾ cup margarine or butter, softened

1 12-ounce package semi-sweet chocolate chips

- ◆ Preheat oven to 350°.
- ◆ Combine the caramels with ⅓ cup evaporated milk in top of double boiler and stir until melted. Set aside.
- ◆ Combine cake mix, ⅓ cup evaporated milk, and margarine.
- ◆ Blend until the mixture holds together.
- ◆ Stir in the nuts.
- ◆ Press HALF of the cake mixture into a buttered 9x13-inch pan and bake for 6 minutes.
- ◆ Remove from oven and sprinkle with the chocolate chips.
- ◆ Cover all with the caramel sauce.
- ◆ Crumble remaining half of the cake mixture over the top.
- ◆ Bake 15 to 20 minutes. Cool and cut.

Add one teaspoon vanilla extract to a boxed cake or brownie mix for a more fresh made taste.

Shortbread

Makes 3 to 4 dozen

2 sticks butter
¾ cup confectioners'
   sugar

1 teaspoon vanilla
   (optional 1 extra
   teaspoon vanilla for
   extra flavor)
1¾ cups flour
¼ cup cornstarch

- Cream butter and sugar until light.
- Add vanilla.
- Add flour and cornstarch. Blend until combined.
- Wrap in wax paper and refrigerate for 1 hour.
- Roll out pieces until ⅜-inch thick.
- Cut with small cookie cutters.
- Place on ungreased sheet (they do not spread) and bake at 300° for 20 minutes or until a pale gold on the edges.

This recipe is easy for "little hands" to do—it is impervious to handling.

Fruit Pizza

1 18-ounce roll
   refrigerated sugar
   cookies
1 8-ounce package
   cream cheese,
   softened

⅓ cup sugar
1 pint strawberries
2 to 3 bananas, kiwis, grapes
   or peaches

- Preheat oven to 375°.
- Slice cookies ⅛-inch thick and arrange on lightly greased pizza pan ¼-inch away from edge. Press to seal.
- Bake 10 to 12 minutes or until lightly browned. Cool.
- Blend cream cheese and sugar.
- Spread on cooled crust.
- Arrange different fruits on top.
- Keep refrigerated.

Lemon Mousse

Makes 8 to 10 servings

1	pint heavy cream	1⅓	cups sugar
2	¼-ounce envelopes	½	cup fresh lemon juice
	unflavored gelatin	4	tablespoons lemon
½	cup water		peel, grated
8	eggs, separated		

- Whip cream and refrigerate.
- Dissolve gelatin in ½ cup hot water; let cool.
- In a large bowl, beat egg yolks and add sugar gradually (about 5 minutes) until smooth and lemon colored.
- Add gelatin, lemon juice, and grated peel to yolks and mix.
- Beat egg whites until stiff.
- By hand, fold egg whites into the yolk mixture, then fold in the whipped cream.
- Chill at least 2 hours.

Easy Chocolate Mousse

Serves 4

1	6-ounce package semi-sweet chocolate bits	1½	tablespoons rum or orange-flavored liqueur
2	eggs	¾	cup milk, scalded
3	tablespoons VERY STRONG and HOT coffee		whipped cream or non-dairy topping

- Combine chocolate bits, eggs, coffee, and rum or orange-flavored liqueur and milk in blender. Blend for 2 minutes.
- Pour into four small bowls or stemmed glasses.
- Chill, undisturbed, for at least 24 hours.
- Serve topped with dollop of whipping cream or non-dairy topping.

This MUST chill undisturbed for at least 24 hours to set up.

Elegant Dessert

Makes 8 to 10 servings

6 eggs, separated
½ cup bourbon or coffee-flavored liqueur
½ pound butter (do not substitute)

1 pound powdered sugar
1 cup pecans, chopped
4 3-ounce packages ladyfingers
1 pint whipping cream

- Beat egg yolks.
- Add liquor. Set aside for ½ hour.
- Cream butter and sugar.
- Stir in egg yolk mixture and nuts. Fold in well-beaten egg whites.
- Make layers (in greased glass bowl) of ladyfingers, separated, and mixture.
- Chill overnight.
- Unmold and ice with whipped cream.

Very rich, but delicious and truly elegant.

Lemon Cups

Serves 8

2 tablespoons butter, melted
1 cup sugar
4 tablespoons flour
5 tablespoons lemon juice

rind of 1 lemon, grated
pinch of salt
3 eggs, separated
1½ cups milk

- Preheat oven to 350°.
- Add sugar to melted butter.
- Add flour, lemon rind, lemon juice, and salt.
- Add milk to beaten egg yolks.
- Add to sugar mixture and beat well.
- Beat egg whites until stiff and fold into mixture.
- Pour into 1½-quart casserole or individual cups.
- Place in pan of water and bake about 45 minutes.
- If using casserole, cut in wedges and serve.

Kiwi Dessert Tart

Serves 8 to 10

Crust

2 eggs
½ cup sugar
¼ teaspoon vanilla

⅓ cup flour
2 tablespoons butter or
   margarine, melted

Filling

8 ounces cream cheese
⅓ cup confectioners'
   sugar

½ teaspoon vanilla
1 pint strawberries
3 kiwis

Glaze

½ cup orange juice
¼ cup sugar

2 tablespoons lemon
   juice
1 tablespoon cornstarch

- Preheat oven to 350°.
- For the crust, in a small bowl, beat eggs and sugar until thick.
- Beat in vanilla.
- Add flour and margarine. Mix until smooth.
- Pour into greased 10-inch tart pan or pie plate.
- Bake 15 to 20 minutes. Cool completely.
- For the filling, in small mixer bowl, beat cream cheese, confectioners' sugar, and vanilla until smooth.
- Spread over cool crust.
- Arrange fruit in 2 or 3 circles on cream cheese layer (or any arrangement).
- For glaze, in small saucepan, combine all glaze ingredients and heat to boiling. Boil and stir 1 minute.
- Remove from heat. Cool to room temperature.
- Pour glaze over fruit and spread around.
- Refrigerate at least 2 hours.

Uncomplicated and very pretty.

Brandied Oranges

Makes 6 to 8 servings

8 oranges	¼ cup orange-flavored
1 cup sugar	liqueur
⅔ cup water	vanilla ice cream
¼ cup brandy or cognac	

- Peel and pith oranges using small serrated knife.
- Cut oranges between membranes into segments (work over bowl so juice is not lost).
- Place segments in bowl.
- Place sugar and water in small saucepan; cook and stir over medium-low heat until sugar dissolves.
- Heat to boiling and boil uncovered 2 or 3 minutes. Cool. Stir in brandy and liqueur.
- Pour over orange segments.
- Refrigerate for several hours (actually better the next day.)
- Serve topped with ice cream in parfait glasses or large wine glasses.

Very easy, light and refreshing.

Lazy Lady's Lemon Ice Cream

Makes about 1 quart

1 12-ounce can
evaporated milk
1 cup fresh lemon juice

1 cup sugar (more if
desired)
rind from 2 lemons,
grated

- Place evaporated milk in freezer until about half frozen.
- Beat with electric beater until slightly thickened.
- Slowly add, alternating, lemon juice, and sugar. (Mixture will thicken.)
- Fold in grated lemon rind.
- Pour into container and freeze (needs no stirring).

This is great served with raspberries and a wafer.

Orange Ice Cream

Makes about 1 gallon

1 2-liter bottle
carbonated orange
drink
1 20-ounce can crushed
pineapple (optional)

1 14-ounce can
sweetened
condensed milk

- Put all ingredients in ice cream cylinder and churn until firm, approximately 1 hour.

Quick and easy to make. A delicious summer dessert.

Schaum Torte

Makes 6 servings

6 egg whites	1 teaspoon vanilla
1⅓ cups sugar	vanilla ice cream
½ teaspoon cream of	strawberries
tartar	whipped cream
pinch of salt	

- Preheat oven to 450°.
- Beat egg whites until stiff.
- Add cream of tartar and salt.
- Add sugar gradually.
- Beat until mixture forms stiff peaks.
- Add vanilla and beat again.
- Pile high in a buttered 10x6-inch pan.
- Place in oven.
- Turn off oven immediately and leave in the oven overnight (or about 8 hours).
- Cut into squares, serve with vanilla ice cream, strawberries, and whipped cream.

Almond-Crusted Chocolate Torte

½ cup butter
1 cup flour
½ cup sugar
½ cup almonds, sliced, chopped and toasted
1 quart chocolate ice cream

2 tablespoons light rum or ¼ tablespoon rum flavoring
1 cup frozen whipped topping, thawed additional whipped cream (optional)

- In a large skillet, melt butter.
- Stir in flour, sugar, and almonds.
- Cook over medium heat, stirring constantly, until mixture is golden and crumbly.
- Remove from heat.
- Reserve ¾ cup of the crumb mixture.
- Pat remaining mixture on the bottom and 1 inch up the rim of a 9-inch springform pan which has been sprayed with cooking spray.
- Cover springform pan with plastic wrap and freeze crumb crust for at least 2 hours.
- In a large mixing bowl, melt ice cream slightly.
- Gently but quickly fold whipped topping and rum into ice cream.
- Spoon mixture into the crumb crust.
- Sprinkle with reserved crumb mixture, and cover tightly with plastic wrap.
- Freeze for 6 hours or overnight.
- Cut into wedges to serve.
- Serve frozen, with a dollop of whipped cream, if desired.

This recipe was a prize winner for one of our contributors. Definitely a "special occasion" dessert.

Coffee Torte

Serves 8 to 10

Meringue

6 egg whites
¼ teaspoon cream of
   tartar
1 cup granulated sugar
1½ cups confectioners'
   sugar

1 teaspoon almond
   extract
dash of allspice
dash of mace

Filling

9 egg yolks
¾ cup granulated sugar
¾ cup strong coffee,
   cold

1½ tablespoons flour
¾ cup soft butter
½ pint cream, whipped

◆ Preheat oven to 250°.
◆ Beat egg whites until foamy. Add cream of tartar. Continue beating until egg whites hold stiff peak.
◆ Slowly add sugars, 1 tablespoon at a time, beating well after each addition.
◆ Add almond extract, allspice and mace. Beat 2 minutes longer.
◆ Cut four 8-inch circles from heavy brown paper. Divide meringue into 4 parts and spread evenly over the circles of paper which have been placed on baking sheets.
◆ Bake for 1 hour and 15 minutes.
◆ Cool and remove paper.
◆ For the filling, combine egg yolks, sugar, coffee, and flour in top of double boiler.
◆ Cook over boiling water, stirring constantly, until thickened. Cool to lukewarm.
◆ Add butter. Stir until blended.
◆ Spoon and spread filling over top of meringue layers, stacking as a layer cake.
◆ Chill, then decorate with whipped cream.
◆ Chill again.

White Chocolate Mousse Torte with Raspberry Sauce

Serves 10 to 12

Crust

24 chocolate sandwich cookies

¼ cup unsalted butter, melted

¾ cup whipping cream

8 ounces semi-sweet chocolate, chopped

Filling

1 pound imported white chocolate, chopped

3 cups whipping cream, chilled and divided

1 tablespoon unflavored gelatin

¼ cup water

1 teaspoon vanilla extract

chocolate sandwich cookies, chopped

Raspberry Sauce

2 12-ounce packages frozen unsweetened raspberries, thawed

½ cup sugar

2 tablespoons raspberry liqueur

- For crust, butter a 10-inch springform pan.
- Finely grind cookies in food processor.
- Add melted butter and blend until combined.
- Press crust mixture onto bottom (not sides) of prepared pan.
- Bring cream to simmer in heavy medium saucepan. Reduce heat to low.
- Add chocolate and whisk until melted and smooth.
- Pour chocolate mixture over crust. Chill.
- For filling, combine white chocolate and 1 cup cream in top of double boiler. Stir over simmering water until smooth and melted.
- Cool to barely lukewarm.
- Sprinkle gelatin over ¼ cup water in heavy small saucepan. Let stand 10 minutes to soften.

Continued on next page

- Stir over low heat until gelatin dissolves. Pour into large bowl.
- Add remaining 2 cups cream and vanilla and stir to combine. Beat cream and gelatin mixture to soft peaks. Fold in white chocolate mixture. Pour filling into crust and refrigerate until filling is set, at least 6 hours or overnight.
- Run small sharp knife around pan sides to loosen torte. Release pan sides.
- Sprinkle top with chopped cookies.
- Pre-slice when fully chilled with dental floss stretched tight.
- For the raspberry sauce, combine all sauce ingredients in processor and puree until smooth.
- Strain mixture through fine strainer into bowl.
- Cover and chill.
- Serve mousse at room temperature with chilled raspberry sauce spooned around slices.

Well worth the effort.

Tacy's Torte

Serves 6 to 8

3 egg whites
1 cup sugar
20 round buttery crackers
½ cup nuts, coarsely chopped

½ pint whipping cream
¾ teaspoon instant coffee granules
¾ teaspoon sugar

+ Preheat oven to 350°.
+ Beat egg whites stiff with sugar.
+ Crush crackers. Fold crumbs and nuts into egg whites.
+ Bake in a greased 9-inch pie pan for ½ hour.
+ Combine cream, instant coffee granules, and sugar. Whip to desired consistency.
+ Before serving, top torte with cream mixture.

Recipe doubles well and freezes well. Very easy and delightful flavor. The torte would be a wonderful base for fresh fruit with a liqueur-based yogurt topping.

Microwave Fudge

1 pound confectioners' sugar
½ cup cocoa
¼ cup evaporated milk

¼ cup margarine
2 teaspoons vanilla
½ cup nuts or peanut butter (optional)

+ Grease 8-inch square dish with butter.
+ Sift sugar and cocoa into microwave-safe bowl.
+ Place milk and margarine on top of dry ingredients. DON'T STIR.
+ Cook 2 minutes on high in microwave.
+ Stir immediately until all lumps are gone.
+ Add vanilla and stir. Add nuts or peanut butter, if desired.

An easy way to satisfy a sudden chocolate craving.

Grandma's Fudge

3	pounds brown sugar	1/4	pound butter
1	cup milk	1	tablespoon vanilla
1/2	pound unsweetened chocolate	1/4	teaspoon salt

- Put brown sugar, milk, and chocolate in a saucepan.
- Heat until a medium ball can be formed. Stir frequently.
- Remove from heat.
- Add butter, vanilla, and salt. Beat until stiff.
- Pour into a buttered 13x9-inch pan or cookie sheet. Cut into 2-inch squares.

One tester commented that this may be the only cooked fudge that has ever turned out just right for her, and that everyone thought was delicious.

Chocolate Nut Candy Bits

3/4	cup walnuts, ground	1/2	pound butter
1	8-ounce milk chocolate bar, grated (chill before grating)	1	cup sugar
		1	cup almonds, slivered

- Put 1/2 of the ground walnuts, then 1/2 the grated chocolate in a 9x13-inch pan.
- In a large heavy skillet, melt butter over low heat.
- Turn burner to high and add the sugar and almonds.
- Cook continuously, folding (DO NOT STIR) until golden brown and the almonds are toasted. Be careful that it does not burn! (It foams and increases in volume. Looks thick and caramel in color.)
- Remove from heat and immediately pour into prepared pan. Add remaining chocolate and walnuts.
- Chill.
- Break into pieces to serve.

Beware, you can't eat only one piece.

Caramels

2 cups sugar	1 stick butter
2 cups light corn syrup	1 12-ounce can
1 teaspoon salt	evaporated milk
(optional)	1 teaspoon vanilla

- Mix sugar and corn syrup in a heavy saucepan. Heat to 245°.
- Slowly add butter and evaporated milk. Cook to 242°.
- Remove from heat and add vanilla, stirring quickly.
- Pour into well-buttered 9x13-inch pan.
- Cool, cut in 1-inch squares and wrap each square in wax paper.

Microwave Peanut Brittle

Makes 1¼ pounds

1 cup sugar	1 teaspoon margarine
½ cup light corn syrup	1 teaspoon vanilla
pinch of salt	1 teaspoon baking soda
1½ cups roasted peanuts, mixed nuts, or cashews	

- Spray a 2-quart microwave bowl with non-stick vegetable spray.
- Add sugar, corn syrup, and salt. Mix well.
- Microwave at HIGH for 6 to 7 minutes, or until it is a pale yellow color. Handle carefully.
- Stir in nuts and microwave 1 to 2 minutes.
- Stir in margarine, vanilla and baking soda until foamy.
- Quickly pour onto cookie sheet prepared with non-stick vegetable spray.
- Cool. Break into pieces and store in a covered container.

Great for gifts, plus it's quick, easy and delicious. You may use any mixture of nuts that you would enjoy.

Chocolate Fondue

1 12-ounce package
semi-sweet chocolate
chips
1 14-ounce can
sweetened
condensed milk

1 14-ounce jar
marshmallow cream
2 ounces or more (to
taste) chocolate mint
liqueur

◆ Melt chocolate chips, sweetened condensed milk, and
marshmallow cream in heavy saucepan.
◆ Add chocolate mint liqueur.
◆ Put into a chafing dish and serve warm with assorted fruit.

Also good over pound cake or ice cream.

Hot Fudge Sauce

Makes about 1½ cups

1 cup sugar
2 tablespoons cocoa
1 5-ounce can
evaporated milk

½ teaspoon vanilla
1 tablespoon butter

◆ Combine sugar and cocoa in small pan. Heat over low heat
for 4 minutes, stirring constantly.
◆ Add evaporated milk. Continue stirring and cooking until
sauce begins to thicken. Remove from heat.
◆ Stir in vanilla and butter. Sauce will thicken more as it cools.
◆ Keep refrigerated. Serve over ice cream, cake or fruit.

Pour hot sauce over ice cream and sauce will harden.

White Chocolate Crunch

Serves a crowd

1 pound white candy coating	1½ cups pretzel sticks, broken into ½-inch pieces
¾ cup salted peanuts	
½ cup dark raisins	1 tablespoon vanilla

- Preheat oven to 325°.
- TURN OVEN OFF.
- Put candy coating in a large baking dish.
- Place in oven for 15 minutes until soft.
- Remove and add all other ingredients. Stir until well coated.
- Spread ¼-inch thick on wax paper and refrigerate until solid.
- Break into pieces.
- Store in tight container in refrigerator.

If you would like to thin the melted chocolate, add 1 to 2 tablespoons solid vegetable shortening. Do NOT add water, milk, oil, margarine or butter to this.

CHOOSE LESS FAT

High-Fat Foods	**Lower Fat Substitutes**
Butter, margarine or vegetable oil	Reduce amount, using a margarine made from mono-unsaturated or poly-unsaturated oil, or use reduced-calorie margarine or oil
Lard, meat fat, shortening	Reduced-calorie margarine, vegetable cooking spray
Gravy with meat drippings	Gravy with bouillon, gravy with defatted broth
Regular salad dressings	Lemon, vinegar, reduced-calorie dressings, oil-free dressings
Whole or 2% milk	Skim, 1% milk, or evaporated skimmed milk diluted equally with water
Whipping cream	Chilled evaporated skimmed milk, whipped
Whole milk cheeses	Low-fat cheeses, skim milk cheeses (cheeses with 5 grams of fat or less per ounce)
4% fat cottage cheese	Nonfat or 1% low-fat cottage cheese, or farmer's cheese
Cream cheese	Light cream cheese product, Neufchâtel
Sour cream	Nonfat or low-fat sour cream, plain low-fat and nonfat yogurt
Ice cream	Ice milk, frozen yogurt, sherbet, sorbet
Whole eggs	Egg whites, egg substitutes

Baking chocolate, 1 ounce square	3 tablespoons cocoa plus 1 tablespoon mono-unsaturated or poly-unsaturated vegetable oil or margarine
Fudge sauce	Chocolate syrup
White flour, 1 cup	½ cup whole wheat flour plus ½ cup white flour, or ⅔ cup white flour plus ⅓ cup oat bran
Sugar	Reduce amount by ⅓ to ½; substitute brown sugar or honey when flavor will not be affected
Salt	Reduce by ½ or eliminate
Mayonnaise	Fat-free, reduced calorie, or low-cholesterol mayonnaise
Soups, canned, condensed cream	99% fat-free condensed cream soups
Egg noodles	Noodles made without egg yolks
White rice	Brown or wild rice
Pecans, walnuts	Reduce by ⅓ to ½
Heavily marbled meats	Lean cuts of beef and pork
Bacon, sausage	Canadian bacon, lean ham
Bologna, salami, pastrami, frankfurters	Sliced turkey or chicken without skin, lean roast, beef, lean ham
Ground beef (hamburger)	Ground turkey or lean ground beef
Oil-packed tuna	Water-packed tuna
Poultry	Skinned poultry
Turkey, self-basting	Turkey basted with fat-free broth
Croissants, butter rolls doughnuts, butter crackers, potato chips, corn chips	Bagels, English muffins matzos, air-popped popcorn, pretzels, rice cakes, bread sticks, whole grain breads

INDEX

INDEX

Music, Menus & Magnolias
The Charleston Symphony Orchestra League

Please send me _____ copies of *Music, Menus and Magnolias*.................. @ $17.95 each

Add Postage and handling ....@ $3.00 each

Add Gift wrap (optional)..@ $2.00 each

South Carolina residents add   6% sales tax................................@ $1.08 each

TOTAL ENCLOSED $

Check or money order enclosed.   Make payable to
Music, Menus & Magnolias.

Mail to:
The Charleston Symphony Orchestra League
P.O. Box 22613
Charleston, SC 29413-2613

Ship to:
   Name:..

   Address: ....

   City.......................... State.. Zip....................

   Daytime Phone Number: (   )_____

If Gift, enclosure card to read:_____

Music, Menus & Magnolias
The Charleston Symphony Orchestra League

Please send me _____ copies of *Music, Menus and Magnolias*.................. @ $17.95 each

Add Postage and handling ....@ $3.00 each

Add Gift wrap (optional)..@ $2.00 each

South Carolina residents add   6% sales tax................................@ $1.08 each

TOTAL ENCLOSED $

Check or money order enclosed.   Make payable to
Music, Menus & Magnolias.

Mail to:
The Charleston Symphony Orchestra League
P.O. Box 22613
Charleston, SC 29413-2613

Ship to:
   Name:..

   Address :..

   City.......................... State.. Zip....................

   Daytime Phone Number: (   )_____

If Gift, enclosure card to read:_____